When Prophecy Failed

ROBERT P CARROLL

WHEN

Reactions and responses to failure in

PROPHECY

the Old Testament prophetic traditions

FAILED

SCM PRESS LTD

For Mary Anne . . .
also Finn, Alice and Saul

334 01789 0

First published 1979
by SCM Press Ltd
58 Bloomsbury Street, London WC1

Filmset in 10/12 pt Times
Printed and bound in Great Britain
by W & J Mackay Limited, Chatham

Contents

Preface

I am indebted to the Court of Glasgow University for granting me study leave from January to September 1977 during which I did the groundwork for this book. Without that escape from teaching and mingling with students it would never have been written – yet without all those lectures, seminars, tutorials and interminable arguments with students my original ideas would hardly have matured into a potential book at all.

Naming names can be a specious practice in preface writing but a few individuals have greatly assisted my work and I would wish to place on record my gratitude to them. As head of the department Robert Davidson made my study leave possible by encouraging me to take it and by rearranging the teaching programmes. Alastair Hunter took over the teaching of some of my courses and so made good my absence. Long hours of discussion over a lengthy period of time with Joe Houston, a philosopher from the theology department, helped to clarify and sharpen my thinking on many issues, especially on the philosophical side. I owe a special debt to Professor Peter Ackroyd of the University of London for encouragement by way of correspondence and the use of my published journal articles in his own writings. Such encouragement greatly stimulated my thinking and helped me to apply myself to the wearisome task of writing and rewriting the book. To my wife Mary Anne, who took the children away on holiday for two summers in order to allow me peace and quiet for writing, this book owes more than I can say.

The writing of it has made me ponder again the argument of Socrates in Plato's *Phaedrus* that as a man's thoughts are much superior to any words he may write writing is a poor reflection of thought. I suspect he may have had a point.

Glasgow   ROBERT P. CARROLL
October 1978

Introduction

On 8 December 1857 Karl Marx wrote 'I am working like mad all through the nights at putting my economic studies together so that I may at least have the outlines clear before the deluge comes.'[1] He need not have been in such a rush to write *Das Kapital* for it was actually some sixty years before the anticipated deluge did come and then it was entirely different from anything Marx had expected. The next sixty years after the Russian revolution of 1917 were to see so many disastrous developments in the course of the revolution that today it is an open question whether the predictions of Marxian theory have been fulfilled or disconfirmed. Yet in spite of all the failures of expectations and the even more disastrous successes of the theory the political philosophy of Marx, supplemented by the work of Engels and Lenin, continues to be a major influence in the contemporary world.[2]

The phenomenon of disconfirmed expectation accompanied by explanatory reaction is not something peculiar to Marxian thought or limited to modern political structures. It goes back much further in time and thought to the early centuries of Christianity when various Christian communities struggled to come to terms with the failure of the parousia and to interpret their own structures as the fulfilment of even earlier predictions. For the problem has its roots in the prophetic traditions of ancient Israel and has arisen due to the failure of the prophetic visions of the future to materialize. The visions and their failure to be realized gave rise to the need for interpretation of the traditions so as to justify them in the light of what had *not* happened.

This book is an attempt to examine the prophetic traditions in terms of their predictive elements and the responses to the failure of the expectations aroused by them. It is necessarily a hermeneutic work because the interpretation of texts is the central concern of any group facing disappointment of expectations – interpretation designed to protect the original premises and also, if possible, to explain the present state of the group. In my analysis hermeneutic indicates the interpretation of texts, and occasionally, in keeping with modern philosophical usage, the theory of the interpretation of texts. Originally it was planned to deal more specifically with the theory of interpretation but that would have involved a much larger book and would have delayed further the actual exposition of the relevant texts.[3]

The approach taken to the interpretation of prophecy is essentially a cross-disciplinary one using the findings of social psychology in relation to attitude change and expectation response. I have used the theory of cognitive dissonance as a means of analysing the prophetic texts because it provides an account of how people react to the failure of their expectations and therefore it might illuminate some elements of the biblical traditions in terms of response to the failure of the prophetic visions to be realized. Cross-disciplinary studies are always vulnerable to criticisms directed at having failed to be expert in one or both fields but the alternative monomania is too narrow a view of complex structures to be worth pursuing. In this study it has been necessary to consider a wide range of disciplines, including psychology and philosophy, in order to do justice to the complexities involved in discerning the reactions to failure of expectations in the prophetic traditions. All predictive prophecy is vulnerable to failure, the biblical prophets no less than any other prophets, but what is most interesting about their failure is the way it was transformed within the traditions to contribute to the hermeneutic process.[4] Although this book is limited to a treatment of prophecy in terms of dissonance response it is hoped that it will also underline the richness and complexity of the prophetic traditions. As a preliminary hermeneutic statement it is but a scratching of the surface of the texts.

One bane of modern biblical scholarship is the footnote. So often the text is prescript to the footnote. I have tried to avoid that state of affairs but have not been able to eliminate the footnote altogether. It is a necessary evil. Necessary in the sense that the work of other scholars should be acknowledged whenever used and that sources of further information should be indicated. The use of the comprehensive footnote wherein appears everything ever written on the specific point has been avoided deliberately. I realize that every judgment or interpretation offered, especially in part I, is only one possible way of treating the material and that often the view taken is controversial. However, as is to be expected in a hermeneutic essay, I have tried to concentrate on presenting my own particular interpretation of the data. Too detailed a bibliographical footnoting system would divert attention from that specific interpretation in order to listen to a cacophony of Babel. I am also aware of the double bind involved in the footnote business – if a work is not mentioned it is because it has not been read or the writer is unaware of its existence, so in order to prevent that misapprehension arising it becomes necessary to list everything ever consulted or read. Thus the growth of the footnote is fostered and the footnote as art form maintained. The massive footnote assures academic respectability and orthodoxy but deters the publisher because of the length of book necessitated by such diligence. Hence the double bind. In pursuit of my analysis I have limited my footnotes to the strictly relevant (in my judgment) and have tried to minimize the number of discussions of and references to German works so as not to exasperate the general reader. The thesis about dissonance must be judged in terms of the sense it makes of the textual evidence rather than the number of other scholars who are inclined to support similar interpretative approaches to the texts.

Biblical quotations are usually from the RSV with a minor adjustment of the divine name from Lord to Yahweh in keeping with critical orthodoxy. In reading the prophetic traditions it is advisable to keep in mind the ancient Chinese proverb: 'Prediction is a very difficult business, especially predicting the future.'

PART I

The Prophetic Traditions

1

Interpreting the Prophetic Traditions

The interpretation of biblical prophecy is a very complex matter involving the analysis of multiplex traditions and the multiple factors that gave rise to and maintained those traditions. Such traditions and factors reveal prophecy to have been a network rich in utterances and interpretative reflections constructed over many centuries of ancient Israelite history. Though my concern is with the predictive element in prophecy it is a prerequisite of understanding that element properly that the other elements constitutive of prophecy in general should be clarified sufficiently to illuminate the nature of prophetic prediction. As this clarificatory process forms the necessary background of interpretative procedure for my analysis of prophecy this opening part is devoted to it. There is, of course, a direct relation between the predictive element and the other elements of prophecy for the part must always be understood in terms of the whole. This reciprocal relationship between the part and the whole, or the particular and the general, is known in interpretation theory as 'the hermeneutic circle'.[1] However as there is already an adequate supply of general accounts of prophecy available on the market it will not be necessary to provide yet another one here.[2] It is only essential to consider those factors that bear directly on the understanding of prophecy, in particular its predictive element and the development of the traditions in response to expectations created by such an element.

The setting of prophecy

There were many movements in the societies of the Ancient Near

East devoted to divination, the manipulation of fortunes and speculation about the future using various techniques of augury, sooth-
saying and sorcery. Some of the functionaries involved in such
divination were ecstatics of a type similar to the prophets of Israel.[3]
However in ancient Israel most forms of divination appear to have
been regarded with suspicion and so few thrived as legitimate
expressions of Israelite culture, except for the simple forms permitted to the priests (cf. Deut. 18.9–14; 33.8–11). Movements and
groups of prophets, i.e. ecstatics and mantics, which were common
in the various cultures of the Ancient Near East were accepted as
legitimate media of revelation in Israel. Indeed it is possible that
some of the ancient traditions regarded prophecy as the equivalent
for Israel of divination in other cultures (cf. Num. 23.23 and the fact
that the prohibition of divination in Deut. 18.9–14 is immediately
followed by regulations on prophecy vv 15–22). These prophets
provided mantic insights, worked miracles, proclaimed messages,
visions and revelations at sanctuaries, royal courts and in public
throughout the monarchies of Israel and Judah. My concern, however, is not with the obscure prehistory of prophecy (cf.
Num. 11.24–30; 12.1–8), nor with the earlier orgiastic movements
of prophecy from Samuel to Elisha but with prophecy as embodied
in the books devoted to the oracles of the named prophets from
Isaiah to Zechariah (the second half of the traditional division of the
Hebrew Bible known as 'the prophets' (*hann^{e}bī'īm*)). It is fully
recognized that these prophets were but the later part of a much
larger prophetic movement in Israel and the Ancient Near East.

Little is known about these individual prophets or of their circumstances so it is necessary to place them in a setting depicted by
broad brushstrokes from what we know already about ancient
Israelite society and from what we can extrapolate from the literary
traditions associated with them. Apparently lacking in organization
they emerged in a period of relative affluence about the middle of
the eighth century before the Christian era. They preached against
social injustice and oppression, warned of imminent catastrophes
and occasionally sought to change the community's attitudes. For
more than two centuries the movement lasted until it slowly faded
into the background again and was transmuted into other forms of
activity. If we may take as representative of the movement the main
features of the traditions from Amos to Zechariah against the

backgrounds provided by those traditions then we may say that the
movement flourished during the period when Assyrian domination
was beginning and declined as the Babylonian hegemony declined.
Thus it was bound up with the fortunes of Israel and Judah in
relation to the larger fortunes of the empires and was inextricably
involved in the disintegration and ultimate collapse of its two patron
states. This overview of its political setting provides the first important feature that I want to emphasize about the interpretation of
prophecy: *crisis produced critique.*

Crisis and critique. The larger prophetic movement had emerged
in Israel during the Philistine crisis (I Sam. 1–7), had regularly
surfaced during crises associated with the monarchies of Israel and
Judah (cf. I Sam. 15, 16; I Kings 11.26–40; 17ff.) and its history
may be seen as a manifold response to various political and religious
crises. Of a piece with this summary observation is the fact that
prophecy faded out of public notice during the relative stability of
the Persian period. If crises were the occasioning of prophetic
appearances what caused them to emerge as critics of their communities? Questions about social causation are very complex problems and hardly to be dealt with in a few sentences. However, it
seems clear from the trenchant denunciations of society in the
oracles of Amos that the prophet was outraged by the corruption
and oppression he witnessed in the various towns of Israel and
among neighbouring communities. Similar reactions among many
of the other prophets, e.g. Isaiah, Micah, Jeremiah and Ezekiel,
suggest that the prophets were spokesmen for the laws prevailing in
their time. Although the origins of many of the laws may well go far
back into Israel's past it may well also be the case that the laws as a
collected body of written legislation may have been recently prom-
ulgated.[4] If they had been so produced during the period which saw
the emergence of these prophets then we would have a partial
explanation for the appearance of the prophetic movement at this
particular period in history. Of course it may be the case that the
growing affluence of the nation caused by the lengthy prosperity of
Jeroboam II's reign had begun to reveal more clearly the enormous
social and economic gap between various groups within the nation.
These two possibilities may be taken together as providing one
scenario for the sudden irruption into Israelite society of men such

as Amos and Isaiah. The growing power of Assyria and its destructive threat to Israel provided the prophets with the necessary crisis against which to launch their critique of society. They addressed communities guilty of failing to live by the laws of the land in a time of grave crisis (to a certain extent Amos anticipated this crisis) and accused them of being intent on their own destruction.

The importance of this particular feature of prophecy is that it emphasizes the fact that the prophets functioned in a context of political crisis and responded to events and processes of their time. This factor of response to crisis not only constructed their preaching it also contributed significantly to the subsequent treatment of their oracles. The prophets responded to various internal (personal) and external (social) stimuli and pressures and their responses took the form of public proclamations or performances of symbolic actions. Crises tend to produce immediate reactions and often such reactions involve short-term resolutions designed to meet the exigencies of the moment. The immediate, short-term diagnoses and responses of the prophets were to be preserved by subsequent generations and were often transformed into long-term possibilities and even programmes. We shall see later to what extent these transformations subtly changed prophecy.

The cult. If the political crises of their day constituted the larger background to the prophets' work then the more immediate context of their activity was provided by the cultic life of the Jerusalem community (or a somewhat similar cultic life in other towns for Amos and Hosea). The religious centre of any community is its cultus and ancient Judah was no exception. The cultus was the location where the particular deity of the community was worshipped in accordance with the traditional ritual gestures and structures of that society supervised by a professional priesthood. In the Ancient Near East such locations were centred on temples where legitimate priesthoods officiated at services and sacrifices. The cult centre of Judah was the great Solomonic temple at Jerusalem and this sanctuary became a focal point of much prophetic activity.

Although much biblical scholarship has been devoted to describing and analysing cultic forms little has been done in terms of explaining its contribution to the way Israel saw the world. In much of the literature the cult is seen as relating to Israelite religion but not as an important nexus of Israelite theology, thus its treatment tends to be descriptive and static rather than structural and dynamic.[5] There are welcome signs that a more realistic assessment of the cult is now emerging in recent studies.[6] Although this is not the place to essay a full picture of the cult in the life of ancient Israel it is important to note that it provided the fundamental background for the whole prophetic movement, from its beginnings in the time of Samuel through its shamanistic period to the proclamation of the word of Yahweh from mount Zion in the mid-eighth century and beyond.

The cult was concerned with the ritual ordering of the world in accordance with whatever was the prevailing mythology of the cult. It presented a view of man in relation to the world which was the basis for the life of the community. Apart from the ritual observances related to the times and seasons of the year, the ordering of specific sacrifices for specific occasions and offences and the maintenance of the traditions of the community the cult can be seen to have had a very strong influence on major areas of biblical literature. The account of the national origins of Israel and its laws associated with the exodus and Sinai are cultic in presentation (Ex. 12.1–15.18; 19.1–24.11). Although the epic poetry and legends about the ancestors were probably part of Israel's oral traditions the locations of which remain unknown, its historians, the deuteronomists, centred much of their writing on the Jerusalem cult.

The existence of the cult prophet in ancient Israel is now a well established datum of contemporary scholarship though it remains an open question whether the canonical prophets were cult prophets or not.[7] It is not important at this stage of my argument to resolve this question but the connections between the prophets and the cult should be noted. These connections may not have been all that important for their thought but they must be kept in mind as contributory factors exercising some influence on them. They may have been as casual as an area in which to preach as was the case with Jeremiah (and possibly Amos), or as important as the matrix of Isaiah's call to be a prophet. For Amos and Isaiah Zion was the nexus of the divine dwelling and proclamation (Amos 1.2; Isa. 8.17; cf. Jer. 7.3, 7). The book of Ezekiel is encapsulated by accounts of the divine presence (1–3) and the reconstructed temple (40–48).

The post-exilic prophets Haggai and Zechariah were heavily involved with the company rebuilding the temple. Other prophets such as Joel, Habakkuk and Zephaniah are perhaps best seen as cult prophets.[8] As many of the prophets were often located at the temple or preaching in its precincts it is hard to resist the general thesis that the fundamental background of most of the prophets was the cult itself. Little may follow from this connection between cult and prophecy but it remains a necessary element in any interpretation of prophetic oracles, especially those relating to salvation and the future. The cultic connection of prophecy can be exaggerated but it can also be ignored so the point being made here is that it should be seen as a backdrop to their work and as a fixed point in the interpretation of their oracles.

At the same time it is also necessary to stress that many of the oracles preserved in the prophetic traditions are virulently against cultic structures (cf. Isa.1.10–15; 58.1–5; 66.3; Jer.7.21–26; Ezek.8; Hos.6.6; 12.11; Amos 4.4, 5; 5.25; Micah 6.6–8). So we must allow for a strong tension within prophecy between the roots and social context of the movement and its perception and critique of society. The preaching against cultic structures is probably indicative of a different view of man than that maintained by the cult and so the cult provided the negative element for the prophetic dialectic. Perhaps prophecy attempted to add, or at least stress, the ethical dimension to the cultic construction of reality. The ethical element found elsewhere in cult liturgies (e.g. Ps.15; 24) may have been original to the cult or have come about due to the influence of prophecy. Whatever the case may have been with reference to an ethical dimension it is clear that the eighth- and seventh-century prophets rejected the large scale sacrificial rituals they encountered in the cult. This rejection was part of their critique of the community and may well have stemmed from their own involvement in, or sympathy towards, the cult. It hardly alters the fact that prophecy itself had a strong cultic dimension.

The structure of prophecy

A complete analysis of the structure of prophecy would take a book in itself so here I must be content to make a number of observations relevant to my general thesis, particularly in their bearing on the problematics of interpreting the traditions.[9] In limiting myself to these specific aspects of prophecy it is my intention to treat them as the essence of biblical prophecy. The subtle interactions of prophet and community or prophet and cult escape our historical research so it is necessary to plot the general presuppositions and stances of the prophets from their own work in order to estimate the structure of prophecy.

The domain assumptions of prophecy. The notion of domain assumptions comes from modern sociology and refers to assumptions made about man and society.[10] Domain assumptions are the things attributed to the members of a domain. A simple example will illustrate the principle behind the term. If I believe that men are irrational and that therefore their behaviour in society will be irrational, then I will also believe that heavy state control is required to restrict their actions. My political outlook may be said to be constructed by a domain assumption that men are basically irrational. Applied to prophecy such a concept as a domain assumption might be the belief that men are wicked, immoral or idolatrous. What the domain assumptions might be has to be investigated in the texts and if there were any prophetic domain assumptions then they should become apparent by reading the texts. Normally such assumptions are not factual beliefs based on evidence but prior beliefs that govern one's outlook on and understanding of society. The empirical evidence may be to the contrary but as Gouldner observes about domain assumptions 'they are often resistant to "evidence"'.[11] Of course this means accusing the prophets of having prejudices! Yet it is difficult to ignore the fact that prophets could, on occasion, be extremely prejudiced as may be seen in a careful reading of Jer. 1–25. A classical example of a prophetic domain assumption must be Jeremiah's belief that *everybody* in Jerusalem and Judah was completely corrupt, wicked and incapable of becoming otherwise (Jer. 5.1–5; 6.13; 8.4–7; 9.4, 5 (Heb. 9.3, 4); 13.23). Now what kind of *evidence* could possibly be produced for such a belief? Not only was it based on presupposition rather than empirical evidence it was actually resistant to contrary evidence. For Jeremiah was often saved from near disasters by the intervention of such 'corrupt' people (26.24; 38.7–13, 14–28; 39.11–14). The recognition of such beliefs or prejudices in the prophets is more important than whether we call them theories, dogmas or domain assumptions. Their existence as part of the background of prophecy must be taken into account when interpreting the traditions.

The general beliefs of the prophets belonged to the common theology of the Ancient Near East.[12] Thus they believed in a deity active in history and saw in the political movements of their time the hand of Yahweh (cf. Isa. 10; Jer. 34; Ezek. 21; 28). This belief in a divine activity in history was common to most of the religions of the area and can be illustrated clearly from such sources as the Moabite Stone and the Esarhaddon treaties.[13] I mention this common belief to show the prophetic solidarity with ancient modes of thought – the content of their beliefs may have been distinctive but the structure was not. In so far as they differed from their contemporaries this would appear to have been in the general interpretation of phenomena, events and processes in relation to the worship of Yahweh. Extrapolating from the prophetic critique it may be surmised that contemporary Israelites and Judaeans had a syncretistic religious outlook, i.e. they worshipped and were loyal to Yahweh but often under the guise of forms derived from foreign cults or alongside of other gods. The prophets however had a rigid Yahweh alone outlook and did not tolerate any obviously syncretistic understanding of Yahweh.

Although the prophets shared a common pattern of belief in divine activity in political history and so saw Yahweh as involved in or behind the rise and fall of the Assyrian and Babylonian empires it should be pointed out that there were other beliefs available in Israel which did not so read history or politics as the arena of divine activity. The wisdom literature depicts a view of the world which did not use such a motif. For the wise men Yahweh may have been present in the world in many subtle ways but he was not a manipulator of empires in relation to Israel, nor was he known by specific acts in the nation's past. I mention this alternative worldview in order to put on record the fact that such did exist and that modern problems with the prophetic belief in the myth of divine instrumentality are partly derived from a careful reading of the biblical text itself. The serious defects in the prophetic conviction about history and politics as the stage of divine operations will become clearer when we consider the problems of failed expectations and prophetic conflict.

A distinctive belief of the prophets was their conviction that they had been called and commissioned as prophets (Isa. 6.1–8; Jer. 1.1–10; Ezek. 1–3; Amos 7.14, 15). As Lindblom observes 'the prophets claimed to be considered as authoritative messengers from Yahweh bringing forth a divine proclamation. The certainty of being sent by God is everywhere a characteristic element in the self-consciousness of men and women who belong to the prophetic type.'[14] Their apperception of their own preaching was that it was inspired by Yahweh and that therefore no distinction could be made between the word of the prophet and the word of Yahweh. That this was the case is clearly established in the oracles and statements throughout the traditions, but it was to pose some fearful problems for the later stages of Judaean prophecy. For the authority of the prophet inherent in this apperception was inevitably bound to conflict occasionally with other figures of authority in society, e.g. priest and wise man (cf. Isa. 5.18–23; Jer. 8.8–12).[15] Furthermore the inevitable subjectivism implied by private inspiration was to become a dominant factor in late seventh-century prophecy and any attempt to delineate the relationship between prophecy and society, or between prophecy and other social authorities, must take full cognizance of this problem. The unsatisfactory, even if inevitable, nature of the prophet's authority resting on his private experiences is not simply a matter of modern categories of thought being unsuitable for interpreting ancient data but is built into the very nature of prophecy itself. This is self-evident from the biblical accounts of prophetic polemics (see below ch. 6). If men may claim to be inspired by God and therefore equate what they say with the words of God then there will be no protection against any number of so inspired persons proclaiming any number of discrete, and even incompatible, messages in society. The question posed to prophecy is not a modern one but an ancient one given classical form by Zedekiah ben Chenaanah 'how did the spirit of Yahweh go from me to speak to you?' (I Kings 22.24). Attempts to answer that question became more hysterical as the state of Judah neared its political end (cf. Jer. 23.9–40; 27–29; Ezek. 13.1–14.11; Lam. 2.14).

It may not be out of place to say something here about prophecy in relation to the notion of covenant. The tendency of modern scholarship is to see the prophetic critique of society as a critique of a society that had broken the divine covenant made at Sinai.[16] This

may be a fair reading of the late seventh-century prophets such as
Jeremiah and Ezekiel but even a cursory reading of the eighth-
century prophets will show a complete absence of the term 'covenant' and very little evidence implying the existence of such a
covenant. I am of the opinion that a further and deeper reading of
the evidence will confirm that impression. Covenant as a category for
describing the past history of the people of Israel in relation to
Yahweh seems to be most clearly expressed in Deuteronomy and it
was the deuteronomists who used covenant as a regulative principle.[17] The absence of covenant terminology or theology in the
eighth-century prophets is due to their not having had access to
categories not utilized until at least the following century. There is
little substance to the claim that the prophets used the theology of
covenant but not its terminology because they did not wish to
encourage wrong ideas associated with the covenant in the popular
mind. The eighth-century prophets showed no such reserve when
using metaphors drawn from the marital sphere to describe the
relationship between nation and Yahweh (cf. especially Hosea's use
of erotic language). Yet such ideas reflected the Canaanite fertility
cults and were drawn from the overcharged eroticism of that
religion. If such considerations did not prevent their use by the
prophets it is hardly likely that popular beliefs about covenant
would have prevented them using covenantal language.

The field of metaphor used by these prophets was that of familial
and personal relationships (e.g. Isa. 1.2–4; 30.1, 9; Amos. 3.2;
Hos. 1, 3; 11.1–4; 13.13). This relationship between Yahweh and
the people had been established at the time of the exodus and was
the most characteristic feature of Yahwism,[18] but the husband-wife
metaphor, found in Hosea and Jeremiah, would seem to have been
prophetic developments of that basic relationship. It has no necessary connection with covenant formulations.[19] The aggressive critique of society propounded by the prophets was essentially a spelling
out of the broken condition of that relationship – 'sons have I reared
and brought up, but they have rebelled against me' (Isa. 1.2); 'go
again, love a woman who is beloved of a paramour and is an
adulteress; *even as* Yahweh loves the people of Israel' (Hos. 3.1).
Broken relationships are entities that can be repaired and made
whole again. Now if repentance was an important feature of
prophecy, and many scholars would assert that it was, then the call

to turn from rebellion and to return to Yahweh (Jer. 3.22; 4.1; cf.
15.19) was the prophetic attempt to repair such broken relationships. If, on the other hand, it is insisted that covenantal theology
played a large part in prophetic thinking then there was no ground
at all for such an attempt. The extra-biblical sources for treaties
clearly show that breaches of the obligations laid down in the
agreements entailed summary punishment of a catastrophic nature.
The notion of repentance does not belong to a covenant paradigm at
all! The broken covenant meant the *end* of the covenant.[20] Thus
covenant was too rigid a concept for the prophets to have worked
with and we should see in their proclamation of a possible change of
direction (cf. Isa. 1.16, 17; Amos 5.14, 15, 21–24) a flexibility
drawn from human and social relationships rather than political-
juridical treaties. The most I am asserting here is that covenant as an
ideological factor was not used by the eighth-century prophets and I
leave open the possibility that various covenants may have been
known to the prophets (e.g. agreements between clans or between
communities and their kings). It was not until the late seventh
century, at least, that the deuteronomists created a covenant paradigm as an overview of the history of Israel.
    So in my reading of the prophetic traditions covenant was not one
of the prophetic domain assumptions. This diversionary discussion
of covenant has been necessary in order to rule out an inflexible
category that would not have permitted the very important prophetic motifs of repentance and a future hope to have been fully
utilized. It also has allowed some emphasis to be given to the
personalist field of metaphor used by the prophets as the basis of
their preaching.

The dialectic of prophecy. I use the term dialectic to describe the
positive and negative attitudes to society expressed by the prophetic
oracles. Although the term has become rather vacuous in modern
usage it is used here as a term of convenience. Its original use in
Greek philosophy referred to reasoned argument, particularly of
the question and answer type. In pre-Socratic times it related to the
tension between opposites (especially in Heraclitus) and allowed
for dialogical discussion. It also could describe the Socratic mode of
reasoning by questioning and was used by Plato and Aristotle as
part of their philosophical methods. In medieval scholasticism

dialectic mainly referred to logic. Fichte introduced the thesis-antithesis-synthesis triad into modern philosophy and was followed in this by Schelling (contrary to popular belief Hegel did not actually use this particular triad!). Transformations of the dialectic are to be found in Kant and Hegel. Karl Marx's inversion of the Hegelian dialectic produced dialectical materialism.

In the thought of Kierkegaard dialectic as the tension between opposites was introduced into theology and dialectical theology has become a very important part of twentieth-century theological thought. In Barth's early theology dialectic means working with opposites and his great stress is on the yes and no of God to man.[21] For my purposes the prophetic proclamation can be seen as a dialectic of yes and no to Israelite society. There was therefore a dialectical tension between positive and negative analyses of the community in which it is often difficult to decide whether the material involves a genuine dialectic or is merely paradoxical. The use of the term allows for an analysis of prophetic preaching that highlights a major feature of prophecy as a predictive critique of the community.

A reading of the traditions associated with Amos, Hosea, Isaiah, Micah, Jeremiah and Ezekiel reveals quite clearly the twofold aspect of their preaching. Many oracles, indeed the bulk of their work, were proclaimed against their society depicting it as a corrupt, oppressive and unjust community. Judgment was declared against that society in no uncertain terms. Judgment of a catastrophic nature which would reduce land and people to ruins and decimation (e.g. Isa. 1.7–9; 6.11, 12; Amos 7.7–9; 8.1–3; 9.1–4; Hos. 10.13–15; Micah 1–3; Jer. 4.18–26; 15.5–9; Ezek. 9). The detailed analyses of the corruptions of society provided the grounds for such devastations (Isa. 2.6–11; 3.9–15; Amos 2.6–12; 4–6; Jer. 2–9). These announcements of broken relationships, corrupt practices and imminent disasters represented the negative pole of prophecy, its NO to Israelite society. Proclaimed as the word of Yahweh against his people it was the NO of God against the community.

The positive pole of the dialectic is more problematic. Running through the prophetic traditions are a number of oracles of a decidedly positive nature. They are salvationistic in tone and proclaim a future determined by well-being and prosperity (cf. Isa. 2.2–4; 4; 9.2–7 (Heb. 9.1–6); 11.1–9; 12; 40–55;

Amos 9.11–15; Hos.2.14–23 (Heb.2.16–25); Micah 4.1–4; 5;
Jer.23.5, 6; 31; 33; Ezek.34; 36; 37). They indicate that the
prophets also envisaged a future time when the devastations
suffered would be reversed and both land and people would enjoy
peace and prosperity. Taken at face value the expectations
represented the positive aspect of the dialectic, the YES of
prophecy to the community. And therefore the YES of Yahweh for
his people.

The strong tensions within the traditions of judgment (negative)
and salvation (positive) warrant the description of the prophetic
preaching as dialectic. Showing that the two elements were both
part of the same prophetic proclamation, particularly in the eighth-
century prophets, constitutes a serious problem for the analysis of
prophecy. If both elements belonged together and were not contradictions within the prophetic thinking then their dialectical status
may be sustained. In order to sustain that it has to be shown that
both elements subsisted together for specific prophets and were not
a second order dialectic provided by later tradents.

Various solutions have been suggested for relieving the tensions
created by attributing judgment and salvation announcements to
the one prophet. One main approach is to delete all salvation
oracles in the eighth-century prophets as secondary (editorial)
material (i.e. Amos 9.11–15; Isa.2.2–4 (= Micah 4.1–4); 4; 9.2–7;
11.1–9; Micah 5).[22] This would effectively deny the description of
these prophets as dialectical figures. They announced an impending
judgment that was virtually inevitable. Thus Amos announced the
lament 'Fallen, no more to rise, is the virgin Israel' (5.2). Their
analysis of society convinced them that it was too late for a corrupt
people to be saved from disaster. It is immaterial whether the
oracles of salvation were added to their collected sayings by their
followers or the cult officials who may have had a hand in the
preservation of the oracles or even by later theologians seeking to
make them relevant for new generations.[23] I will not deny that there
is a case to be made out along these lines which would exclude the
dialectical tension between judgment and salvation as an authentic
element in eighth-century prophecy but it is not one which I feel
really gets to grips with the nature of dialectical prophecy. I grant
that there are obvious secondary additions in Isaiah, e.g. 4; 12;
possibly 2.2–4; 11.1–9; perhaps 9.2–7, and possibly Amos

9.11–15; Micah 5 but I think that a good case can be made out in the following way for maintaining that the eighth-century prophets (some of them at least) took a dialectical view of judgment and salvation.

If some of the salvation oracles are treated as genuine to the prophets in whose traditions they are found (e.g. Isa. 9.2–7) the surface tension of apparent contradiction could be relieved by the suggestion that the woe oracles and announcements of judgment were given in public to the community but the oracles and hints of future wellbeing were limited to the intimate associates of the prophet as private sayings.[24] Then it would have been a case of public doom and private hopes with a controlling hermeneutic (perhaps) explaining to the followers just how the two elements were to be related to one another. It is a seminal suggestion and could relieve some of the tension inherent in the traditions as they now stand.

A consideration of the oracles of Amos (leaving aside the vexed question of the authenticity of 9.11–15) shows that the prophet gave Israel very little hope for the future. The most that can be derived from his work is the possibility of divine grace: 'Seek good, and not evil, *that you may live*; and so Yahweh (the God of hosts) will be with you, as you have said. Hate evil, and love good, and establish justice in the gate; *it may be that Yahweh* (the God of hosts) *will be gracious to the remnant of Joseph*' (5.14, 15). The call to 'let justice roll down like waters, and righteousness like an everflowing stream' (5.24) may be of a piece with this possibility of grace. The command to change is there but there is no articulation of salvation or promise of wellbeing. The prophet left such possibilities barely open – but it cannot be denied that a hint was given, a future contingency mooted. The oracles of Amos the Judaean were limited to the northern kingdom but his theological centre was clearly Jerusalem (1.2).[25] So although he may have regarded salvation as a most unlikely eventuality for Israel he may not have been so negative in his outlook on Judah. We do not know. The addition in 9.11f. might point in that direction but without knowing the relation between the editor who appended it and the thought of Amos little more can be said of it.

That Hosea believed in a positive future for Israel would appear to be the case from 2.14–23, or at least the genuine elements in that

section, and possibly 6.1–3; 11.8, 9.[26] Hosea's hope for the future
was based on a very strong emotional conviction that because the
relationship between Israel and Yahweh was based on love there
would be no ultimate destruction of the people. There would be
serious trouble and many disastrous encounters with their enemies
(cf. 2.1–13 (Heb. 2.3–15); 9; 10) but the people would survive
because Yahweh's love for them was too strong to permit their
destruction. There was certainly a dialectic tension between punishment and salvation in Hosea's preaching even though we cannot
see how he resolved the tension.

Isaiah's appeal to the community 'Wash yourselves; make
yourselves clean; remove the evil of your doings from before my
eyes; cease to do evil, learn to do good; seek justice, correct oppression; defend the fatherless, plead for the widow' (1.16, 17) is
evidence that the prophet held out the possibility of change for the
community and that therefore his fierce attacks against injustice and
oppression did not necessarily mean that destruction was inevitable.
In the exchanges with Ahaz (7.1–17) the possibility of salvation was
held out so again we must recognize that Isaiah maintained an open
outlook on the direction the future might take. Whether he ever
resolved this dialectic of judgment and salvation remains an open
question but for the moment the relevant concern is just showing
that such a dialectic did belong to some of the eighth-century
prophets.

The importance of the cult for prophecy has already been
asserted and its role has some bearing on this issue of expectations
of salvation in the prophets under consideration. The cult was the
place where the kingship of Yahweh was celebrated (cf. Isa. 6.1–4),
where Israel's saviour God was encountered. There the sacral traditions of Yahweh's acts of vindication on behalf of his people were
preserved and regularly commemorated. The fact that Isaiah was
associated with the temple to some degree must strengthen the
likelihood that he also believed (to a certain extent at least)
or shared in that salvation tradition.[27] His very name Isaiah
(*yĕšaʿyāhū*) carried the conviction of Yahweh as saviour. If the cult
had any involvement in the preservation of the prophetic oracles
then it is unlikely that it would have preserved purely negative
material. Judgment might have been a feature characteristic of the
temple cult but it was always judgment within the context of the

vindicating God of Israel. Whether that is an argument for Isaiah having originally included the possibility of salvation in his preaching or for the cult having edited his oracles to include such a motif that was found to be lacking in the first place I must leave open to debate. The matter will be raised again at a later stage in the book.

I think it is fair to say that the evidence for a dialectical factor in eighth-century prophecy is of the following order. For Amos it was an unarticulated possibility, for Hosea a definite conviction and for Isaiah a distinct possibility. Apart from the disputed authenticity of such passages as Micah 4.1–4; 5 Micah did not entertain any such hope for the nation. His view of the matter may be summarized in his assertion 'Zion shall be ploughed as a field; Jerusalem shall become a heap of ruins, and the mountain of the house a wooded height' (3.12). The four prophets would appear to have covered the spectrum of possibilities with their individual stances. The real force of the dialectic becomes clear when we attempt to work out how the trenchant predictions of doom uttered with such certitude by the prophets were to be reconciled with the much more modest hopes of prosperity. Working towards such a resolution of the dialectic will be one of the main strands of part three.

It has been necessary to devote some space to arguing for taking seriously the view that the prophetic preaching was dialectical in nature in order to make space for two further important considerations. One is a matter of major principle for the interpretation of prophecy, especially for the predictive aspect of prophecy. The second is a minor motif which became important for later prophecy and which may have something to contribute to resolving some of the dialectical tensions in the traditions. For the arguments of this book the principle of repentance is of fundamental importance and the motif of the remnant may provide some useful second order observations. Both ought to be touched on at this stage of the interpretative process.

Repentance. For Martin Buber the true prophet was the one who posed question and alternative to the community. There was no proclamation of an immutable decree but the prophet 'speaks into the power of decision lying in the moment, and in such a way that his message of disaster just touches this power. The unformulated primal theological principle of the Garden of Eden story about the

divine-human relationship, namely that created man has been provided by the Creator's breath with real power of decision and so is
able actually to oppose YHVH's commanding will – this mysterious
article of faith rises now to awfully practical force. The divine
demand for human decision is shown here at the height of its
seriousness. The power and ability are given to every man at any
definite moment really to take his choice, and by this he shares in
deciding about the fate of the moment after this, and this sharing of
his occurs in a sphere of possibility which cannot be figured either in
manner or scale. It is to this personal decision of man with its part in
the power of fate-deciding that the prophetic announcement of
disaster calls. The alternative standing behind it is not taken up into
it; only so can the prophet's speech touch the innermost soul, and
also be able to evoke the extreme act: the turning to God.'[28] This
turning (šūb) was the essence of the prophetic concept of repentance.

Stated in this way the prophetic proclamation becomes a moral
force seeking to change society in a particular way. The oracles of
doom may then be taken as analyses of the community aimed at
making the people turn *away* from their current social patterns and
turn *to* a different way of life that was appropriate to the familial
relationship between Yahweh and Israel. The summons to decision
became the driving force of prophecy and the terrible visions and
threats of destruction must then be seen as having been in the
service of that call to decision. The point of the denunciations of
Amos was to reinforce his invitation 'Seek Yahweh and live' (5.4, 6;
cf. 5.14, 24). Isaiah's analysis of the breakdown of society (3.1–12)
and indictment of corrupt practices (1.10–15, 21–23; 2.6–8;
3.13–15; 5.8–25; 9.8–21 (Heb.9.7–20); 10.1–4; 28.7–22) was
designed to shock the people into an awareness of their plight and to
drive them to repentance. Micah's denunciations of a corrupt leadership were also intended to have such an effect on the community
and a later generation understood his threats in such a way (cf.
Jer.26.17–19). This is an account of the matter which provides a
way of treating the dialectical tensions between salvation and judgment. Because the call to repentance allowed the possibility of
change being introduced into the community it also guaranteed the
moral freedom of that community and preserved in some sense the
sovereignty of Yahweh to withdraw the word of judgment.

The matter is more complicated than Buber's reading of prophecy suggests. It is very difficult to decide whether the eighth-century prophets voiced a clear appeal to repentance as a positive element of their preaching or even that it was an *implicitum* of their work.[29] Amos certainly accused the people of failing to return (4.6, 8, 9, 10, 11). Hosea probably thought that the community's wicked ways prevented them from returning (5.4) but may have held out some hope that after a period of punishment they would return to Yahweh (3.5).[30] If Micah offered any possibility of repentance it must have been either implicit in his oracles or such oracles have not survived. Isaiah may have spelled out the benefits of returning to Yahweh, 'In returning (*bᵉšūbāh*) and rest you shall be saved' (30.15), but he was equally certain that the people had refused to do so (30.15–17). Furthermore he later saw his mission as having been one of preventing the people from returning (6.10).[31]

The notion of turning, changing direction, making a decision, repentance or whatever it may be called did not have to be expressed solely in forms of the word *šūb*. The appeal to cease from evil in order to do good, to desist from oppression in favour of vindicating the oppressed, to seek Yahweh rather than the other gods or cults, to let justice roll like waters or to love kindness (*ḥesed*) all made the same challenge to turn from the community's current way of life to a different and proper form of living (Isa. 1.16, 17; Amos 5.4–7, 24; Micah 6.6–8). This much is clear from the eighth-century prophetic oracles. It has to be recognized that these prophets were generally sceptical that the community would so change. The corruption and injustice had become such a way of life that the community indulged itself in waywardness and was virtually incapable of changing (cf. Amos 4.4, 5, 6–12; 5.10–13; 8.7–10; 9.1–4; Isa. 3.9; 30.8–14). Such scepticism was unlikely to have spelled out the benefits of turning from evil in the glowing terms used in the various salvation oracles scattered throughout the prophetic traditions but I suppose that possibility should be allowed to stay on the books at the moment.

The seventh-century prophets, particularly Jeremiah, used the notion of repentance or turning from evil much more frequently than the earlier prophets but also maintained a similar sceptical view of the nation's capacity to respond to such a possibility (cf. Joel 2.12–14; Zeph. 2.3; Jer. 3.22; 4.1; 5.3; 8.4, 5). In Ezekiel's preaching there was a monotonous usage of the notion of either turning from evil or from good (e.g. 3.16–21; 14.6; 18.21–32). The deuteronomic editing of the book of Jeremiah also used the notion of returning to Yahweh frequently but in keeping with that school's approach to editing texts the motif had become a formal device for writing history. The regulative nature of the principle is made clear by the statement 'If at any time I declare concerning a nation or a kingdom, that I will pluck up and break down and destroy it, and if that nation, concerning which I have spoken, turns (*šāb*) from its evil, I will repent of the evil that I intended to do to it. And if at any time I declare concerning a nation or a kingdom that I will build and plant it, and if it does evil in my sight, not listening to my voice, then I will repent of the good which I had intended to do to it' (18.7–10).

This is a schematic organization of material which was to produce a mechanical account of history typified by the Chronicler's treatment of Manasseh's long reign as justified by an act of repentance (33.10–20; cf. II Kings 21.1–18).

The paradigm case of prophetic preaching of repentance that effectively warded off the threatened destruction is the book of Jonah.[32] But even that paradigm poses problems that will have to be examined at a later stage in this book. Ideas about repentance in the prophetic traditions though complex have a great bearing on the analysis of predictive prophecy. The origins of the notion of repentance being a sufficient response to the practice of evil are obscure and such a concept itself not at all easy to grasp.[33] It can hardly have been a legal doctrine for Israelite case law laid down fairly precise penalties for offences (e.g. Ex. 21–23). I suspect that it may have been a prophetic invention put forward as a last ditch possibility for a corrupt society and one which took until the deuteronomists to become a formal principle. The paucity of references to a positive view of repentance in the eighth-century prophets might have been due to reticence and a conviction that such gross social corruption had to be wiped out by disasters. The past was not to be entirely determinative of the future so they allowed a certain possibility of change. This possibility of openness towards the future became more formally articulated as the doctrine of repentance. As such it may provide a part resolution of the dialectic of judgement and salvation.

The remnant. But what might have been the synthesis of

catastrophic disaster (thesis) and possible salvation (antithesis)? The surface reading of the traditions as a totality might suggest that the synthesis was a devastated land reoccupied by deportees and a few remaining inhabitants awaiting the salvation of Yahweh. Such a group of survivors would be the remnant. The remnant then is the resolution of the dialectic. This makes for a neat reading of a patchwork of sources and it probably does represent the interpretation made of prophecy by later communities of Jews seeking to understand their own position in relation to the traditions. Outside the various secondary additions to the traditions it is very difficult to find this synthesis in the eighth-century prophets. To be sure a similar synthesis can probably be drawn from Jeremiah, Ezekiel and Second Isaiah but that would not resolve the dialectic in Amos, Isaiah or Micah.[34]

In Amos the remnant motif is purely a negative one, it was used by the prophet to indicate the scale of the disaster (3.12; 5.3), to assert complete destruction (1.8; 9.1), and to maintain that the remnant had no future meaning as a nation (4.1–3; 6.9, 10). Of course the prophets were not thinkers so neither articulation or consistency should be demanded of their oracles. The negativity of some of his statements may not have prevented Amos from entertaining a hope that the appeal to seek Yahweh and live might be responded to by some Israelites. However it is going far beyond the evidence of the text to claim that the remnant of Joseph would be the Israel of the day of Yahweh and would consist of those who had returned to Yahweh.[35] Even accepting the disputed text in 9.11, 12 as part of the genuine oracles of Amos would hardly provide sufficient evidence for such a claim. The most that can be derived from 9.11, 12 is that Amos shared Judah's view of itself and its monarchy as the rightful rulers of a vast territory. The old kingdom ('the booth of David') had never conceded much power to Israel (hence the disruption detailed in I Kings 12) so it is unlikely that a future restored kingdom would have modified the claims of the house of David in favour of an Israelite remnant. The oracle is more in keeping with the Judaean gloss of Hos. 3.5 than with the highly dialectical message of Amos.

The evidence in the Isaiah traditions for a remnant is rather ambiguous. That Isaiah had a negative view of the remnant is clear from 1.9 where the few survivors of the devastation of the land are addressed by an oracle beginning 'Ah, sinful nation, a people laden with iniquity, offspring of evildoers, sons who deal corruptly!'. This to the so-called 'holy seed' (cf. 6.13c) as remnantalists insist on calling Isaiah's positive doctrine of the remnant! If judgment distinguished between Judah and the cities of the plains (Sodom and Gomorrah) only in terms of a few survivors then Isaiah can hardly have maintained a remnant doctrine wherein there would be a nucleus of faithful Yahwists distinguishable from the seed of evil-doers (1.4 *zera' m^{e}rē'im*). This points to the main difficulty with the remnant concept: how to identify it in actual historical terms (rather than in ideological or theoretical terms). If Isaiah did entertain a positive notion of a remnant at what stage in the experiences of Judah in his time could the remnant be pointed to in the community? Did the survivors of the Assyrian onslaught of 701 constitute that remnant? Hardly likely if 1.4–9 was addressed to those survivors. If a second Assyrian onslaught resolved by the miracle of II Kings 19 is posited then was the delivered community of that period the remnant?[36] Surely Manasseh's Jerusalem was not the referent of Isa. 4.2–6? As each generation of seventh-century Judah is paraded we are forced, like Samuel, to say 'Yahweh has not chosen this one'. What then was the prophet talking about? That is the crux of this whole remnant discussion in modern biblical scholarship. In order to make sense of it some scholars are forced to discern two remnants – the remnant mentioned in various statements in Isaiah and a further *eschatological* remnant arising out of that first remnant.[37]

The references to a remnant in Isa. 4.2–6; 10.20–23; 11.11–16; 28.5, 6 are probably better seen as secondary material used in the editing of Isaiah by later tradents holding a positive doctrine of the remnant.[38] The phrase 'the holy seed is its stump' in 6.13c poses a serious problem of attribution. It could belong to the oracle or be a later gloss. If taken as genuinely Isaianic then it must be associated with the prophet's conviction that after terrible destruction something positive will survive. As an unarticulated statement it is impossible to develop its implications. Isaiah's son's name Shear-yasub (7.3) has been seen by many as further evidence for a positive remnantal belief in that its meaning 'a remnant shall return' explicitly points to the remnant motif. A name and an obscure final phrase hardly amount to a positive doctrine though both are obscure and ambiguous enough to permit major eisegetical readings.

The language of 4.2–6; 10.20–23; 11.11–16; 28.5, 6; is sufficiently distinctive to be considered secondary reconstructions of Isaianic material. These reinterpretative elements will be considered more fully in chapter 4. This largely negative treatment of the remnant in Isaiah is partly caused by the difficulty of showing a coherent account in the traditions of the relation between the prophetic demand for turning from evil and the remnant as such a group of changed people. The son's name only asserted that some would survive, it carried no further information about the status of those survivors. If those survivors turned to Yahweh from their wicked ways perhaps they would have been saved (cf. 30.15). Isaiah certainly accepted the fact that there were survivors of the catastrophe (1.9) but to equate those survivors with a positive nucleus for salvation is to go far beyond the warrant of the texts. This is a crucial point for the understanding of eighth-century prophecy having had a sharp moral thrust in the community. That Isaiah believed the faithless city would eventually be redeemed seems clear (cf. 1.21–26) though he may not have retained that belief all his life (cf. 30.8–14, 15–17). The problem of the dialectic is getting from that insistence that change is necessary to the hope that city and people will be redeemed in the future. A coherent account of the remnant might well resolve the dialectical tension but it is far from clear that Isaiah of Jerusalem provided such a coherent account.

As the subsequent experience of first Israel and then Judah was one of destruction and deportation the notion of what was left became increasingly important. This may be seen in the editing processes of the book of Isaiah. The remnant came to be seen as the object of Yahweh's salvation. A salvation not made dependent upon repentance. In so far as the remnant motif had any moral dimension it presumably involved the notion that the exile (or a similar period of destruction and deportation) had constituted sufficient punishment for offences committed (cf. Isa. 4.4; 40.2; 46.3, 4). Such a notion lacks the particularity of each person turning from his or her own wicked ways and tends to assume that survival is the equivalent to expiation or repentance. Although such a view of the remnant is especially associated with the Isaiah traditions it does appear in some of the later prophets (cf. Jer. 23.3; Hag. 2.2; Zech. 8.6; also in Micah 7.18).

Neither Jeremiah or Ezekiel appears to have believed in a

remnant as such though both prophets believed in a future for the community, a future in some sense ruled over by a member of the house of David (cf. Jer.23.5, 6; 31.17, 31–34; Ezek.11.14–21; 34.20–24; 37). For them the term remnant indicated the survivors of the nation after the various Babylonian attacks (cf. Jer.39.10; 40.6; Ezek.11.13). In one vision Ezekiel did make a distinction between the good and the bad in Jerusalem so that the righteous were spared and the wicked killed (9.3–6) but this in no way constituted a righteous remnant being saved from the catastrophe which destroyed the wicked (the opposite view would appear to have been current in Jerusalem cf. 11.15!). For Ezekiel did not have a coherent view of what the impending disaster would entail for the wicked or the righteous. In one place he allowed the righteous to escape (9.4–6), in another one-third of the wicked escape death by being scattered (5.12 cf. 6.8–10) and in yet a third place he has the deity kill both the righteous and the wicked (21.2–4). Such a prodigality of options hardly allows the modern interpreter sufficient data for establishing a coherent account of what the prophet thought on that particular subject.

A good deal of space has been devoted to discussing the two motifs of repentance and the remnant. Yet they are very important aspects of the dialectic of prophecy and will figure largely in this account of the predictive element in the prophetic traditions. Some of the difficulties involved in interpreting this dialectic must be apparent by now. The bulk of the material in the prophets from Amos to Ezekiel is quite clearly negative, but there are some positive elements, elements which assumed greater importance in some of the cult prophets and particularly in Second Isaiah and the post-exilic prophets. Both the negative and positive elements had their counterparts in the cultic view of the community but whereas the cult possessed techniques and rituals of expiation and purification prophecy only had its insistence on the necessity of changing attitudes and practices. In the long run the doctrine of repentance failed to change the community sufficiently for it to avoid the disasters of invasion and destruction. In the subsequent reconstructed community of the fifth century contemporary prophecy had little part to play. The dialectic had ceased to be a vital force in the community. So the traditions of the prophets were edited, preserved and utilized in the subsequent centuries of the Jewish community in and around Jerusalem. In such activity we may discern a belief that the dialectic had worked and might yet still work.

Predicting the future. If the critique of society was the fundamental activity of the prophets then the predictive element in their preaching could be regarded as secondary. However many of the oracles criticizing the community included threats and warnings that associated the corruption of society with the impending doom announced. There was in the prophetic critique a causal connection between the coming disaster and the people's behaviour. Therefore many of the oracles were predictive in nature, or, at least, contained a predictive element as part of the social analysis. The accounts of prophecy given by the deuteronomic historians included the notion of history as the unfolding of the prophetic word (I Samuel – II Kings). Such statements as 'and Samuel grew, and Yahweh was with him and let none of his words fall to the ground. And all Israel from Dan to Beer-sheba knew that Samuel was established as a prophet of Yahweh' (I Sam. 3.19, 20), and 'Now Elijah the Tishbite, of Tishbe in Gilead, said to Ahab, "As Yahweh the God of Israel lives, before whom I stand, there shall be neither dew nor rain these years, *except by my word*"' (I Kings 17.1), clearly show the importance attached by the historians to the fulfilment of the prophetic word. The regulation of prophecy in the seventh century by Deuteronomy included the coming to pass of the word spoken by the prophet as a mark of the authentic prophet (18.21, 22). An important part of Second Isaiah's proclamation was the belief that Yahweh knew the future and this knowledge distinguished him from the other gods (41.21–24; 44.7, 24–26; 45.21; 46.9, 10; 48.3–8; cf. 55.10, 11). The relationship between Yahweh and his prophet was such that the prophet could assert 'I am Yahweh . . . who confirms the word of his servant, and performs the counsel of his messengers' (44.24, 26). There can be little doubt that the biblical traditions reflect a firm belief that the prophet was capable of predicting the future. Such a belief was also characteristic of later periods and has passed into popular beliefs about prophets in general as foretellers of the future.

The notion of predicting the future raises a number of problems of understanding for us. What is meant by predicting the future? What in fact is meant by the future? Does the future as such exist?

Can men predict the future? If men *can* predict the future what is so
special about biblical prophecy? These questions pose difficulties
for the interpreter of prophecy that are both philosophical and
theological. It is a commonplace of criticisms of the historical critical approach to biblical studies that it operates with an *a priori*
rejection of the possibility of predictive prophecy.[39] Some scholars
may operate with such an *a priori* but many scholars certainly do
not. The issue is a good deal more complicated than the accusations
of concealed *a prioris* would lead one to expect. Without digressing
too far I must touch on some of these problems in order to clarify
certain aspects of understanding the prophetic traditions and also to
discuss the predictive element which is so seldom examined in
treatments of biblical prophecy.

The question about the future is not an easy one. Augustine had
great difficulties understanding what time was, particularly the
status of the future.[40] For him the future did not exist yet it was
possible to think and talk about it. There could be expectations of
the future, expectations foretold from things which are present but
what does not exist cannot be revealed. To talk about the future as if
it existed is to reify an abstraction. To talk about predicting the
future then has to be carefully qualified so as not to indulge in such
reification.

One's model of the universe is an important feature of the discussion at this stage. If the universe is conceived of as a block universe
then its future can be known. The analogy here is that of a cinema
screen on which is projected the film. As the film is projected the
audience witness its contents unfolding relative to their own time –
the events on the film are all in the past but they are also in the
audience's future. In such a deterministic universe it is possible to
know and predict the future. But if a different model is used then
this analogous possibility must be discarded.

Yet the behaviour of the physical world can be predicted. If
calculus is applied to the smooth motions of the earth, sun and moon
the next eclipse of the sun can be accurately predicted. This
achievement of modern physics would appear to be a case of regular
successful prediction of future events. Of course it is based upon
mathematical calculations, careful observations and involves knowing the paths of particular bodies and particles so as to be able to
predict precisely where they are all going to be at any time in the

future. In physics the future of certain things can be known because general rules apply and prediction entails extending lines from the present to any number of points along such extensions. In this context the past determines the present which determines the future because of the stability and regularity of the system which is the universe.

In certain senses human societies may generally be described in terms of a present determined by factors in the past and of having a future that will be determined by the present. But only in the most general terms and in ways seldom susceptible to accurate prediction. In spite of millennia of attempts to predict or forecast the future human groups have seldom successfully gathered together all the variables of individual and group possibilities, discerned which invariables were involved and made the correct predictions. It is obviously possible for people to attempt to predict the future but the marked lack of success of such attempts hardly indicates a particular human aptitude for successful predicting of the future. Primitive systems of divination, witchcraft and astrology testify to the human concern with knowing the future. Modern society depends largely on the ability of social scientists to forecast future trends in order to plan complex movements of urban and industrial expansion, economic growth and social mobility. But such forecasts depend upon extrapolating from present data factors which are then assumed to be invariables of the future. This 'art of conjecture' as it has been called is familiar to most people and much of the blight of modern life is ample evidence of how inaccurate it can be.[41]

The findings of research in parapsychology suggest that some individuals may be capable of clairvoyance or possess extra-sensory perception. The precise relationship of such findings to the human ability to predict the future is not yet clear. It may be strictly irrelevant in relation to predicting events or it may prove to be an interesting anomaly but beyond any rational control. There is great difficulty in pinning down this material as it tends to be very vague and indefinite. But allowing for the possibility that some people, under less than strict conditions, may be able to see things that are about to happen, i.e. premonitions, also raises some problems for biblical prophecy. For if we assume that there are some grounds for believing that it is within human capacity to predict accurately (even if only on occasion) the immediate future then we have a naturalistic explanation for prophecy. In being open to the possibility of living in a more complex universe than the sceptic permits we have also removed the need for the prophet's attribution of his ability to a transcendental source.

The possibility of accurately forecasting the immediate future is only part of the larger issue of prediction. A very important aspect of the subject is the effect of any prediction on the person or group to whom it is addressed. Prediction is not an isolated activity independent of human response. The human response is fundamentally a part of the prediction. Thus a prediction may be ignored, acted upon or counteracted by its recipients. Such responses can have very significant consequences for predictions. Predictions may be of the self-fulfilling type in which the prophet ensures the accuracy of his prediction by fulfilling it himself (cf. Isa. 7.14; 8.3) or it is deliberately fulfilled by somebody who hears the prediction (cf. Macbeth's response to the predictions of the three witches). One might call this the Turnbull effect after Anthony Trollope's character of whom he wrote: 'Mr Turnbull had predicted evil consequences, both in the House and out of it, and was now doing the best in his power to bring about the verification of his own prophecies.'[42] It is a very common phenomenon. On the other hand a prediction might have the effect of causing people to do the opposite in order to frustrate it (cf. Jonah's fleeing to Tarshish) or reacting in such a way as to render it inoperative. Suppose Cassandra had specified that Troy would fall when a wooden horse was brought within its walls. The Trojans, had they believed her, would have left the horse outside the city and her prediction would have been falsified. Then a supposedly 'necessary' event would not have taken place and that implies a logical contradiction.[43] A prediction can have the opposite effect if people attempt to create the opposite. An example of this might be seen in the attempt by Haggai and Zechariah to make one of Coniah's descendants the anointed king in spite of Jeremiah's prediction that Coniah's descendants would not succeed to the throne (cf. Hag. 2.20–23; Zech. 4.6–10; 6.10–14; Jer. 22.28–30). Their failure confirmed Jeremiah's prediction but falsified their own!

G. K. Chesterton defined one of the games people play as 'Cheat the Prophet'. 'The players listen very carefully and respectfully to all that the clever men have to say about what is to happen in the next generation. The players then wait until all the clever men are dead, and bury them nicely. They then go and do something else. That is all.'[44] In spite of Chesterton's typical form of overstatement the notion of cheating the prophet does illustrate the principle of predictions having such effects on the events of which they are predictions that we should see predictions as being part of a complex process involving reciprocation and feedback. These facets of response (intentional and otherwise) may be termed the 'Oedipus effect'.[45] Oedipus knowing that he was supposed to kill his father and marry his mother took steps to avoid such terrible actions but only succeeded in achieving them. The knowledge of the predictions became a necessary part of the fulfilling of them. Thus prediction can be the cause, in some sense, of the event it predicts. The Oedipus effect can be seen in modern society in such self-fulfilling predictions as 'it is not safe to go out on the streets at night', 'if the blacks get into a neighbourhood the value of property there will plummet', or 'if any more immigrants are allowed into the country there will be bloodshed'. By suggesting the reactions such predictions help to create them. Thus predicting the future can be an attempt to create that future. A very complex network of factors is involved in the primary arousal of predictions and in the social responses to such forecasts.

Prophetic predictions. All these factors have direct bearing on the interpretation of biblical prophecy. If people can predict the future and regularly do so with varying degrees of success it would be uncritical and irrational to deny the same possibilities to the prophets. However because there is a complex relation between prediction and its fulfilment the prophet should be seen as attempting to create certain responses in the community. When that attempt failed, as often it did for all the prophets, it was more a case of failing to persuade the community to change than of the failure of prediction. Thus the prophet was a creative force in society. To analyse such a force purely in terms of prediction-fulfilment paradigms may be to miss the proper dimension of prophecy in ancient Israel. It is, of course, what the traditions did with prophecy but such traditions were governed by other considerations of function for subsequent generations and therefore need not be regarded as the most perceptive commentators on prophecy.

Biblical prophecy included divination of the future by means of inspiration and observation. Its sources are never presented as simply naturalistic but always in terms of divine transcendence in which the prophet as messenger was sent to proclaim the given word for specific occasions. The prophet announced the judgment of Yahweh against a community for various breaches of just relationships within that society. That judgment usually consisted of dire threats against the continued well-being of the people and their land. If that threat failed to materialize then the prophet could be said to have been wrong. Such is essentially the problem of unfulfilled predictions. But it is much more complicated than that. Only a naive biblicistic outlook could possibly treat the matter in such unreflective terms. The types of prediction and the structure of prophetic activity have to be clarified before it can be established that failure of prediction has occurred.

In the first place it must be admitted that the manuscripts of the prophetic traditions are centuries younger than the events discussed in those traditions. All such documents may represent *post eventum* statements and we have no controls by which we could guarantee that any predictive oracle was given before the events to which it referred. There is a fair amount of evidence in the literature of the Ancient Near East for the genre of *vaticinia ex eventu* 'predictions after the event'.[46] However if all the prophetic oracles were of this kind there would be no problem about lack of fulfilment. The presence of oracles lacking clear fulfilment is evidence against historical scepticism about some of the oracles, though not necessarily all of them.

The kinds of arguments used in some theological circles to secure the authenticity of prophecy as genuinely predictive and also as incapable of being wrong need not concern the argument here. They are based on a number of dogmatic positions that are not open for critical discussion. These positions include the notions that God knows the future, he reveals it to the prophets and as such the revealed word cannot be wrong. These archaic metaphors belong to a discarded form of theological discourse and raise far more problems than solutions for the understanding of prophecy. To equate *simpliciter* the words of men with the word of God is to saddle the deity with the errors of men. Talk about God knowing the future is unnecessary even for theological thought as process theology makes so clear.[47] The hermeneutical gymnastics required to give any coherence to the notion of God knowing and revealing the future in the form of predictions to the prophets does no religious community any credit. Furthermore the account of prophecy produced in such circles is banal beyond belief and on a footing with astrological charts and other such diversions of irrationalism.

An important feature of prophetic statements is the fact that they were inevitably short term in outlook. They were delivered to specific communities on specific occasions and therefore any expectations created by them could be confirmed or otherwise by the passage of time (cf. Deut. 18.21, 22). Any prophet whose words were not so confirmed encountered a good deal of scepticism from the public (cf. Isa. 5.19; Jer. 17.15). Later editing may have been designed to make prophecy relevant for another generation but the real impact of prophecy was in the immediacy of its proclamation.

A reading of the prophetic traditions will show that they have a great generality of language which often obscures more precise statements of what would constitute the fulfilment of such expectations in the first place. General oracles of woe or salvation can be found throughout the traditions and lack specificity (cf. Amos 9.11–13; Zephaniah). This generality of language makes it too difficult to show failure of expectations because any invading force or particularly good harvest would sufficiently meet the terms of the oracles. The sum total of all the metaphors and the rhetoric may be expressed much more simply: there will be a period of destruction or there will be a time of prosperous well-being. Where such is the case there can only be a vague approximation between language and event. Such vagueness will protect many oracles from outright failure.

There are also very many particular predictions in the traditions (e.g. Isa. 45.1, 13; Jer. 22.18, 19; Ezek. 26.7–14; Hag. 2.21–23; Zech. 4.9, 10; 6.10–14). Such specific statements do admit of failure or success. Many of the oracles against the nations (e.g. Isa. 13–19; Jer. 46–51; Ezek. 25–32) had specific objects of reference. If checks for fulfilment were limited to oracles of a specific nature it might be possible to work out which had been fulfilled, which had not and which were incapable of being verified or falsified due to lack of historical information.

This distinction between general and particular predictions is simply intended to make the analysis of prophecy more precise. A further refinement may be noted in the fact that the bulk of oracles directed against Judah and the nations concern destruction. This negative dominance in prophecy may be explained by the critical attitude the prophets took towards various communities. Furthermore in the geopolitical context of their activity the smaller nations were constantly vulnerable to the invasions of the larger imperial powers *en route* to Egypt or Assyria. The prophets did not make such connections but linked such inevitable invasions with their analyses of the corruption of the societies condemned by them. They were moralists who related impending disasters to oppression and injustice in the community. The success of their predicting disaster cannot be separated from the political context of their time. To what extent there was any actual connection between the immorality of their communities and the eventual destruction of those communities by the Assyrians and Babylonians is open to debate. I suspect that the causal connection made by the prophets cannot be sustained.[48] Small nations have always been subject to the whims of large nations. In this century Belgium has played the role that Israel played millennia ago. There is no evidence that the Belgians were more immoral than the Americans but Germany invaded Belgium not America. So with ancient Israel the prophetic critique of its wickedness leading to destruction was one of the domain assumptions of prophecy which cannot be empirically verified. It was the short-term good fortune of prophecy that its diagnosis of Israelite society should have been underwritten by the political expansionism of Assyria and Babylon but it had long-term deficiencies.

One grave deficiency of the prophetic critique was its inability to be as equally successful in prophesying salvation for the future. It is open to debate whether this failure should be attributed to the major prophets, i.e. Isaiah, Ezekiel and Jeremiah, or limited to the lesser prophets and the tradents who regularly worked over the traditions. But there are sufficient hints about the future in Jeremiah and Ezekiel (not to mention Second Isaiah) to involve them in this failure. Their ability to analyse their own period was not matched with a penetrating foresight which could anticipate the shape of the future and so their predictions for the post-catastrophe community were often banal and lacking in specific content. Part of the problem was the fact that the political organization of the Persian period differed so much from the Assyrian and Babylonian hegemonies that the prophets failed to make allowances for such changes. For them the future was really the past writ large with various contemporary defects removed from the community. As analysts of society they were the conscience of their time. As forecasters their visions were defective. But failure is a relative thing. In subsequent generations the visions of the prophets were to become the stimuli of many groups and in terms of seminal influences they were immensely important.

A final point about the nature of fulfilled predictions must be made in relation to the motif of repentance. In so far as the prophetic proclamation was conditional in its utterance it could hardly be said to have been a proper prediction. The call to turn from evil, to seek Yahweh or to return to him made the future of the community dependent upon what the people did not upon what the prophet said. The possibility hinted at by Amos 'Hate evil, and love good, and establish justice in the gate; it may be that Yahweh will be gracious (*'ūlay yeḥ'nan yhwh*) to the remnant of Jacob' (5.15) was not a prediction. No event was predicted by such invitations though there may have been an implicit 'but if you do not seek good then Yahweh will bring destruction upon you'. Thus the principle of repentance or turning can modify the prediction-fulfilment paradigm sufficiently for it to be unclear as to what precisely was being said. Later generations were able to account for failures in prophetic expectations by reference to repentance (Jer. 26.19). How the deity would act in the future was of course always beyond the prophet's prediction. If any emphasis is put on the transcendental element in prophecy then all predictions must be held to have been both conditional and open to being set aside by the deity. But to pursue that particular path is to run the risk of emptying prophecy of all content whatsoever.

Prophetic eschatology. If eschatology is understood in its literal sense as the doctrine of the last things, or the final things, or even the ultimate things then prophecy had no eschatology.[49] If eschatology is understood in a much weaker sense as talk about the future in terms extrapolated from the present and the past and indicative of a belief and a hope in the future then biblical prophecy had an

eschatological dimension.[50] This broader approach yields the
definition of eschatology as 'a vision of God's final provision for his
people, the farthest future of his dealings with them within history,
the definitive consummation of his purposes for them beyond which
no further development was envisioned or expected'.[51] It might be
more accurate to describe such beliefs as futurism or future hope so
as not to confuse prophetic motifs with later apocalyptic eschatology. Prophecy did not talk about the last things but about a day or
period in the near future when the present troubles would be over
and the more positive aspects of Israelite life would be enjoyed
without hindrance from any source. It was a fairly modest dream of
a small nation used to living on the periphery of the larger empires
and regularly subjected to invasion or the threat of invasion (cf.
Isa. 2.4; 9.5; Zech. 8.4, 5). The Davidic dynasty would still control
the fortunes of Judah, either a member of the dynasty as it was then
constituted or of the dynasty restored to its former proportions (cf.
Isa. 9.6, 7; 11.1–5; Jer. 23.5, 6 (33.14–26); Ezek. 34.23, 24;
Amos 9.11, 12; Micah 5.2–4 (Heb. 5.1–3)). Some of the hopes put
the emphasis on the temple rather than the dynasty (Isa. 2.2–4 =
Micah 4.1–4; Ezek. 40–48) and Second Isaiah appears not to have
had any place for the Davidic house (Isa. 55.1–5). The pictures of
the future also included a belief in the transformation of nature so
that there would be no more antagonism between men and animals
(Isa. 11.6–9; cf. Ezek. 34.25), incredible rates of productivity from
the land (Ezek. 36.30; Amos 9.13–15), and the desert would blos-
som (Isa. 35.1, 2). There would also be complete loyalty to Yahweh
(Jer. 31.31–34), a healing of the divisions between Israel and Judah
(Ezek. 37.15–23), and a sharing of power with the imperial powers
(Isa. 19.23–25). Various images of the future hope could be multi-
plied from the numerous oracles and fragments scattered throughout the prophetic traditions but what have been referred to are
sufficient to indicate the nature of the future hope.

The details of that future hope show that the prophets enter-
tained rather conventional expectations about the future. They
accepted the current view of the Davidic monarchy as the divinely
appointed source of authority in the community. Whatever defects
the dynasty might have had it still provided the model for the future.
Catastrophe might occur but after a period of suffering throne and
temple would constitute the centre of a renewed land and people.

Thus their hopes (in so far as we can discern these hopes as specifically prophetic) were a mixture of popular beliefs and transformational elements characteristic of the prophetic critique of society. The roots of such hopes were in the cultic view of reality. For part of the mythology of the cult in Jerusalem was the importance of the city as Yahweh's residence and the king as Yahweh's son (cf. Ps. 2; 45; 46; 48; 72; 110; 132).[52] The association between prophet and cult has already been noted and with the exception of Amos, the main traditions used by Isaiah belonged to the David-Zion cycle of traditions, as did those used by Jeremiah and Ezekiel (with the supplementation of the exodus traditions).[53] A good deal of the incidental images of the future was probably provided by later editors and cult prophets but it is unlikely that they distorted the original holdings of the prophets. Rather they expanded them along cultic lines so as to supplement the paucity of such references and to balance the substantial amount of critical oracles in the traditions. However it is no easy task to separate original vision from editorial addition and expansion.

If it is accepted that most of the prophets had a future hope and on occasion expressed such a hope in formal terms then it has to be admitted that their expectation was not realized historically. The state of Israel disintegrated under Assyrian pressure and the collapse of Judah in 587 meant the end of the Davidic dynasty. Attempts to revive that dynasty supported by the prophets Haggai and Zechariah came to nothing. The larger hopes for peace and prosperity also were substantially unrealized. The two nations did not merge but rather the survivors of both became more sharply separated. The only elements of the general hopes that could be said to have been realized in any sense were the survival of a community centred on Jerusalem and a rebuilt temple as its focus. It may be that originally the prophets despaired of the community ever achieving any level of independence of the Assyrian empire and so began to project their hopes beyond what they saw as a policy leading to disaster (cf. Isaiah confronting Ahaz in Isa. 7) to a time when a chastened community would come to its senses and devote itself entirely to the service of Yahweh. As it became steadily more apparent (in the days of Jeremiah) that Judah's scope for becoming independent was diminishing such hopes were pushed further into the future.[54] Of course they believed that eventually the deity would act on behalf of the community and make good these hopes (cf. Isa. 9.7), even after the disaster had occurred (cf. Isa. 37.30–32; Jer. 42.1–17). Unless that transcendental conviction was subject to the conditionality of community response it has to be admitted that their vision was mistaken. They do not appear to have considered the possibility that after catastrophe the surviving community might display all the faults of the pre-disaster period. However the very failure of prophecy was to become the necessary condition for the growth of subsequent movements of reinterpretation of the traditions. Such reinterpretative activities are the clearest evidence that the problem of unfulfilled predictions was recognized by the communities and that it was felt to be a serious flaw in the prophetic proclamation. Whether the original prophets were also aware of some of these problems is part of the inquiry of this book.

The status of the prophet

In spite of prophecy having been a widespread phenomenon in ancient society it is still necessary to ask after the status of the prophet within Israelite society. The important question here is: what legitimated a prophet for any given community? The question is set against a background of the acceptability of prophetic groups located at specific sanctuaries or in accredited coenobia but is directed to those prophets who periodically emerged as preachers of particular messages from the mid-eighth century onwards. What legitimated their messages? Did they derive their authority or acceptability from the prophetic communities well known in the district (cf. Elisha)? The incident in II Kings 9.1–13 suggests that that may have been the case for the earlier period. Such communities will have legitimated themselves over a lengthy period of time in particular regions. Associated with a notable leader, displaying the accompanying signs of prophecy (ecstatic behaviour cf. I Sam. 10.5–13) and making regular intrusions into society such prophets will have become accepted as weird but legitimate. They may have been regarded as 'mad' (cf. *mᵉšuggā'* II Kings 9.11; Hos. 9.7; Jer. 29.26) but their utterances were accepted as authoritative under certain conditions. Such social acceptance was conditioned by prevailing cultural norms many of which are now inaccessible to us because texts seldom convey the subtle interactions that constitute social relations in any society.

The prophet was a holy man honoured by the community and visited by individuals with requests for help (cf. I Sam. 9.5–21; 19.18–24; 28.8–14; II Kings 4; 5). Often he was an advisor of kings (II Sam. 7; I Kings 1.11–14, 22–27, 32–48). Over centuries such roles will have become fixed points in society though each individual prophet may well have had to earn his reputation as a particularly effective prophet.[55] Elements of this need may be seen in the account of Samuel's developing reputation in I Sam. 3. The young Samuel emerged as a prophet after the reception and delivery of a specific message (vv 2–18). As he grew older the continued reception of messages and their confirmation proved that he was a genuine prophet (vv 19–21). The account is essentially an ideal one included by the deuteronomistic historians reflecting their ideas about what constituted a prophet. Similar features may be seen in the account of the call of Moses which displays features of the prophetic call.[56] In Ex. 3, 4 Moses is called by Yahweh and a number of signs are carried out by him in order to confirm the truth of his call and to provide models for his future work. Thus for the major editors of the biblical traditions the performance of signs and the relation between word and its fulfilment were legitimating aspects of prophecy. Of course these are neat, tailored accounts in line with certain beliefs about prophecy but some such relation between word and event was required to establish a prophet. Without such a relation it is very difficult to see how any particular prophet could have become established in the community. Only by showing a distinct connection between his proclamation and the subsequent development of events for the community could a prophet hope to create for himself a specific identity and reputation for reliability.

Whatever the relation between the canonical prophets (i.e. the named prophets of the Amos, Isaiah, Hosea, Micah, Jeremiah, Ezekiel and other traditions) and the sons of the prophets (*b⁽nē hann⁽bî'îm*), or the cult prophets, or the court prophets may have been the call motif came to be seen as very important. Thus the response of Amos to Amaziah's criticism stressed the fact of his call. 'Then Amos answered Amaziah, "I am no prophet, nor a prophet's son; but I am a herdsman, and a dresser of sycamore trees, and Yahweh took me from following the flock, and Yahweh said to me, 'Go, prophesy to my people Israel'." (7.14, 15). The vexed problem of determining the precise meaning of the phrase *lō'-nābî'*

'ānōkî wᵉlō' ben-nābî' 'ānōkî indicates something of the ambiguity
of prophetic speech. It may be taken as 'I *am* not a prophet', or 'I
was not a prophet' (but now am one), or 'am I not a prophet?', or
even as an emphatic 'I *am* a prophet'.[57] Amos could point to a
specific experience which accounted for his presence in Bethel.
Similar call experiences appear in the traditions of Isaiah, Jeremiah
and Ezekiel as well as those of Moses and Samuel. Whether every
prophet had such a call or only those for whom there is posited a call
in the texts is open to question. We do not know what made a cult
prophet, i.e. whether he attached himself to a sanctuary and went
through a specific training which equipped him to be such a prophet
or whether he also was required to produce evidence of a call. This is
an area of prophecy that we know very little about and therefore our
knowledge of what legitimated the prophet is defective.

In the process of preaching the prophet will have gained the
attention of the authorities in society (assuming he was not a
member of such strata by birth or profession) and also have
attracted some following among those who heard him. The
significant details of the interaction between prophet and listeners
are not known to us, but we may make some observations that may
not be too wide of the mark. A prophet's ability to express his
visions in powerful language (rhetoric) that knitted together observation, experience and insight with analysis of the contemporary
fortunes of his community will have commended him as a prophet to
some in that community. This poetic power of expression (see
especially Isaiah and Jeremiah) allied to the ability to translate his
words into dramatic actions (cf. Isa. 8.1–4; 20.2–5; Jer. 13.1–11;
19; 27; Ezek. 4; 5) was the prophet's main resource for persuading a
community to heed him. Such ability was set in a society familiar
with the prophetic mode and already possessing beliefs and traditions with which to assess the prophet. Confirming signs may or may
not have accompanied the prophetic proclamation (cf. Isa. 7.11, 14;
20.3) but signs in themselves were of little value. The regulation of
prophecy in Deut. 13.1–5 recognized that the fulfilment of a predicted sign should not be taken as the authentication of a prophet.
The content of the message was paramount for determining the
authenticity of the speaker (cf. the duplication of signs by the
Egyptian magicians in Ex. 7.14–8.19).

There is some evidence in the traditions for the existence of followers of particular prophets. The clearest example is Isaiah. There is reference to his disciples (*limmudîm* 8.16), though these could have been his followers or his children (cf. 7.3; 8.18), and also to his support from at least two reliable people in Jerusalem society, Uriah the priest and Zechariah ben Jeberechiah (8.2). As their support was given to a specific predictive activity it indicates an approval of Isaiah as a reliable prophet. There is a good deal of evidence in Jeremiah for social support of the prophet. The support may not have come from followers but it certainly came from important people in the community – Baruch the scribe, the powerful family of Shaphan and, on occasion, the king himself (cf. 26.24; 36; 38.14–28). The fact that Jeremiah survived a career characterized by strife and contention (15.10) and lived to be old whereas the prophet Uriah, who proclaimed a similar harsh message (26.20–23), was extradited from Egypt and executed by the king indicates that Jeremiah had effective support in high places. Without such support it is difficult to see how the prophet would have survived his differences with so many authorities. The support may not have constituted discipleship (there is a fine distinction between support and agreement) but it did give the prophet's message some standing in the community. Without some social elements responding to the prophet's preaching a prophet would have had little legitimate status in society.

A further element of this support must have been the survival, maintenance and transmission of the various prophetic oracles. For a prophet's words to have survived his death by many centuries surely indicates that somebody or some group or institution was prepared to maintain and transmit them for various reasons. Again we do not know why or how this came about. If a prophet had followers then they would have been responsible for recording and handing on his oracles. But such a practice would have required a continual succession of such followers to go on maintaining the tradition (i.e. a school). Unless at some stage the collection had become significant enough to be taken over by the temple authorities, members of the temple staff or some body or school of theologians. In the case of Jeremiah it is fair to say that the deuteronomists were able to use his work to illustrate their thesis about the relation between history and prophecy. So his oracles were preserved, edited and expanded in an enlarged edition representing the triumph of the deuteronomistic programme of prophetic history in the closing decades of Judaean history. In the case of the cult prophets, e.g. Habakkuk, Joel, Nahum and Obadiah, it may be surmised that the temple cult, or the cult prophets in the temple, preserved their work. The importance of the temple in post-exilic society probably had much to do with the survival of collections of prophetic oracles. For other prophets among the twelve, e.g. Amos, Hosea, Micah, we do not know why they survived or who maintained their oracles. The traditions of Isaiah and Ezekiel have been enlarged greatly in the course of their transmission. The Ezekiel material probably was maintained by priestly groups, particularly those interested in programmes of restoration after the exile. The Isaiah traditions present an example of the growth of traditions by accumulation and a multiplex reinterpretative process. The basic core of Isaiah of Jerusalem's work was reinterpreted at various periods (e.g. 24–27) and then supplemented by 40–55 and later 56–66. Again we must assume that Isaiah's original vision was such that groups deliberately maintained it by adding further insights to it over a lengthy period of time.

The maintenance of the traditions cannot be separated from the belief that the prophetic works so maintained were important to the community and that they represented the work of legitimate prophets. The essentially negative visions of Amos, Isaiah, Micah, Jeremiah and Ezekiel had been confirmed by the disasters that befell Israel and Judah. They were therefore authentic prophets. The maintenance of collections of their oracles with added oracles of salvation spelling out the hints already found in the original oracles may have been designed to keep alive hope for the future of the hard pressed community living in the period of reconstruction. Perhaps by an inductive argument it was hoped that the positive aspects of prophecy would be equally confirmed as the negative aspects had been (cf. Isa. 55.10, 11).

An account, therefore, of the status of the prophet would have to be an interactionist one. A subtle blend of factors and circumstances relating to the techniques and message of the prophet, his reading of the social and political circumstances of his time, the response of the community to him and the survival of his oracles after his death. The oracles had to be recorded when spoken or remembered by hearers who were prepared at some stage in the future to commit what they had heard to others or to writing. Without some such structures a prophet's preaching would die with his death.[58] Perhaps this factor will have assisted the rise of prophetic legends or the type of prophetic story typified by the book of Jonah in which a historical figure is transformed into the protagonist of a strange prophetic legend (cf. II Kings 14.25). Beyond such possible schemes of survival we must recognize just how little we know about the production of prophetic traditions in ancient Israel and all the factors, chance and intentional, involved in the eventual emergence of the larger prophetic tradition. The interactionist account also has to acknowledge the reciprocal relationship that probably existed between how a prophet was legitimated in the community by his own convictions, words and actions and how the community accepted his status by its responses to him, thereby demonstrating that he was a legitimate prophet.

Prophecy and tradition

The records of the sayings and deeds of the prophets have come down to us as traditions about various individuals in relation to their own time along with editorial comments, additions, organization and processing. They belong to a lengthy process of editing and transmission which contributed significantly to the development of the prophetic traditions themselves. The Reformed distinction between scripture and tradition is, so far as I can judge, a distinction without a difference. For my purposes tradition is what has been handed down from the past, whether written or oral, by communities concerned to preserve it, understand it and to pass it on to the next generation. As tradition it has to be located within a particular cultural stream or community. As a cultural deposit of the community it is maintained and explained by the group and becomes part of the hermeneutic process by which the community understands itself. To see the documents of the prophetic movement as traditions entails a number of features about them of relevance to the interpretation of prophecy.

The nature of tradition. The word tradition (Latin *traditio*) is derived from *trado* (*tradere*) meaning 'give up', 'hand on', 'deliver', 'transmit', 'surrender', 'consign'. It may be the handing on of something tangible or abstract (e.g. teaching). It is a bequeathing of something to someone else. The equivalent Greek word is *paradosis* (from *paradidomi* 'give', 'hand over', 'transmit') meaning 'what is bequeathed' or 'transmitted'. It can refer to the transmission of legends, doctrines or teachings (it is used in the New Testament to describe the core of the apostolic teaching (I Cor. 11.2; 15.3; II Thess. 2.15; 3.6)). In Jewish terminology tradition is called *masora* but its meaning and derivation are disputed.[59] The word *masoret* occurs in Ezek. 20.37 but its form is disputed and the LXX has a different reading.[60] If the present textual form is accepted it may be derived from *'sr* 'bind', 'tie', 'imprison' so tradition would be that which binds. As the Torah was binding with the force of law in later Judaism such a meaning may be a good description of tradition. Tradition came to be seen as that which protected Torah 'tradition is a fence for Tora' (*massōret s*ᵉ*yāg latōrāh* Avot 3.17). Others relate *masoret* to the root *msr* (**ysr*) 'hand over' (cf. Num. 31.5) which would give it the force of *traditio* and *paradosis*. The scribal activity of rabbinical Judaism involved the preservation and transmission of the sacred texts (hence the Masoretic Text). The whole history of Israel was seen as the continuous transmission of the revelation received by Moses at Sinai and the rabbis maintained the handing on (*msr*) of that revelation (cf. Avot 1.1).

Tradition is what is handed down and what is binding on the community to which it is transmitted. Tradition relates to identity, continuity, direction and limitation. That is, it helps to contribute to the construction of the group's identity and its transmission processes help to preserve the identity and continuity of the group. It provides the direction for the community as it understands and responds to the received tradition. It also limits the group by defining boundaries and identifying legitimate and illegitimate uses and transformations of the tradition. Limiting processes contribute to identity by protecting the discrete nature of the group. As such the formation and maintenance of tradition are complex features of any community and the continuity of that tradition's interpretation an intricate network of checks and balances.

The origins of a tradition relate to a person, an event or a series of relations between persons and events or things. In Judaism the tradition began with Moses and his promulgation of Torah so the whole rationale of Judaism was seen as commentary on this basic revelation. Each generation was concerned with the understanding of Torah, the practice of it and the transmission of it. In this sense Israel might be termed 'the people of the tradition' rather than 'the people of the book'.[61] In Christianity the tradition centred on Jesus of Nazareth, his life, activities and teaching. Karl Popper's observation that 'A tradition is, as it were, capable of extending something of the personal attitude of its founder far beyond his personal life.' is applicable to the major biblical traditions of Judaism and Christianity and also pertinent for the prophetic traditions.[62] The individual prophetic traditions had their origins in the utterances of specific prophets whose activities seized the attention of various elements in the community and were remembered sufficiently to be written down at a subsequent stage of the community's life. As the community found the prophet's sayings illuminating their circumstances the more likelihood there was of the tradition being preserved and developed.

Tradition is not only an intrinsic part of religion it is also fundamental for other categories of human activity. It plays a large part in science, in literature – be it a particular tradition such as the comic tradition or Leavis's great tradition or Thomas Mann's use of tradition – in art and philosophy.[63] It may not always be called tradition but whether as paradigm or *epistémé* or whatever it provides the context for asking questions about basic data and affords ways of reading that data so as to make sense of the world. Tradition can also contribute towards the answers to the questions it raises. Tradition then is the context in which a community has its existence. Hans-Georg Gadamer makes the point well: 'We stand always within tradition, and this is no objectifying process, i.e. we do not conceive of what tradition says as something other, something alien. It is always part of us, a model or exemplar, a recognition of ourselves which our later historical judgment would hardly see as a kind of knowledge, but as the simplest preservation of tradition.'[64]

If the importance of tradition cannot be gainsaid for so many dimensions of human existence it also has to be observed that tradition can also be dead. The 'dead hand' of tradition can paralyse the community as easily as living tradition maintains the life of that community. Karl Marx's famous observation is to the point here: 'Men make their own history, but they do not make it just as they please; they do not make it under circumstances chosen by themselves, but under circumstances directly encountered, given and transmitted from the past. *The tradition of all the dead generations weighs like a nightmare on the brain of the living.*'[65] What makes one tradition living and another dead or how traditions die are complex issues for analysis but the history of religious and political traditions is partly the history of the death of such traditions and the restrictive role played by such dead elements in the surviving structures. Tradition can become overbearing and burdensome, it can paralyse thought and force life into preconceived moulds which thwart rather than enhance growth.

The negative and positive aspects of tradition make for a dialectical understanding of the place of tradition in human structures. Different traditions may criticize, modify or transform other traditions. Some of the tensions within tradition may be seen in the synoptic accounts of a discussion between Jesus and the Pharisees where the Pharisaical oral law 'the tradition of the elders' (*paradosis tōn presbyterōn*) is unfavourably contrasted as 'the tradition of men' (*paradosis tōn anthrōpōn*) with the word of God, namely the written biblical tradition (Matt. 15.1–9; Mark 7.1–13). One set of traditions had become fixed as scripture and this was held to outrank a later set of traditions which functioned as the interpretation of the first set. Change comes about when movements critical of tradition attempt to destroy such traditional structures (anarchism) or reject traditional positions in favour of immediate decision making (existentialism). Yet such radical moves tend to be deeply traditional. A good example of the radical rejection of tradition in favour of the deeply traditional is the statement in John the Baptist's preaching: 'and do not presume to say to yourselves, "We have Abraham as our father"; for I tell you, God is able from these stones to raise up children to Abraham,' (Matt. 3.9; Luke 3.8). In the prophetic traditions the critique of the cult and the transformation of popular beliefs represented the dialectical handling of traditions. These preliminary remarks must serve as an indication of the nature of tradition and as an intimation of some of the complexities involved in the approach to prophecy as tradition.

Prophecy and tradition. The appearance of the canonical prophets in a society which had been settled in the same geographical area for centuries meant prophecy of this kind emerged into a context of existing beliefs and ideologies. This context of world-view, outlook and belief conditioned prophecy to a great extent and in its relationship with such traditions the dialectic of prophecy was partly constructed. It may be surmised that tensions within society, dissatisfactions with current community structures, economic and political factors within and outside the community and a distinctive vision of their own helped to bring about the emergence of this type of prophet in the mid-eighth century. The religious traditions of the community were the necessary background for the prophets but they were soon to reshape them in a number of ways.

With the exception of Hosea and the sphere of activity of Amos the prophetic traditions belong to prophets and their editors who worked in Jerusalem and Judah. So the main traditions inherited by them and central to the understanding of their work were those associated with the Jerusalem cultus, especially the David-Zion complex of motifs. The prophets will have shared a common belief in Yahweh the God of Israel and his special relationship with the community. The legitimacy of the house of David was a central feature of their preaching and the later prophets came to believe in the shared heritage of Judah and Israel expressed by the hopes that one day both kingdoms would be reunited under a Davidic king (e.g. Ezek. 37.15–28; cf. Hos. 3.5). After the promulgation of Deuteronomy and under the influence of the deuteronomic school, itself heavily influenced by prophecy, the more specialized Jerusalem theology was broadened by amalgamation with the greater Israelite traditions of the exodus.[66] It was part of the real achievement of the deuteronomists that they applied the *language* of election, previously used in the royal theology of Jerusalem, to the nation of Israel as the elect people of Yahweh (cf. Deut. 7.6, 7).[67]

The prophets provided their own interpretations of the traditions they inherited and often these interpretations conflicted with popular beliefs about them. This was probably the case with the transformation of the day of Yahweh from a day of light to one of darkness by Amos (5.18–20).[68] They opposed the massive scale of cultic offerings which represented the popular devotion to the sacrificial system of worship (Isa. 1.10–15; Amos 4.4, 5; 5.25; Micah 6.6, 7; Jer. 7.21–23) and attacked the community for practising idolatry (cf. Isa. 2.6–8). Strangely it is only in Hosea that a trenchant criticism of idolatry was maintained by an eighth-century prophet (4.12–19; 8.4–6; 10.2, 5, 6, 8; 11.2; 13.2; cf. the editorial additions in Micah 1.7; 5.13, 14). The prophets of that period were more intent on condemning social injustice than on criticizing idolatry. However the later prophets, particularly Jeremiah and Ezekiel, saw Jerusalem society as idolatrous to the core (cf. Jer. 2.20–28; 3.1–5, 21–23; 5.7–9; 13.25–27; Ezek. 8; 14.1–11; 16; 20.32; 23). In the closing decades of the Judaean monarchy various cults flourished (cf. Jer. 7.17–20; 44.15–30; Ezek. 8) as part of popular religion. There is some difficulty with the accounts of such practices because if Ezekiel's account of the bizarre cults that operated in the temple precincts is an accurate one then it means the Jerusalem cult itself was by its very nature corrupt.[69] For such cults to have used openly the temple area (Ezek. 8.3–6, 14–17) they must have had priestly authority for doing so (this need not have been so for the esoterical practice depicted in vv 7–10 but the presence of the Israelite elders at such a ceremony suggests that even such a ritual had official blessing).

This sharp difference between particular cultic practices and the prophetic understanding of tradition demands further comment. Allowing for the exaggerations of prophetic rhetoric and polemical enthusiasm it seems to be the case that Ezekiel had a radically different view of what took place in the temple cultus than did the Jerusalem priesthood. How are we to account for such a disagreement between prophecy and tradition? Without explaining away the tension it may be possible to account for this polemic in one of two ways. On the one hand, the cult may have been worshipping Yahweh but in forms not acceptable to the prophet because the forms were derived from pagan religious structures. The prophetic charge against the cult was that it was syncretistic. In using Canaanite forms of worship the cult was guilty of participating in pagan religion. The origins of many of the cult rituals were undoubtedly pagan, e.g. sacrifice, passover, the temple structure (Solomon had used Canaanite experts who had inevitably built a Canaanite shrine – I Kings 5–8), but in the past they had been transformed into Yahwistic elements and used in the service of Yahweh (cf. Ex. 12.11; 25–31). However the prophet was not prepared to accept such transformations but insisted on treating the practices in terms of their origins: origin indicated nature (cf. Ezek. 16.1–5 where the nation's origin was seen as the ground of its subsequent rebellions against Yahweh). For the priests in the cult the origin and nature of the rituals would have been less important than the attribution of such rituals to the commands of Yahweh and their integration into his service over a lengthy period of temple worship. Both prophet and priests will have had substance in their viewpoints but the incompatibility between the views will have made strife inevitable. A comparable example of such incompatible beliefs about a common religious holding would be the objection some pious Christians have towards celebrating Christmas because they regard it as originally having been a pagan festival with no connection whatsoever with the birth of Jesus. Technically they are correct but the transformational factor in the Christian religion has taken over such pagan festivals and baptised them into the appropriate Christian rituals. A similar clash of *interpretations* may lie behind the polemic in Ezek. 8. For many of the issues between prophecy and tradition were matters of interpretation. The facts may have been common to prophet and priest or community but the interpretation put upon the facts was the crux of the issue.

On the other hand, the prophets may have represented a Yahweh-alone party in ancient Israel which dissented from the more dominant party of Yahweh-but-under-many-discrete-guises worship and possibly in association with other gods.[70] Up to the exile the temple cult may have been controlled by such a party and the prophetic critique may have been issued on behalf of all those in Judah and Jerusalem who supported the Yahweh-alone principle of worship. The deuteronomic drive against the rural sanctuaries may have been the first stage of a movement against the majority party which attempted to destroy the popularity of such nature cults (cf. II Kings 23.4–25). Perhaps Ezekiel's condemnation was directed against the pre-reform state of the temple but if it were not then the reform must have been a serious failure.

A variation on this account is to make a distinction between the official worship of Yahweh and popular Israelite religion.[71] Popular religion emphasized the role of women in the cult, magical practices and the noise of solemn assemblies where many sacrifices were offered and great festivities celebrated (cf. Isa. 1.11–15; Amos 4.4, 5; Jer. 7.17, 18). It blurred the distinction between Yahweh and the local baals and worshipped 'upon every high hill and under every

green tree' (Jer. 2.20). Because the priesthood depended for its
livelihood on the economics of a well patronized cult popular religion was tolerated within the temple courtyards. During certain
regnal periods such cults may have been more than tolerated (cf. II
Kings 21) and even dedicated reforms may not have been capable
of ridding the temple complex of all the multitudinous cults. Hence
Ezekiel's identification of specific cultic practices within the temple
and his association of such abominations with the destruction of the
polluted temple (8; 9).

The importance of these considerations for the relation between
prophecy and tradition should be fairly clear. Apart from the central interpretative role they posit for the prophets as interpreters of
the Yahwistic traditions of the nation they provide for a continuity
link between prophecy and the earlier traditions. The attacks on
idolatry, the polemic against the temple cult and the opposition to
popular religion suggest that prophecy should be seen as the continuation of the Mosaic polemic against idolatry by other means.[72]
An aspect of the prophetic activity was concerned with identifying
the real significance of the nation's religious traditions and relating
that meaning to the contemporary situation. Often that meant
criticizing the community for its lack of understanding of its condition, for its unawareness of the true nature of its position before
Yahweh – 'Israel does not know, my people does not understand',
'the whole land is desolate, but no man lays it to heart' (Isa. 1.3;
Jer. 12.11). In its interaction with tradition, both its advocacy and its
critique (hence the dialectic of prophecy), the prophets found their
own identity and advanced the understanding of the traditions
(often adding to and developing them) for later generations. The
richness of the hermeneutic additions to the prophetic traditions is
ample evidence of their achievements.

The transmission of prophecy. The phrase prophecy and tradition
has two references – one as prophecy in relation to the traditions of
Israelite religion and the other as the development of prophecy into
the prophetic traditions.[73] We know very little about the processes
behind the growth and transmission of these traditions so what
follows is inevitably the patching together of hints and inferences
with a few assumptions derived from reading the texts.

If we accept that an individual tradition had its origins in the utterances and activities of a particular prophet then the first stage in the formation of his tradition would have been the collecting together of his oracles and sayings. This might have been done orally or have used written forms. Whether this was done by the prophet, one or more of his followers, interested parties among his listeners, or a later group cannot now be answered from the sources. On occasion a prophet might write something himself (cf. Isa. 8.1–3; 30.8; Jer. 29.1–28; Hab. 2.2; I Chron. 21.12).[74] In the case of Jeremiah his writing may have been done by his amanuensis Baruch (cf. 36.1–8), whereas the complex literary structure of Ezekiel's visions may point to the prophet himself as writer. In spite of the difficulties of attribution in these texts the purpose of the written forms is fairly clear: the written word testifies to the prophetic message, especially after it has been fulfilled (cf. II Chron. 21.12–20). In the case of Ezek. 43.11 the intention of the writing was to keep the community mindful of its duties.

None of these instances can be generalized into a theory of how prophecy came to be recorded. The individual books all have notes indicating some details about the subsequent oracles and these details imply some editorial activity. Collections were made and grouped together under brief titles such as 'the word of Yahweh that came to Micah of Moresheth in the days of . . .' (Micah 1.1), 'the vision of Isaiah the son of Amoz, which he saw concerning . . .' (Isa. 1.1), 'the words of Amos . . .' (Amos 1.1), 'the oracle of God which Habakkuk the prophet saw' (Hab. 1.1), '. . . the book of the vision of Nahum of Elkosh' (Nahum. 1.1; cf. Jer. 1.1; Obad. 1; Joel 1.1). In some cases a follower or disciple may have been responsible for the collection because some of the prophets had such disciples (cf. Isa. 8.16, 18) or officials at the court (as in the case of Jeremiah) or in the temple (for cult oracles).

Originally the words were spoken in specific circumstances for particular reasons. Once delivered they had served their purpose. As such there was no cause for writing down such specific statements. On occasion the writing of a particular saying may have added significance to what was said or preserved it as a witness for the future occurrence of the word uttered (cf. Isa. 8.1–4; 30.8). Perhaps memories of what a prophet had said were revived when something occurred to remind people that recently such and such a prophet had spoken of events rather like the ones they were then witnessing. An example of such a possibility must be the introduction to Amos 'the words of Amos . . . which he saw . . . *two years before the earthquake*' (1.1). It would be carrying prophetic powers of prediction too far to claim that the time indicator was part of the original message rather than an editorial note! The earthquake, perhaps catastrophic, may have seemed to some people to have been a foretaste (if not the actual fulfilment) of what Amos had warned the community would be the consequences if it continued its present way of life (cf. Zech. 14.5). The sudden disaster may have enhanced the reputation of the prophet (whether living or dead) and have led to an initial collection of his oracles. We do not know whether such oracles were retrieved from memory or had some existence in written form. In order to account for the survival of any genuine material from Amos it may be necessary to postulate a small group of people originally either associated with Amos or so impressed by his preaching that they banded together to preserve the tradition of what he said.

Much stress has been put on the role of oral tradition as the creative force giving rise to the preservation of the biblical traditions in the first place (particularly associated with Scandinavian scholarship).[75] In the absence of firm knowledge it is difficult to be as confident of the matter in view of the fact that the analogies used to establish the practice are taken from cultures quite different from ancient Israel. Whether the role of memory for preserving traditions was as strong in urban cultures as it may have been in nomadic cultures is a matter for debate but urban cultures afforded resources for the written preservation of traditions. As much of the prophetic proclamation took place in the sanctuary the cult was the most likely place for the conservation of their oracles. The recording of *tōrōt* ('decisions', 'directions', 'rulings') was a normative cultic practice therefore a similar practice may have been applied to the preaching of the prophets.[76] The third person accounts in the prophetic books point to recorders other than the prophets themselves.

In the heavily edited book of Jeremiah elements of the complex process of editing prophecy may be seen in the accounts given of the temple sermon (7.1–15; 26). Sayings of Jeremiah (possibly some fragments of his *ipsissima verba*) have been added to a deuteronomistic sermon and a number of prophetic forms have been combined with priestly traditions.[77] The catastrophe of 587 did much to preserve the memory of Jeremiah and his words through the long exile and his work found editors prepared to organize his oracles and supplement his visions with sermons and other material updating his message for a later period. Such a process can also be seen in the Isaiah traditions where major additions and many subtle changes developed the work of Isaiah of Jerusalem into the most substantial of all the prophetic traditions.[78]

The preservation and transmission of prophecy were not done for antiquarian reasons but because the prophets were seen as astute analysts of their own time and preachers of the word of Yahweh. Their critique of society retained its element of warning for the later communities but the schematic interpolation of salvation oracles into the traditions turned them into words of hope for the hard-pressed communities of the post-exilic age.

Traditions and the tradition. The centuries long process of editing and enlarging the individual prophetic traditions led to the formation of a collection of prophetic books which may conveniently be called the prophetic tradition. This tradition was made up of all the individual traditions and in later Jewish thought was known as the 'latter prophets' (*n^ebî'îm 'ah^arōnîm*). This designation was due to the belief that the books of Joshua, Judges, Samuel and Kings were prophetic, either by authorship or because they displayed fundamental principles similar to those in the prophetic oracles, and so were known as the 'former prophets' (*n^ebî'îm ri'šōnîm*). In order to understand biblical prophecy properly it is often necessary to use the material in Samuel and Kings (also Deuteronomy) but generally the presentation of prophecy in these books is too ideologically schematic. The attempt to regulate prophecy in Deut. 13.1–5; 18.15–22 belonged to the period of prophetic conflict towards the end of the seventh century and therefore is really only relevant to that issue. The extent to which the variety of discrete prophetic traditions constituted a unified tradition is debatable but in so far as it is legitimate to refer to the prophetic tradition then it is a reference to the collective traditions of the prophets who worked from the mid-eighth century until the post-exilic reconstruction period.

Interpreting prophetic language

The central element in the hermeneutic process is understanding the nature of the language used in the prophetic traditions. As my concern is specifically with the predictive element in prophecy I will restrict my considerations to that aspect of the language. However it should be noted that the predictive element cannot be isolated from prophecy in general but was just one aspect of the prophet's preaching. Therefore the language of prediction was not distinctive but used similar sets of metaphors, grammatical construction and references as the rest of prophetic language. Often it turns out to be the case that what appears to have been a prediction was in fact a *vaticinium ex eventu* or simply part of the warning metaphors designed to turn the community towards a different course of action. The oldstyle 'prophetic perfect' referred to the nation's immediate future in terms of destruction or salvation: e.g. the nation has fallen (*nāf'lāh* Amos 5.2), the cities laid in ruins (*nitṣū* Jer. 4.26), or the redemption of the nation (*g*ᵉ*'altîkā* Isa. 43.1). The catastrophe can be spoken of in the future (cf. Isa. 8.7, 8; 10.3; Amos 7.11) as could the hope for the future (cf. Isa. 9.7 (Heb. 9.6)). A careful examination of the language of prophecy will show that the grammar of the future is not specifically tensed but perfects, participles and imperfects were used freely to depict the immediate future, whether disaster or salvation was the content of the vision.

What were the prophets doing when they predicted or saw visions of a specific future? Was it simply forecasting the future? Obviously they were making utterances which they expected would have clearly identifiable links with events that would occur soon. Without some such equivalence or similarity between word and event there would be no prediction. The generality of their images of destruction (or of salvation wherever these are authentic predictions and not cultic glosses) would have made for a broad range of fit between word and event. The problem for interpretation is clarifying those oracles which were genuine predictions and those which were post hoc adjustments to match word and event (cf. Ezek. 26.7–14; 29.17–20). Whatever the precise nature of these activities may have been it has to be accepted that the contemporary perception of the prophet was that of one who predicted the future (cf. Deut. 18.22; Jer. 28.9). Subsequent Judaean communities also believed that to have been the case and prophecy was preserved on that basis.[79]

Accepting prediction as an integral part of prophecy leads on to recognizing that, apart from pseudo-predictions, many of the predictions made failed to be fulfilled. The necessary equivalence between word and event did not occur. This failure does not pose a problem for the modern interpreter. Men may predict the future without a guarantee of being right on every occasion. Individual skills, the circumstances governing the events being predicted and the probabilities of success all have to be taken into account when judging the failure rate of prophets. However such a rational account of the matter does not do justice to the levels of material in the traditions. The prophets did not see themselves, nor did their followers or the editors of their work see them, as engaging merely in the human activity of predicting the future with a greater probability of getting it wrong. For them their activities were the proclamation of the word of Yahweh announcing his will for his people. They spoke the word of Yahweh and that shaped the future itself. It was in agreement with that basic religious attitude that their traditions were created and maintained. What then are we to make of their failures? Are we to conclude that the word of Yahweh can be wrong? Expressed in such forms the prophetic activity is vulnerable to radical criticism. Indeed it could be argued that the failure of the prophets in the matter of creating a viable future for the community was the main factor in the demise of prophecy as a dominant force in the post-exilic community.[80] In accepting a dialectic of destruction and salvation we have saddled the prophet with the responsibility for being wrong. The more sceptical approach which sees only judgment in the great prophets at least exonerates them from serious error. Despite this way of absolving them from self-deception and mistakes it is still a more adequate account of the traditions to see in them a struggle on the prophets' part to turn the community from disaster and to maintain faith in Yahweh as the saviour of the nation.

I do not wish to exonerate the prophets from the true but trivial accusation of having been wrong in many of their predictions. That all the prophets who believed in the future triumph of the Davidic dynasty were wrong is self-evident. As also must be the case with all the prophetic hopes that a reunited Israel and Judah would plunder their enemies (e.g. Isa. 11.12–14). Although some of the prophets can be absolved of holding such beliefs the communities that produced the prophetic traditions did so because they shared many beliefs with the prophets. The emergence of the prophetic traditions was due to a commonalty of conviction, a shared theology linking prophet with tradent. The important task of interpretation is not demonstrating that the predictions were wrong but showing how they were treated by the later communities as ongoing possibilities for their future. Had being right or wrong been the main consideration then perhaps the traditions would never have survived but small groups went on reinterpreting those traditions because they kept alive the vision of the earlier prophets. That vision was to have creative significance repeatedly in the following centuries.

Over the centuries of the post-exilic period it must have become clear to many that the prophetic expectations of a transformed nature with Israel sovereign in its own land had not been realized. Did awareness of such failure find its way into the edited traditions? Can we detect responses to regular frustration of hopes in the texts? This is the central thesis of this book: the reinterpretation of prophecy as response to failure of expectations. The principle of this approach can be criticized if it can be shown that the predictive element of prophecy was not predictive but some other linguistic usage. So in order to avoid an initial flaw in the argument I must consider some of the possible ways in which the prophets may have used language so as to clarify the linguistic turn of the traditions. Such linguistic analysis is a very necessary part of the hermeneutic process.

Magical language. The legends about the prophets in the volumes of Kings reveal magical features in the activities of the prophets. The prophet was expected to wave his hand in order to cure sickness (II Kings 5.11), he could make water drinkable by using salt (II Kings 2.19–22), or counteract poison in food (II Kings 4.38–41), or cause an iron axehead to float (II Kings 6.1–7). He could feed large numbers of people with very little food at his disposal (II Kings 4.42–44), increase the contents of one jar of oil until it filled many vessels (II Kings 4.1–7), and guarantee that a small amount of meal and oil would be daily renewed throughout a long famine (I Kings 17.10–16). Even the bones of a dead prophet had magical properties (II Kings 13.20, 21). Such were the magical powers popularly believed to belong to the prophet that he was a figure to be feared. He could transfer leprosy from one person to another (II Kings 5.27), strike an army with blindness (II Kings 6.15–19), cause bears to savage children (II Kings 2.23, 24), destroy contingents of men with fire from heaven (II Kings 1.9–12), cause a king's arm to be withered and destroy an altar simply by means of word and sign (I Kings 13.1–5). It was believed that the prophetic word had great power to achieve whatever it predicted, whether destruction (cf. I Sam. 2.27–34; 4.11; I Kings 2.26, 27) or deliverance (cf. II Kings 19.6, 7, 35–37; 20.1–11).

There are signs in the traditions that such magical powers were attributable to the prophet as the servant of Yahweh so that it was the word or will of Yahweh that achieved some of these magical acts (cf. I Kings 13.2, 3, 5; 14.5; 17.1, 14, 16; II Kings 3.13–20; 4.33, 43; 7.1, 2, 19). This was a process of transforming the primitive magic of early prophecy into an account of the rational activity of the prophet as spokesman of Yahweh. Yet magic is an essential component of religion so this transformation may have been more apparent than real.[81] The magical approach to life was dominated by rituals of manipulation whereby specific goals were sought. In ancient Israel many of these rituals were prohibited (cf. Lev. 20.27; Deut. 18.9–14) but other manipulative rituals, e.g. sacrifice, were accepted as legitimate means of approaching the deity. These ancient magical rituals may have been carefully controlled to fit in with a rational account of the divine will but they retained their magical status for the masses (hence the strong prophetic protest against the popular cult of sacrifice). In a sense the later priestly authorities were able to bypass such opposition to magical activities by incorporating the complicated ritual legislation (Lev. 1–16) into the narrative of the exodus and Sinai legends. Thus a deeply magical way of achieving certain ends, e.g. expiation by blood sacrifice, was legitimated as the revealed word of Yahweh (Torah).[82]

The roots of language belong in magic and all language usage tends towards the bewitchment of reality.[83] That the word was considered powerful in itself in ancient Israel may be seen clearly in the popular view of prophecy whereby the prophet spoke the word and things happened (cf. II Kings 5.11; I Kings 13.1–5; Jer. 38.4). The preservation of the prophetic traditions may have been due to a similar belief in the effective force of the word of Yahweh. For if the spoken word was a powerful force in the world how much more powerful was the word of Yahweh. 'Israel's theologians and prophets were, of course, certain that, for all the mysterious possibilities inherent in every word of man, the word of Jahweh towered incomparably high above them.'[84] Late prophecy clearly held such a belief: 'For as the rain and the snow come down from heaven, and return not thither but water the earth, making it bring forth and sprout, giving seed to the sower and bread to the eater, *so* shall my word be that goes forth from my mouth; it shall not return to me empty, but it shall accomplish that which I purpose, and prosper in the thing for which I sent it' (Isa. 55.10, 11).

Whatever the magical roots of language may have been the genuinely effective word for Israel was the divine word, usually mediated by the prophet. In the account given of the conflict between Elijah and the prophets of Baal (I Kings 18.20–40) both sides used words and rituals but only Elijah's were effective because they were in line with Yahweh's will – 'I have done all these things *at thy word*' (v 36). Behind the speaker, whose status was important for the outcome, had to be the power that made the speaker's utterance operative. Thus of Samuel it was said 'Yahweh was with him, and let none of his words fall to the ground' (I Sam. 3.19). It was what Yahweh had determined that made the spoken word effective, rather than just the word in itself (cf. Num. 22.12, 18, 35, 38; 23.11, 12, 25, 26; 24.13; I Sam. 2.25). The Balaam oracles indicate the belief in the magic power of words when expressed by the right person (Num. 22.6) but were designed to show the controlling power of Yahweh. The belief in the effective word remains as an element in the narrative for Balaam has to bless what is blessed, i.e. the spoken word has to agree with what was the case.

This last point is important. Simply to have spoken in the name of Yahweh was not sufficient for many of the prophets, if not all, did that without being effective (cf. Deut. 18.20). The conflict between the prophets (cf. I Kings 22.5–28; Jer. 27–29) was a struggle to proclaim the effective word while using similar prophetic techniques. The formulas of prophecy, e.g. *kō 'āmar yhwh* 'thus says Yahweh', *nᵉ'um yhwh* 'oracle of Yahweh', were common to the different prophets (cf. Jer. 23.31; 28.2, 4). In making the effective word the distinguishing mark of the word of Yahweh we have only succeeded in aligning genuine prophecy with what was happening in the real world, i.e. the historical world. None of the prophets declared that effective word regularly, though some were more successful than others. The problems of unfulfilled prediction remain whether we operate with a magical power inherent in language model or an effective word of Yahweh model.[85]

The consideration of prophetic language as magical offers as an explanation for the failure of prediction the possibility that the prophetic activity was viewed as a magic force operating independent of human factors and that therefore the various hopes of salvation were believed to be guaranteed an inevitable fulfilment. Such a view would at least account for the preservation of the oracles and their expansion by further images of salvation. Their failure to be realized in the empirical world was due to the imperfect match between the world and the magical approach to reality. The conviction of the prophet that he spoke the word of Yahweh, a conviction shared by the tradents and the communities that later preserved the traditions, must also be seen as a poor fit between belief and reality. However if the prophetic words are limited to the oracles of destruction then at least for Amos, Isaiah and Micah it can be said that they proclaimed the word of Yahweh. For the real crux of the matter concerns the positive visions scattered throughout the traditions (and certainly genuine to Jeremiah, Ezekiel, Second Isaiah and Zechariah to say the least). Beliefs about the earlier prophets, e.g. Elijah and Elisha, constructed accounts of their activities as effective whether in destruction or salvation of the nation. Similar beliefs could only preserve the oracles of the later prophets in the knowledge that the disasters had befallen the nation as announced by the prophets (cf. Lam. 2.17), perhaps the more positive elements would also be realized. That conviction may have been a completely wrong reading of the traditions but if so the misreading may have been due to residual elements of the older magical view of the effective word still surviving in the community.

Cultic language. The cult was the place where the kingship of Yahweh was celebrated (cf. Ps. 93; 97; 99) and his mighty acts on behalf of the nation remembered (cf. Deut. 26.5–9; Ps. 106; 136). The traditions of the early history of the nation were preserved in the sanctuary and in many cases the narratives owed their structure to the liturgical organization of the material (e.g. Ex. 12; 13; 19). The cultic view of reality would appear to have been one of reading behind empirical reality a different order of things. During the exodus from Egypt the clans had had to fight the Egyptian border guards in order to make good their escape. The account of this battle has been so overlaid with a different story about Yahweh's power on behalf of his people that it is now very difficult to provide a coherent account of what might have happened (cf. Ex. 14).[86] The episode was linked to a celebration of Yahweh's power culminating in the nation's settlement around the sanctuary (Ex. 15.1–18). The cultic tendency to attribute human achievements to divine acts can also be seen in the reading of the conquest as a divine rather than a human military triumph (cf. Ps. 44.1–3 (Heb. 44.2–4)).

The Jerusalem cultus was devoted to the worship of Yahweh and the maintenance of the royal theology of the house of David. A striking feature of the royal psalms is the elevated view they present of the king and the city over which he was king. The king was the son of Yahweh (Ps. 2.7) who posed the threat of annihilation to the kings of the other nations (cf. 2.8, 9; 110.5, 6). The city where he was king was Yahweh's city and impregnable against the attacks of foreign armies (cf. 46.4–7 (Heb. 46.5–8); 48.1–8 (Heb. 48.2–9); Lam. 4.12). Yet apart from a brief period in the early part of the monarchy the Judaean king was regularly subjected to the domination of foreign powers (e.g. Assyria, Egypt, Babylon). In 701 the Assyrians almost destroyed Jerusalem (cf. Isa. 1.7–9; II Kings 18.14–16) and in 587 the Babylonians sacked the city (II Kings 25; Jer. 52). So how are we to explain the discrepancy between the high chauvinism of the psalms and the bitter reality of history? The concern of the cult was with depicting the world in terms of its ideology (mythology or theology) so the kings of the world were mere puppets operated upon by Yahweh. The king who had real power in the world was Yahweh's anointed one in Jerusalem. Thus did the small nation of Judah come to terms with its beleagured situation in the world. What was believed of the deity was posited of the king. This representation of reality dominated the royal cult in Jerusalem. It was so strong that even the eighth-century prophets accepted it (cf. Isa. 8.18) and only Jeremiah seems to have protested seriously against some of the occupants of the throne (cf. 22.13–19). So it appears to have been part of prophetic mythology as well (cf. Isa. 6.3).

The contrast between historical reality and the cultic view that these references seem to indicate may contribute to an understanding of the salvation oracles in the prophetic traditions. The association of prophecy with the cult has already been noted so here it is only necessary to observe that the various prophetic traditions attributed to cult prophets also show a tendency to stress salvation for the community (e.g. Hab.3; Zeph.3.8–20; Joel 2.12–3.21 (Heb.2.12–4.21)). The lengthy addition to the oracles of Micah in Micah 7.7–20 also has all the marks of a liturgy of salvation.[87] Such liturgies were no doubt composed by cult prophets and reveal the cultic concern with salvation. Classical prophecy may have been a highly negative movement in Judah and Israel but the cult had to be positive. It was too central to the community's existence for it not to have had a positive image both of its being and its future. The prophets may have had an open view of the future but later communities needed to fill in that openness with definite images of salvation. This may partly explain the substantial expansion of Isaiah's oracles by the work of a cult prophet in Isa.40–55.[88] When we compare the discrepancy between history and the view presented in the prophetic liturgies of salvation we find the same kind of disparity as we find between the ideology of the royal psalms and the historical experiences of the Judaean monarchy.

The cult was the place where difficult problems could be resolved (cf. Ps.73.16, 17), it was where the assurance that Yahweh was Israel's powerful God working on its behalf was maintained (cf. Hab.3.12–15). The earlier prophets had tried to breach that assurance by insisting that only a community that turned from its evil could have any hope of deliverance and in the failure of the people to turn their destruction was assured. The cult, on the other hand, emphasized the redeemer God who had delivered the people from Egypt against the might of Pharaoh, an act not dependent upon a prior work of repentance – it stressed the sovereignty of Yahweh to redeem. Prophecy had stressed the sovereignty of Yahweh to destroy (cf. Amos.3.2; 4.12). The dilemma for prophecy was reconciling those two aspects of the divine. Thus for Hosea the way out of the dilemma was to opt for the redeemer aspect of Yahweh: 'I will not execute my fierce anger, I will not again destroy Ephraim; for I am God and not man, the holy one in your midst, and I will not come to destroy' (11.9). The sentiment does the prophet credit but it was a vain hope for the Assyrians destroyed the nation of Israel. The lack of clear statements indicating that Yahweh would save his people in the traditions of Amos and Isaiah may have been due to their inability to see how the inevitable disaster could be prevented without the turning of the community to Yahweh.

Jeremiah and Ezekiel appear to have held some hopes for the future but after the catastrophe and only in limited and conventional ways. It may be that those prophets accepted the destruction of land and community as the equivalent to turning (cf. Isa. 27.7–9 whatever it may mean).[89] If Jer. 31.31–34 is to be attributed to Jeremiah then we have an example of how that prophet gave up the attempt to resolve the dilemma of the nation's turning and made the future dependent upon a divine act. However such a resolution was a counsel of despair and represented the prophetic loss of nerve brought on by the catastrophe of 587. The moral demand for turning to Yahweh was scrapped and a miraculous act substituted in its place. Thus did late prophecy concede its brilliant vision to a more cultic understanding of the future.

The cultic interpretation of prophetic language relieves the pressure of understanding the predictive language in historical terms. The grandiose liturgical resonances of the salvation oracles referred to the cult ideology of how the community stood in relation to the world (cf. the realized eschatology of later Christian communities for a similar phenomenon). When reality in the form of the Babylonians destroyed city and cult the shock was enormous (cf. Lamentations). The post-exilic cult developed much stronger emphases on purificatory and expiatory rituals and the prophetic community faded into the peripheries of that cultic community (cf. II Kings 23.2 with II Chron. 34.30). Separated from the cultic dimension these salvation oracles look like predictions having reference to the real world but that may have been an accident of social history. Taken along such lines the prophets could be exonerated from false predictions because of category confusions in the work of the later tradents. It is a possibility but one unlikely to recommend itself to many because it cannot be ruled out that the cult prophets may well have believed that these visions would have a real fulfilment in due course in the territory of Judah. Furthermore it is fairly clear that later communities took such a view.

Symbolic language. One level of prophetic language was quite clearly rhetorical with a frequent use of metaphor and hyperbole. The clearest examples among the prophets of the rhetorician were

Ezekiel and Second Isaiah. Ezekiel produced lengthy statements full of purple prose and bizarre images (e.g. 16; 20; 23). Second Isaiah described the redemption of the nation in inflated terms that included the trembling of the ends of the earth at the approach of Cyrus (41.5), Israel's crushing of the mountains (41.15), the transformation of the desert into a pool of water (41.18; 43.19, 20), the servant Israel as a covenant to the nations (42.6), and the transformation of nature (55.12, 13). These extravagant metaphors add up to very little: no more than 'your time of exile is over, you may return home if you wish'. For that was precisely the outcome of the fall of Babylon to the Persian Cyrus: a few exiles returned to Palestine. Of the magnificent designs proclaimed by the prophet little was seen. The metaphors and figures were symbols of the prosaic observation: captivity is finished, return is possible.

If we treat all the futuristic oracles of hope as such symbolic statements then we have a clear indication of the content of the positive side of prophecy. It was a reassurance that there would be a future for the community, a future in their own land and with their own cult. All the oracles may be reduced to Jer. 31.17 (whatever its original context may have been): 'There is hope for your future, says Yahweh, and your children shall come back to their own country.' Ignore the images of a restored Davidic dynasty, a reunited Israel and Judah, a triumphant demolition of the nations, a transformed nature or a Jerusalem temple to which stream all the nations in order to learn peace and Yahweh's Torah. In retrospect all those images carry only one message – the survival of a community centred on Jerusalem. No other elements turned out to have any lasting significance therefore they may be considered to have been redundant elements in the message.

Such would be the effect of treating the prophetic language as symbolic. It rescues prophecy from the charge of failure but at the cost of being highly reductionistic and denying any cognitive content in the oracles except the anticipation of a future. Yet reductionism cannot be avoided for so many of the metaphors and details actually referred to nothing that developed in the subsequent reconstruction period. Judah survived the catastrophe but in such a diminished way that one more triumphant redemption like that and it would have become extinct. However the symbolic handling of the language does rescue an element in the oracles and so may be a way of understanding the language of prophecy so as to retain something of its original force.

Apart from the objection that such a treatment of the language involves too great a cognitive loss there is also the fact that the need to treat the language as symbolic only arises because of the failure of the predictions in the first place. Prophetic rhetoric was equally present in the oracles of doom but because of the correspondence between word and event it was not necessary to treat them as symbolic statements. This hermeneutic shift from literal to symbolic understanding of language is an old principle of biblical interpretation. Pascal has epitomised it in one of his *pensées: Quand la parole de Dieu, qui est véritable, est fausse littéralement, elle est vraie spirituellement. Sede a dextris meis, cela est faux littéralement; donc cela est vrai spirituellement.*[90] 'When the word of God which is true, is literally false, it is spiritually true; when it is rightly read so that it is literally false; then it is spiritually true.' My treatment of prophetic language as symbolic is not an attempt to rescue the biblical text from error but an enquiry into the nature of the language used by the prophets. The hermeneutic task involves understanding the language as it was intended by the writers rather than maintaining some theory about it. Literally understood the prophets were wrong; the question remains: should we modify our approach to their language by accepting a reduced level of meaning for it or not?

There is one important problem connected with interpreting the language as symbolic and that relates to the precise limits of symbolic interpretation. How are symbolic equivalences of literal terms to be determined? The symbolic interpretations I have offered of the future hope oracles have been straightforward because they have been reductions of the various terms to the general summary of the thrust of each oracle governed by the subsequent historical outcome. New terms or concepts have not been introduced and the interpretations have been strictly controlled by the historical circumstances of the prophets. Too often in the past biblical interpretation has indulged in typology, allegory, and christology as means of understanding the texts and have therefore introduced many anachronistic concepts into the interpretation of the biblical traditions. To avoid language losing its connections with reality it is necessary to recognize that limits should be imposed on the possible range of symbolic interpretation.[91]

Conditional language. Earlier statements about the importance of repentance for the prophetic proclamation have indicated that the language of prophecy was necessarily conditional. As such it can hardly have been straightforwardly predictive in nature. Statements to the effect 'this city or community will be destroyed if the people do not turn from evil' are not predictions but hypothetical declarations. Contingent language is not directly predictive but is threatening or warning. It is not designed to forecast the future but to create responses. If we accept this contingent nature of some prophetic statements then it would be more accurate to describe it as warning or threatening language than predictive. It aimed to achieve changes in the community rather than make predictions and as such should be regarded in terms of failure or success in accomplishing change rather than as true or false forecasts of the immediate future.

If the future is indeterminate then any proclamation about that future must have been conditional. If the prophetic call to turn is understood as belonging to the sphere of decision making then it will necessarily have been a message contingent on the people's response. The outcome of the warnings depended upon what decisions the community made. So prophecy as summons to decide cannot have been simply prediction followed by fulfilment. That the deuteronomistic historians often presented history as the unfolding of fulfilled prophecy means that there were at least two models of prophecy operative in the various traditions. One model depicted the prophet as the announcer of Yahweh's judgment against a specific individual or house, e.g. the denunciations of Ahab and Jezebel's political hegemony (I Kings 21.20–26), the other model presented the prophet as the one summoning the community to turn to Yahweh, e.g. Elijah's performance on mount Carmel (I Kings 18.17–40). Yet for the deuteronomists the motif of repentance was a dominant element in prophecy so even a king as corrupt as Ahab (I Kings 21.25, 26) could be portrayed as responding to the prophetic denunciation so as to avoid the threatened destruction (I Kings 21.27–29). Such a picture of response was in keeping with the deuteronomistic principle that turning from evil averted destruction (cf. Jer. 18.7, 8). The actual destruction of Israel by the Assyrians forced the deuteronomists to operate that principle on an individual, rather than a communal, basis so that Ahab did not experience the evil but his descendants did. The similar collapse of Judah forced them to provide the same explanation with reference to Josiah (II Kings 22.14–20).

The dialectical tension between the call to turn (contingent message) and the announcement of Yahweh's decree of destruction (absolute message) was resolved by limiting the contingent word to the individual and applying the absolute word to the community. This resolution of the tension was available to the historians because they had the benefit of knowing how the community's fortunes had finally turned out with the destruction of Jerusalem. For the individual prophets the tension between absolute and contingent words had to be maintained without such knowledge. The motif of the divine council where absolute decrees were handed down by Yahweh to the prophet (cf. I Kings 22.19–23; Amos 3.7; Isa. 6.8–13; Jer. 23.18–20) structured the proclamation of the absolute will of Yahweh. The prophet mediated that decree to the community. The call to repent provided an outside possibility that the decree could be suspended – hence the 'perhaps' (*'ûlay*) of Amos (5.15; cf. Gen. 18.24, 28). That contingent possibility gave prophecy its conditional aspect.

The motif of repentance cannot be absolutized in the way that the deuteronomists or the author of the book of Jonah constructed it. In the preaching of the eighth-century prophets it had a place but the emphasis put on it varied from prophet to prophet. Jeremiah's early preaching accepted the possibility that repentance could be achieved but later gave way to an extremely pessimistic outlook that it was no longer possible for the community to change (cf. 3.22; 4.1; 13.23; but see the deuteronomistic editing of 7.3, 5–7). Yet even the deuteronomists had to accept that certain forms of repentance were a sham: 'Judah did not return to me with her whole heart, but in pretence, says Yahweh' (Jer. 3.10 *lō' šābāh 'ēlî ... yᵉhûdāh bᵉkol-libbāh kî 'im-bᵉšeqer*). The necessity for introducing a distinction within returning so as to be able to designate one false and the other authentic suggests a growing awareness that repentance could not be simply equated with formal communal rituals (the deuteronomic reform?) and that perhaps it was not an adequate protection against disasters in the community (the death of Josiah?). The banal type of national repentance presented by the reaction of Nineveh to Jonah's preaching (Jonah 3.6–10; cf. I

Kings 21.27) could not avert the fate of Judah so it had to be designated 'false' (*šeqer*).

The reflections on the motif of repentance show that it was a complicated notion even for the deuteronomists and that its treatment in relation to prophecy has to be a sophisticated one. The absolutizing of repentance in Jer. 18.7–10 has to be modified by the notion of 'false' turning. Furthermore the question about the effectiveness of repentance (whether genuine or false) in averting national or individual disasters has to be asked. The dogma of turning preventing catastrophe may have been a domain assumption of prophecy or, at least, the deuteronomists but it is far from clear what constituted its grounds. Was it purely a concomitant of belief in divine transcendence? Was it simply a hope that changes within the community would have corresponding changes in the community's destiny? Or was it more linked to change in political policies? It is quite possible that radical changes in political allegiance, e.g. pro-Babylonian support rather than pro-Egyptian support in the time of Jeremiah, would have prevented some of the disasters that befell Israel and Judah from the eighth to the sixth centuries. However the biblical traditions represent the matter in religious rather than political terms so these questions can only be registered rather than answered. Treating prophecy as conditional preaching would ease the problem of unfulfilled predictions by modifying the notion of prediction to one of threat or warning intent on changing attitudes and behaviour. However the contingent aspect of prophecy has to be balanced with the absolute element of Yahweh's sovereignty over everything. Beyond conditionality there was the theology of transcendence in which the decrees of Yahweh functioned as absolutes and man's activity was dismissed as being of no consequence (cf. Isa. 2.22; 40.6–8, 12–17). Such fearful transcendence which rendered human decisions as straws in the wind must severely limit any rational account of prophecy.

Performative language. How language works in any given context depends upon many factors, but particularly on the social context in which it is used. So with prophetic language we must posit for it a context in which it operated conventionally. The notion of the meaning of language being convention derived, i.e. its usage in various contexts is in accordance with a predetermined set of rules, is a very important element in the account of language as performative. According to J. L. Austin performative language involves the use of illocutionary acts. In an illocutionary utterance one does something rather than talks about something. It is the 'performance of an act *in* saying something as opposed to performance of an act *of* saying something'.[92] Common examples of illocutionary acts are 'I do' said in a marriage ceremony, 'I give and bequeath' said in dictating a will, 'I name this ship . . .' said when smashing a bottle of champagne against the vessel. As such they are performatives: one is actually *doing* something by these utterances, i.e. getting married, making a will, naming a ship. Provided the proper circumstances, i.e. the conventions, are observed these forms of words achieve something. The conventions are fundamental for they determine how the statements are to be treated; without them the phrases become confusing or meaningless.

As well as illocutionary acts there are perlocutionary acts. A perlocutionary act involves consequences: 'By doing *x* I was doing *y*', e.g. 'I embarrassed him by saying that.'[93] It involves the production of some effect whereas illocutionary acts do not. An illocutionary act can be the means to a perlocutionary act but not *vice versa*. Examples of illocutionary verbs include report, announce, predict, reprimand, order, express, promise, exhort; perlocutionary verbs include deceive, persuade, encourage, inspire, distract, embarrass, attract attention, get *x* to do something.

Austin distinguishes five classes of illocutionary forms: verdictives, exercitives, commissives, behabitives, expositives.[94] Verdictives are typified by the giving of a verdict and include acquit, convict, grade, rule, value, diagnose and calculate. Exercitives are the exercising of powers, rights or influences and include appoint, dismiss, sentence, levy, proclaim, pardon, advise, announce. Commissives are typified by promise or undertaking; they commit one to doing something and are typified by such examples as promise, covenant, contract, undertake, vow, oppose, guarantee. Behabitives have to do with behaviour and attitudes and include apologise, thank, commiserate, resent, welcome, bless, curse, wish and challenge (behabitives include special scope for insincerity). Expositives are more difficult to define but are used in acts of exposition or argumentation such as repudiate, testify, rejoin, agree, demure to, conclude by and deduce.

If the question of truth or falsity is a mark of statements (or locutions) then a mark of performatives is what Austin calls 'the doctrine of the Infelicities' rather than of being true or false.[95] When the performative act goes wrong it is not false but unhappy, it is a failure. There may be misapplications, misinvocations or hitches of one kind or another. An example of such an infelicitous performative would be the saying of 'I do' in a marriage ceremony when one of the performers was already married. Such an example poses the interesting problem of rendering the ceremony inoperative and yet at the same time making the act a bigamous one. Legally the bigamist would be charged with having married twice whereas the second party would not be married at all! Statements made on stage during a theatrical performance would not be performative – these are covered by conventions distinguishing acting from real life. Where the conventions are not observed the performatives do not work: they become infelicitous.

This very brief account of performative language will have to serve as an introductory approach to treating prophetic language as essentially performative. Taking language as having a performative dimension it is necessary to read prophecy as not only saying things but also doing and achieving things. Such a performative element in prophetic language would make it less prone to analysis in terms of true-false categories and more appropriately open to being considered in terms of happy-unhappy possibilities. The success or failure of various prophetic performatives would then be related to their ability to persuade the community to follow them rather than to a capacity for seeing the future before it came into being. It would provide a more adequate account of the complexities of prophecy than the traditional foreteller of the future approach.

The performative dimension of prophecy can be clearly seen in a number of statements in the traditions. Jeremiah's commission was 'to pluck up and to break down, to destroy and to overthrow, to build and to plant' (1.10). Preaching accompanied by dramatic actions was his technique for achieving these ends. Elijah accounted for the absence of rain in terms of his preaching (cf. I Kings 17.2). The commission of Isaiah is particularly instructive in this matter. After preliminary purification the prophet received the following instructions: 'Go, and say to this people: "Hear and hear, but do not understand; see and see, but do not perceive." Make the heart of this people fat (*hašmēn lēb*), and their ears heavy (*wᵉ'oznāyw hakbēd*), and shut their eyes (*wᵉ'ēnāyw hāša'*), lest they see with their eyes, and hear with their ears, and understand with their hearts, and turn (*wāšāb*) and be healed,' (6.9, 10). The use of the causatives ('make fat', 'make heavy', 'besmear') indicates the performative thrust of the prophetic word. The preaching of Isaiah was intended to cause these effects in the community: it had a perlocutionary force. The opening phrases of Second Isaiah's oracles had a similar performative force: 'Comfort, comfort my people, says your God. Speak tenderly to Jerusalem, and cry to her that her warfare (*ṣābā'h*'hard service') is ended, that her iniquity is pardoned, that she has received from Yahweh's hand double for all her sins' (40.1, 2). The declaration of pardon was intended to comfort the nation, indeed in performative terms was the comfort.

The general terms used to describe the prophetic preaching such as proclamation, announcement, threat, warning, opposition, pardon all indicate that the very core of prophetic language was performative. In behaving in such ways the prophets performed the tasks of challenge, indictment of community, repudiation of its behaviour, conviction of crimes and offences, announced the people's guilt and passed sentence of death on it. On other occasions they commiserated with the community, pardoned it, promised it prosperity and blessed it. The perlocutionary aspects of their preaching may be seen in their encouragement and inspiration of the people, their persuasion of the people to act in certain ways and, on occasion, their deception of the community.

Performative language is convention bound and so to treat prophetic language as performative entails showing that it operated in terms of well established conventions of linguistic use in ancient Israel. This is perhaps the most difficult part of dealing with prophecy as being performative. The traditions present prophecy as generally having been either ignored or rejected by the community. Thus Jehoiakim's response to hearing Baruch read Jeremiah's oracles was to have the scroll cut into strips and thrown into the fire (36.20–26). This contempt for the prophetic word was typical of Jeremiah's public reception throughout his life. It is not clear whether the king's action was designed to convey his contempt for Jeremiah or was an attempt to render the thrust of the oracles inoperative. Clearly the king was not automatically afraid when he heard the words of terrible destruction announced against him, his city, people and land. The deuteronomistic editors however were of the view that the correct attitude to such prophetic words was to be afraid and respond to them by heeding them: 'Yet neither the king, nor any of his servants who heard all these words, was afraid, nor did they rend their garments. Even when Elnathan and Delaiah and Gemariah urged the king not to burn the scroll, he would not listen to them' (vv 24, 25; cf. 26.17–19). In spite of having no standing in the royal court the prophet's preaching was expected to have an effect on those who heard it. The incident in Jer. 36 yields information on certain actual attitudes as well as ideal responses to prophecy.

If there had been a belief in the magical power of the prophetic word or gesture (cf. II Kings 5.11) in ancient Israel then we would have expected the prophets to have been taken more seriously than they appear to have been. Jehoiakim's action was dismissive of Jeremiah's warnings and threats, though there remains an ambiguity about whether it may not have been designed to frustrate that word by destroying it (cf. a similar symbolic action done by Jeremiah himself when he broke the potter's flask thereby asserting the destruction of the community, 19.1, 10). The king opposed the prophet's power with his own power because as king he had the oversight of the community's welfare. The opposition between prophet and king belonged to the deuteronomists' reading of Judaean history as a power struggle between prophecy and royal house in which they supported the ideology of prophecy against the ideology then dominating the house of David. The presence of prophets in the royal court also complicates the issue because in so far as the conventions of prophecy were observed there individual prophets such as Micaiah or Jeremiah were either unconventional or flaws in the system (cf. I Kings 22.7, 8). The conventions of prophetic speech used by the canonical prophets were clearly distinctive from those of the court prophets in terms of being critical of the royal house and announcing the destruction of the nation. The differences between the two sets of prophets were emphasized by the deuteronomists throughout their presentations of prophecy in Kings and Jeremiah.

Performatives such as announcing, warning, threatening allied to the belief that the prophet was the spokesman of Yahweh would have been effective in ancient Israel provided that the community shared the prophetic belief in its own legitimacy and therefore accepted its authority. When the king announced that he pardoned or condemned somebody that was a successful performative because the king held authority legitimately in Judah, i.e. he was the source of effective power. When a prophet declared the king to be illegitimate or doomed then whether that was a successful performative or otherwise will have depended upon the general acceptance of the prophet as a legitimate figure of authority in the community. There can be little doubt that the deuteronomistic historians so presented the prophet and therefore could write their history as the history of prophecy opposing the illegitimate practices of various kings (especially in the Elijah–Elisha sagas where kings were anointed or deposed by prophetic fiat). However hindsight contributed much to the deuteronomistic history and as a way of reading the history of Israel and Judah it sustained the theological dogmas of the deuteronomists. However in the eighth and subsequent centuries prophecy could only announce the destruction of the community as having been caused by its sinfulness but was unable to effectively impose its authority. That authority was regularly fragmented by the presence in the community of other prophets who took a radically different view of the political situation. In such a context of prophetic conflict the effective prophet was the one whose preaching influenced the community thereby confirming the performative force of the prophetic word. Unfortunately for the community the illocutionary and perlocutionary aspects of prophecy were to lead to the verdict: 'Your prophets have seen for you false and deceptive visions; they have not exposed your iniquity to restore your fortunes, but have seen for you oracles false and misleading' (Lam. 2.14).

The tradition that certain of the prophets were rejected by the communities of their own time suggests that that particular form of prophetic proclamation had little conventional force within their society. The inability to persuade king or community to accept their analysis of religion and politics meant that this kind of prophet was essentially ineffectual, though the possibility that a few of them did gain followers or had some influence must be allowed for in view of the preservation of their oracles. Other cultural contexts in ancient Israel used language in a performative way, e.g. the cult where the priestly role involved declaratory statements to the effect that the individual was clean or unclean (cf. Lev. 13.6, 13, 17, 23, 28, 34, 37 (clean); 13.3, 8, 11, 15, 20, 22, 25, 27, 30, 44 (unclean); 14.7, 48).[96] The priest also pronounced over sacrifices whether they were acceptable or not to Yahweh (cf. Lev. 1.3, 4; 19.5; 22.19, 21, 25 (for); Lev. 7.18; 19.7; 22.23, 25 (against)). Given the conventions operative in the cult these declarations had an illocutionary force for the cultic community. However it is far from clear that prophecy functioned in a similar way outside the cultic community. The existence of cult prophets may have carried some of the cultic norms over into the sphere of prophecy but apart from the recognized cult prophets and Second Isaiah there is little evidence to suggest that the other major prophets functioned in such a way. Later prophecy did utilize the blessing and cursing forms but probably under cultic influences (cf. Isa. 19.25; 44.3; 51.2; 61.9; 65.8, 16, 23; 66.3; Jer. 31.23; Hag. 2.19; Zech. 8.13 (blessing); Isa. 65.20; 23.9; Jer. 11.3; 17.5; 20.14, 18; 24.9; 25.18; 29.22; Ezek. 21.26; 22.7; Zech. 8.13; Mal. 1.14; 2.2; 3.9 (cursing)).

Considering the difficulty of establishing conventional procedures for prophetic language because of the way the traditions presented the prophet as speaking against societies which regularly ignored him and given the fact that so many of the positive oracles contained in the traditions were such an infelicitous use of language it may be fair to make the following observation about prophetic language. It was most likely made up of conventional forms and often both illocutionary and perlocutionary in force but where it strayed from prophetic conventions, e.g. in applying cultic language to matters outside the cult (cf. Second Isaiah), it used infelicitous forms and such uses may account for the failure of the salvation hopes of prophecy. However one cannot rule out the possibility that prophecy originally attempted to do something new, namely the prophets sought to translate into the categories of human history the divine activity they perceived on a cosmic scale.[97] What was true from a cultic standpoint they wished to see made historical in the experience of the community. In their failure to achieve such a high vision we have both category confusion and an infelicitous use of performative language.

Reflections on prophetic language. I have devoted a good deal of space to the discussion of ways in which prophetic language may have been used in the traditions. Because we cannot be sure how it was intended originally or how it was heard we must work on the assumption that this multiplicity of levels, i.e. magical, cultic, symbolic, conditional and performative, is the way to approach understanding the prophetic uses of language. If their language can be read so as to yield such a wide range of possible meanings it becomes much more difficult to be precise in our interpretation of it. Such imprecision has the benefit of allowing us to see how many ways it may be handled and the defect of clearly showing the concomitant lack of cognitive force in the language. That the traditions survived and were maintained by other communities suggests that the multivalent levels of prophetic language were very amenable to the reinterpretative processes of the later communities. Such imprecise language with its many possible ways of being interpreted should warn us about attempting to pin down prophetic oracles in rigid true or false categories. The truth-falsity paradigm, although fundamentally important for philosophy, theology and the interpretation of texts, can very easily frustrate understanding any language. The difficulties of applying truth conditions to complex social factors can be seen in the conflict between the prophets that characterized the closing decades of Judaean national life.

The basic thesis being argued for here is that in order to understand prophecy it is necessary to understand the language in the ways the prophets used it. Where there are difficulties of interpretation such as the understanding of prediction and fulfilment we must treat the matter in terms of the language used. This is to seek the resolution of problems in the interpretation of the language. I have in mind Wittgenstein's lapidary observation: 'It is in language that an expectation and its fulfilment make contact.'[98] The context of that remark is a discussion of the nature of the satisfaction of expectations and its point seems to be that how we describe things linguistically is what links an expectation to something of which we are prepared to say that it is the fulfilment or realization of that expectation. The precise meaning of Wittgenstein is not always clear but along such lines it may be possible to link two sets of events and regard them as connected in terms of expectation and realization by the language in which they are both expressed. Later communities were to describe their own experiences and expectations in terms derived from the prophetic traditions. Such a linguistic turn became very important for the interpretation of prophecy and its justification may well have been in the original traditions themselves. For the deuteronomists were quite prepared to apply the same prophetic oracle to three different kings on three separate occasions: 'Any one belonging to Jeroboam who dies in the city the dogs shall eat; and any one who dies in the open country the birds of the air shall eat' (I Kings 14.11; cf. 16.4; 21.24).[99] An examination of the ways the later prophetic traditions reinterpreted the earlier oracles will make the force of this thesis clearer and sounder. In this sense the argument about how language functioned in prophecy is of fundamental importance for the interpretation of prophecy.

The logic of question and answer

There are many ways of approaching and interpreting the prophetic traditions but the ones I propose using in this book are necessarily limited to a few that I regard as important in uncovering the problems of interpretation. One such important and useful approach is what is called the logic of question and answer. This approach sees the text or tradition as the answer, or set of answers, to the question, or set of questions, posed by something not in the text. The questions give rise to the texts in the first place. This means we have to take seriously not only the text but what is behind the text. In the logic of question and answer we may see the text or tradition as the tip of the iceberg, the greater part of which remains unseen. It is for this reason that I have devoted so much space to unravelling the background of prophecy and some of its contextual factors as prerequisites for understanding the traditions.

The logic of question and answer approach comes from the writings of the Oxford philosopher R. G. Collingwood. In his autobiography he wrote: 'I began by observing that you cannot find out what a man means by simply studying his spoken or written statements, even though he has spoken or written with perfect command of language and perfectly truthful intention. In order to find out his meaning you must also know what the question was (a question in his own mind, and presumed by him to be in yours) to which the thing he has said or written was meant as an answer.'[100] He developed this point about asking questions in terms of the Socratic mode of doing philosophy and the Platonic notion of dialogue in other writings.[101] The probe of questioning can illuminate a subject, provided that the questions are put intelligently, in the right order, and are sensible. Sensible questions are questions for which you think you have or are going to have evidence for answering. Collingwood relates evidence to questioning, i.e. something is evidence in relation to some definite question, and the collection of evidence he relates to thinking which means asking questions.

Collingwood never developed systematically the logic of question and answer but his approach has been taken up by Hans-Georg Gadamer and expanded into an important part of his work on philosophical hermeneutic.[102] After discussing the Platonic dialogues Gadamer writes: 'Thus we come back to the point that the hermeneutic phenomenon also contains within itself the original meaning of conversation and the structure of question and answer. For an historical text to be made the object of interpretation means that it asks a question of the interpreter. Thus interpretation always involves a relation to the question that is asked of the interpreter. To understand a text means to understand this question. But this takes place, as we showed, by our achieving the hermeneutical horizon. We now recognize this as the horizon of the question within which the sense of the text is determined. Thus a person who seeks to understand must question what lies behind what is said. He must understand it as an answer to a question. If we go back behind what is said, then we inevitably ask questions beyond what is said. We understand the sense of the text only by acquiring the horizon of the question that, as such, necessarily includes other possible answers. Thus the meaning of a sentence is relative to the question to which it is a reply, i.e. it necessarily goes beyond what is said in it. The logic of the human sciences is, then, as appears from what we have said, a logic of the question.'[103]

Elsewhere Gadamer expands his point about the question giving rise to the statement: 'For no statement has an unambiguous meaning based on its linguistic and logical construction as such, but, on the contrary, each is motivated. A question is behind each statement that first gives it its meaning. Furthermore, the hermeneutical function of the question affects in turn what the statement states generally – in that the statement is an answer.'[104] According to him 'to understand a question means to ask it. To understand an opinion is to understand it as the answer to a question'.[105] This dialectic of question and answer then is an important approach to the understanding of texts.

This approach to the prophetic traditions involves seeing prophecy as the response of the prophets to the questions posed by their time and society and also to the questions raised by their relationship to that society. Their oracles were answers to questions posed by them and to them. Beyond that prophecy was also the questioning of Israelite and Judaean societies by its trenchant critique. There is a multiplicity of levels at which questions and answers were posed and answered in the traditions. There are the obvious surface ones that constitute part of the texts themselves and then the deeper questions to which the traditions were answers in the first place. The various reinterpretative additions to the traditions were attempts to answer some of the questions raised by the continued failure of the prophetic vision to be realized.

The prophetic vision is often presented in the traditions as the outcome of questions thrown up by different events and experiences. Isaiah's commission was the outcome of his response to a question (6.8) and resulted in his having to ask the question 'how long?' (6.11). The initial proclamation of Second Isaiah was the declaration: 'all flesh is grass . . . but the word of our God will stand for ever' which was a response to the question 'what shall I cry?' (40.6–8). The visions by which the prophets mediated so much of their message often were accompanied or stimulated by the question 'what do you see?' (Amos 7.8; 8.2; Jer. 1.11, 13; cf. Ezek. 8). On occasion the vision developed on from the question posed (cf. I Kings 19.9–18; II Kings 2.1–14; Ezek. 37.1–14). The prophetic question could be directed to Yahweh (cf. Amos 7.2, 5; Isa. 6.11) or the proclamation to the nation could take the form of question and answer (cf. Amos 2.9–11; 3.3–8; 5.18–20, 25; 6.2, 3; 9.7). The prophet's inner tensions could result in a dialogue of questioning with the deity (cf. Amos 7.1–6; Hab. 2.1–4; Jer. 12.1–6; 15.15–18). That prophecy could be the attempt to answer questions raised by contemporary disasters would seem to be clearly the case with the oracles of Joel (1.2, 3; 2.11, 17). The task of prophecy could also be seen as the declaration of Yahweh's requirements of the community (e.g. Micah 6.6–8).

The main centre in ancient Israelite culture for dealing with questions relating to the organization of life and occasional crises was the cult. At the sanctuary the priest answered questions and gave directions (*tōrōt*) to enquirers about issues of legitimacy and entrance qualifications for the cultic community (e.g. Ps. 15; 24; 81.8–10 (Heb. 81.9–11)). There the community lamented disasters and sought comfort in times of distress. Thus the question 'how long?' (*'ad-mātay*) had an important place in the worship of the community (cf. Ps. 6.3 (Heb. 6.4); 74.10; 80.4 (Heb. 80.5); 82.2; 90.13; 94.3). The community directed this question to the deity in times of great trouble when its enemies had yet again devastated its land. The continued suffering of the community was cause for grave concern and the cult sought to answer its people's lament. Echoes of this concern can be heard in the traditions of the cult prophets (e.g. Joel, Habakkuk) and in instances where prophets were involved with the sanctuary (cf. Isa. 6.11; Zech. 1.12; Hab. 2.6). Isaiah's use of the lament formula may have had an ironic element in that the formulaic appeal to Yahweh to end quickly the community's destruction was answered by the assertion that the destruction would go on until cities were deserted and the land ruined (6.11–13). In the oracles of Jeremiah the question was addressed to the continued corruption of the community (4.14), the prolonged period of fighting (4.21), and the lengthy period that would need to elapse before the community's purification (13.27; cf. Hos. 8.5). The question was one posed by Elijah on mount Carmel to the Israelites as a challenge to them to choose Yahweh (I Kings 18.21). The thrust of the question was addressed to the community during a period of apostasy or to the deity when catastrophe had hit the nation. Both contexts shared the element of crisis and the question thrown up by such crises.

The crisis of disaster was seen as the anger of the deity directed against the community in the form of foreign invasion of the land and destruction of the temple (cf. Ps. 74.9–11; 79.5–7). Part of the distress caused by the invasion was the failure of the expectations of salvation encouraged by the (cult) prophets. 'We do not see our signs (*'ōtōtēnō*); there is no longer any prophet, and there is none among us who knows how long' (Ps. 74.9). The prophet backed his proclamation with a sign (*'ōt*), the occurrence of which indicated that his prediction was in the process of being fulfilled (cf. Isa. 7.10–16; I Sam. 10.1–7). The prophet was also the authority in the community for answering the critical question 'how long?'. In this instance the failure of the prophetic signs meant either the community's prophets were inadequate to the task of discerning the duration of the crisis or they had been exposed by the crisis so the community lacked any effective prophets.[106] A community without a prophet or that lacked adequate prophets in a time of crisis was in a lamentable position. Such crises posed serious questions for prophecy as well as for the community.

The emergence of the canonical prophets during the period of the Assyrian rise to political domination of the Ancient Near East was partly as a response to the crises of urban settlements in the smaller nations caused by the expansionist policies of the imperial power. In such a context the prophets directed their question to the triumphalism inherent in the traditional cultic presentation of Yahweh's relationship with the nation, especially associated with the day of Yahweh. To the general question of crisis 'what is to become of the nation in such times?' the prophets answered 'Yahweh will sweep away city and people, priest and prophet, rich and poor!' Such a devastating critique of the structures in turn posed the question 'how can Jacob stand? He is so small!' (cf. Amos 7.2, 5). The destruction of the vineyard because the enterprise had failed (Isa. 5.1–7) posed very serious questions for community and prophets. One set of questions led to another set about the continued existence of Israel and the concomitant problem of the relationship between people and deity. That question was posed in the most profound way by Hosea: 'How can I give you up, O Ephraim! How can I hand you over, O Israel! How can I make you like Admah! How can I treat you like Zeboiim!' (11.8). To that question with its deeply disturbing implications the prophets essayed an answer in their proclamations over the next century and a half. Each prophet sought to work out a dialectic of question and answer which would adequately deal with the crisis and the prophetic traditions handed on, with expansions and modifications, various accounts of their responses.

Much more could be said by way of treating the traditions as answers to questions posed by historical events and experiences, by inner tensions between prophets and society, even between prophet and prophet, and by their dialogues with Yahweh but sufficient has been hinted at to indicate the appropriateness of applying the logic of question and answer to the interpretation of prophecy. In my subsequent treatment of prophecy the application of the dialectic of question and answer will be limited to the predictive element in the prophetic traditions and particularly to the problem of unfulfilled predictions. As a way of approaching the analysis of the later traditions which interpreted prophecy in the light of fulfilment problems it has much to recommend it. How are we to understand texts which appear to be saying things for which there was no evidence of any confirming event to justify the continued maintenance of the expectation? What pressures or paradoxes were created by such failures of expectation? Do the traditions give any indication of an awareness of such problems or reveal attempts to respond to or explain difficulties caused by the lack of fulfilment of earlier hopes? How did the later tradents come to terms with the disappointment of their beliefs? What functions did the preservation of the prophetic traditions serve for the communities in which they were kept? Such questions seeking to analyse the traditions are part of the logic of question and answer approach to the texts.

The question about understanding the predictive element in biblical prophecy is not simply one posed by modern interpreters but is also posed within the traditions. The prophets were on occasion confronted by sceptical responses to the effect that their word had not yet come to pass: 'Woe to those . . . who say: "Let him make haste, let him speed his work that we may see it; let the purpose of the holy one of Israel draw near, and let it come, that we may know it!"' (Isa. 5.18, 19). 'Behold, they say to me, "Where is the word of Yahweh? Let it come!"' (Jer. 17.15). Those phrases *tābō'āh* and *yābō'nā*' 'let it come' represent the authentic voice of scepticism directed at the prophets and demanding to see evidence that what they proclaimed would actually occur. The failure to meet such sceptical demands for proof of their predictions must have contributed significantly to the lack of public response to the prophets (cf. Isa. 53.1; Jer. 25.3, 4). For the later groups that preserved and edited the traditions the problem was more one of coming to terms with the failure of the cult oracles of salvation. Their activity was devoted to interpreting those oracles so as to indicate how the hopes expressed therein were still open to fulfilment and provided notes on how to read prophecy in the light of contemporary experiences (cf. Isa. 10.25; 56.1; Hab. 2.3).

It has to be admitted that the Socratic mode of questioning everything, of applying the logic of question and answer can be a sternly critical approach which not only destroys all vestiges of unreflective thought but also can be destructive of all serious enterprise if not carefully controlled. It was Nietzsche who pointed out that the Socratic dialectic destroyed the heart and basis of Greek tragedy because it went on questioning what it did not understand.[107] The dialectic of questioning in order to learn what was the case and thereby replace one's ignorance with genuine knowledge was an epistemology highly inimical to the ecstatic dream world of mythic tragedy. The epistemology of prophecy was essentially inspirational and demanded by way of response what some modern theologians would call 'the logic of obedience'.[108] The theological editors of many of the biblical traditions put great emphasis on obedience as the proper response to divine revelation (cf. Ex. 19.5; Deut. 6.1–3; 7.11; 8.1, 11, 20; 10.12, 13; I Sam. 15.22, 23; Jer. 7.22, 23). The deuteronomists attributed the destruction of Judah to the persistent refusal to obey the prophets (Jer. 7.25, 26; 25.4; cf. 26.17–19; 36.20–26). So the proper response to prophecy was to listen to and obey the prophetic injunctions rather than critically examine what they had to say. For Socrates the ideal response was to confess to ignorance and to go on questioning until true knowledge was attained. To imagine a Socrates encountering the prophets is to see what the real problem is with reference to the analytical tool of the logic of question and answer. Prophecy did not respond to such probings because it asked the questions and did not tolerate opposition of any kind.

The prophet as his own authority and prophecy as a special form of religious authority in the community were two facets of the phenomenon of prophecy that developed in ancient Israel. For the later tradents such authority became normative (cf. Isa. 8.16–20; Zech. 1.4; 7.7, 12). However, as Collingwood noted, the logic of question and answer is an alternative approach to doing history in keeping with the Baconian method of 'putting Nature to the question' rather than the older method of submitting to authorities and accepting their views of the matter.[109] The negative effects of this approach to prophecy provide a number of insights into the nature of the prophetic interaction with society which will be of particular assistance in dealing with the problems of prophetic conflict and the failure of expectations. The Socratic method of asking 'what is it that you know?', with its basic humanist aporias (cf. Montaigne's motto *Que sais-je?*), affords a dialectical foil to the certainties of prophecy and in the conflict of epistemologies may also contribute to our understanding of the tensions within the prophetic traditions.

The lengthy consideration of so many aspects of prophecy along with the discussion of how prophetic language might be interpreted and the dialectical approach of question and answer have been necessary preliminary investigations of the complexities of the hermeneutic of prophecy. The selection of factors has been determined by a concern to understand the ways in which later prophetic circles came to terms with crises of failed expectations, and to monitor such responses in so far as they were registered in their editing of the texts. To achieve such aims more effectively I propose an analysis of the traditions using a theory of cognitive dissonance.

PART II

Dissonance Theory and the Traditions

2

The Theory of Cognitive Dissonance

The theory of cognitive dissonance was first propounded in the 1950s by a professor of psychology, Leon Festinger.[1] In the twenty years since then it has become one of the most influential and stimulating theories in social psychology and has generated hundreds of study projects and research programmes. It would be extremely difficult, as well as beyond the needs of this book, to list all the studies and experiments carried out using its techniques or to survey the vast literature devoted to dissonance theory.[2] However it is fair to say that the general testimony of the literature can be summed up in the statement: 'No theory in social psychology has stimulated more research than the theory of cognitive dissonance . . . If there is any one theoretical formulation that has captured the imagination of social psychologists during this decade, it is beyond any doubt Festinger's theory of cognitive dissonance.'[3]

The theory grew out of work done by Festinger and others in social comparison and communication and belongs to that aspect of social psychology devoted to determining principles of consistency, balance and congruity. Part of its influence is probably to be attributed to its stress on 'a very interesting kind of inconsistency, some interesting aspects of the magnitude of inconsistency and some interesting ways of reducing inconsistency'.[4] The theory is a more sophisticated theoretical treatment of problems arising from consistency-inconsistency, balance-imbalance and congruity-incongruity factors in social psychology. In particular Festinger's formulation of cognitive dissonance relates to explaining problems arising in post-decision making circumstances. This concern with consistency (consonance) between expectation and experience, and the avoidance or reduction of inconsistency, makes the theory eminently suitable for the analysis of predictive prophecy in terms of responses to problems of realized expectations.

An outline of dissonance theory

Cognitive elements are the basic units of dissonance theory. They are the things a person knows or believes about himself, his behaviour and his environment. Conflict occurs when a person has to make a choice among a number of possibilities, each of which offers a desirable option. Once the decision has been made the possibility of experiencing dissonance is created. So dissonance theory is essentially about post-decisional conflict. In Festinger's terminology dissonance is a replacement term for inconsistency, so that instead of behaviour, beliefs or opinions being inconsistent with one another they are now said to give rise to the experience of dissonance. Cognitions are what people know, believe or feel – the term is loosely used in the general theory – so cognitive dissonance arises when two cognitions are inconsistent with one another. Where cognitions are consistent or compatible the relationship is one of consonance (the replacement term for consistency). Between different beliefs, attitudes or patterns of behaviour there are, at least, three possible relationships. They may be *irrelevant* to each other so that they are cognitively neutral in relation to one another. They may be *consonant* with each other. Or they may be *dissonant* with each other, in which case conflict occurs. According to Festinger dissonance is a noxious state that people will attempt to reduce or resolve and his theory is mainly about modes of dissonance resolution.

Dissonance arises in the first place with the acquisition of new information or knowledge (i.e. further cognitive elements). Because it is not possible to control one's environment to the extent that no elements of a disturbing nature can reach one, dissonance may easily arise under any number of circumstances. Dissonance need not be limited to the individual's apperception but can arise between two people who are in regular contact with one another. Furthermore dissonance can be a part of everyday life because very few things are so clear and simple that ambiguities and ambivalences can be avoided. Whenever opinions are formed or decisions have to be made the possibility of dissonance inevitably appears. Dissonance is often unavoidable because after decisions have been made the decision maker can still be aware of the choices refused and also of the defects in the options exercised. Once dissonance occurs it can be a very persistent problem. For Festinger cognitive elements mirror or map reality so therefore 'the reality which impinges on a person will exert pressures in the direction of bringing the appropriate cognitive elements into correspondence with that reality'.[5] He posits a drive to bring all cognitive elements into a consistent relation with one another; a drive which seeks to resolve dissonance and restore the equilibrium of the system. In this sense dissonance reduction 'seems to be the psychological analogue of the physiological mechanisms which maintain homoeostasis in the body'.[6]

Two elements are said to be dissonant if, for one reason or another, they do not fit together. This lack of fit is defined by Festinger as 'two elements are in a dissonant relation if, considering these two alone, the obverse of one element would follow from the other'.[7] To put it in more formal terms x and y are dissonant if not-x follows from y. Dissonance may arise from logical inconsistencies, e.g. if one believed that men would soon land on the moon and also believed that it was impossible to leave the earth's atmosphere. Cultural mores may give rise to the experience of dissonance, e.g. arriving for church in a state of undress. Dissonance may occur where a specific opinion is entailed by a more general belief, e.g. believing in abortion and being a Catholic of unimpeachable orthodoxy. Or dissonance may be caused by past experience being contradicted by a discrete experience, e.g. having always found that the singing of 'Kevin Barry' in hostelries along the Shankill Road area of Belfast produced riots, one would be perplexed to discover a particular occasion on which it did not.

There are degrees of dissonance and the magnitude of the dissonance will depend upon the importance (i.e. the function) of the cognitive elements. The more value the cognition has for a person the greater the magnitude of dissonance will be. So many other cognitive elements have to be taken into consideration in order that the degree of dissonance may be determined. The central element in the theory is Festinger's claim that 'the presence of dissonance gives rise to pressure to reduce or eliminate the dissonance. The strength of the pressures to reduce dissonance is a function of the magnitude of the dissonance.'[8] Action is taken to reduce dissonance just as being hungry leads to action to reduce that hunger. Comparable to drives the greater the dissonance the greater the intensity of action to reduce it. The limits of the magnitude of dissonance are defined as 'the maximum dissonance that can possibly exist between any two elements is equal to the total resistance to change of the less resistant element. The magnitude of dissonance cannot exceed this amount because, at this point of maximum possible dissonance, the less resistant element would change, thus eliminating the dissonance.'[9]

The core of the theory of cognitive dissonance may be stated rather simply in the following terms:

1. There may exist dissonant or 'nonfitting' relations among cognitive elements.
2. The existence of dissonance gives rise to pressures to reduce the dissonance and to avoid increases in dissonance.
3. Manifestations of the operation of these pressures include behaviour changes, changes of cognition, and circumspect exposure to new information and new opinions.[10]

The main experimental work derived from the theory involved questionnaires and tests relating to decision making activities which posed dissonance inducing circumstances for the subjects tested. From these tests it was confirmed that after decision making:

1. There is active seeking out of information which produces cognition consonant with the action taken.
2. There is an increase in the confidence in the decision or an increase in the discrepancy in attractiveness of alternatives involved in the choice. Each reflects successful reduction of dissonance.
3. The successful reduction of postdecision dissonance is further shown in the difficulty of reversing a decision once it is made and in the implication which changed cognition has for future relevant action.
4. The effects listed above vary directly with the magnitude of dissonance created by the decision.[11]

The tests, developments, ramifications and modifications of the general theory have been going on for twenty years now and there is an industry of psychologists producing literature on the subject. It is not necessary to go into the continued streamlining of the theory or its consequences for public behaviour or social responses to advertising schemes which constitute the practical effects of the theory. These are very interesting aspects of the theory and provide employment for many social psychologists as well as affording great opportunities for constructing experiments and tests which tend to confirm the general approach to cognitive change outlined by the theory. My main interest in the theory is to consider the ways in which dissonance is reduced or resolved by individuals or groups confronted by circumstances which threaten their cognitive holdings.

Paradigms of dissonance response

To introduce the complex matter of dissonance resolution the following four cases may be considered as typical illustrations of the problem of dissonance.

Case A. Subject M has just bought a very expensive new car. He can ill afford it but it confirms his self-image and he believes it to be the best car on the market (cognition B). Soon after buying it he reads an article in a car magazine, highly rated by car *aficionados*, that harshly criticizes the model he has acquired and provides facts and figures to back that judgment (cognition C). His friends also inform him that his car is a bad performer and a waste of money (further confirmation of C). The conflict between B and C produces an acute sense of dissonance in M which he must resolve in order to maintain his peace of mind.

Case B. Subject N is a very heavy smoker (cognition D). After reading a good deal of current medical literature on the injurious effects of smoking on health he comes to share that belief (cognition E) but continues to smoke. Between his practice (D) and his newly-formed belief (E) there is irreconcilable conflict that produces disturbing dissonance.

Case C. J and K are friends of longstanding but one day in argument it emerges that J believes that everything wrong with the world is due to the younger generation (cognition F), whereas K believes that the present young generation are a good deal better than their own generation had ever been (cognition G). Their disagreement becomes so intense that the dissonance aroused threatens their complete friendship.

Case D. Subject P believes that black people are dirty, lazy and corrupt (cognition H). This belief is so strongly held that he regularly goes on demonstrations to protest about continued immigration and to demand the repatriation of black people. One day at work he encounters a black person who is clean, hard working and morally attractive (cognition I). To his horror he discovers that most of the black people he now meets are of this type rather than what he believes about them. So in his mind there is conflict between H and I. He must now either resolve the dissonance or change his way of life.

These cases involve fairly common experiences and show how dissonance arises as a conflict between beliefs, practices, experiences or attitudes. The dissonance caused by such conflict can be so strong that it has to be reduced or resolved in order to preserve sanity, peace of mind, friendship or way of life. If the conflict were unimportant the sense of dissonance would be tolerable but where the magnitude of dissonance is great there is an urgent need for it to be modified.

However cognitive elements can be very resistant to change. The degree of that resistance depends upon how such elements relate to reality. If one's general beliefs about the world are such that they appear to be both reasonable and self-evident then change will be very difficult. If change involves pain or loss there will be great resistance to changing. If current behaviour gives much of life its meaning then the incentive to change will be correspondingly weak. Changing beliefs, outlooks or practices may not always be possible. Often certain actions may be irrevocable, e.g. selling a house or having a baby, so change is ruled out. Any one cognitive element is only one among many, therefore changing it may not be in the best interests of the other elements. All these factors make cognitions resistant to change. So the analysis of dissonance resolution involves a network of complex factors being taken into account.

In each of the cases outlined as examples dissonance was caused by the introduction of new cognitive elements into the experience of the subject. The need to reduce that dissonance was created by the desire to retain existent values which were important for the subject's way of life. Obviously such occasions of dissonance could only be avoided if the subjects isolated themselves from the rest of the community but that is a very unrealistic approach to life. In *case A*

M could reduce the dissonance by subsequent avoidance of negative information on his model of car, joining a club devoted to that particular car make (if such existed), and seeking out positive accounts of the car and its performance. Apart from the possibility of selling the car which would resolve the problem but, perhaps, at too great a cost, he must change his social habits in order to confirm cognition B and modify cognition C.

Case B provides a similar set of options. N may either give up smoking or attempt to reduce cognition E. If the habit is ingrained then he may resolve, or at least reduce, the dissonance by ignoring E, associating only with other smokers and restricting his reading on the matter to the publications of the tobacco producers. He may recognize that D is bad for him, that E is correct yet continue with D because it has become too addictive for him to stop. Thus he achieves an uneasy resolution of the dissonance by self-deception or a schizoid attitude to the matter. He could reduce the dissonance effectively by admitting the truth of E but also recognize that the benefits of D outweigh its defects sufficiently for him to persist in it. Those benefits might include social conformity, group identity, the hint of sexual status constantly reinforced by advertising, weight control and a sense of maturity carried over from adolescence.

For *case C* the problem is one of deciding whether a particular belief is more important than a friendship. If the belief is valued higher then the dissonance is resolved by the termination of that friendship. If the friendship is to continue then the belief will have to be modified or J and K will have to agree not to discuss that particular matter whenever they meet. They could, of course, argue the matter out to the point where both reached agreement or understood each other sufficiently for the conflict to cease being a cause of dissonance.

In *case D* the dissonance is caused by a deeply held conviction confronting a new experience. The ensuing conflict can be so strong that the options available to P involve one or other cognition having to be seriously rethought. He may maintain cognition H by denying the reality of cognition I, i.e. he may regard the blacks he meets as not *really* clean, hard working or moral. He may modify cognition I by explanations which show the blacks to be exceptions to the racial norm, in fact that they are exceptional people aspiring to be white in their way of life in order to rise quicker up the social ladder. He may even accord them an 'honorary white' status (cf. South African practice with regard to Japanese people). Or he may reinforce his original cognition by joining such groups as share that belief and campaign more actively on their behalf. In such circumstances he is less likely to meet such disturbing black people and so the dissonance is gradually reduced.

The treatment of these four examples in terms of response to dissonance show at least three important elements. The importance of explanatory or rationalization schemes, the avoidance of sources of dissonance arousal and the centrality of the social group. These categories are fundamental for the theory of cognitive dissonance. Avoidance techniques, explanatory systems and social support are the key moves in the reduction or resolution of dissonance. Abelson makes the point 'dissonance theory does not rest upon the assumption that man is a *rational* animal; rather, it suggests that man is a rationali*z*ing animal – that he attempts to appear rational, both to others and to himself'.[12] Explanatory schemes may often display this rationalization tendency as cognitions are modified to harmonize with each other. Avoidance of sources of dissonance may be achieved by group exclusivity or the evading of individuals or groups whose views are different. The less exposure to dissonant information the less dissonance will have to be reduced. The social group is the pivot of these responses to dissonance for it provides a stock of explanatory schemes and group support to shield from dissonance arousal. The three elements may occur separately or together but the importance of the group is paramount: that is why the theory of cognitive dissonance is essentially a theory of social psychology – it concerns groups and social needs. Man being a social animal, as language and sexuality indicate, has needs and desires that can only be satisfied in community with other people. These three aspects of dissonance resolution will form the central analysis of prophecy for evidence of response to dissonance.

Avoidance of dissonance. Whatever the event, opinion or encounter that produced the experience of dissonance in the past it must be avoided by the subject or group in the future. This may be relatively simple in that the subject need only avoid certain situations in order to maintain present cognitions free from disturbance. But where the beliefs impinge on reality in a major way it is not

possible to avoid dissonance producing confrontations. Such confrontations may be involuntary, i.e. accidental exposure to new
cognitive elements introduced into the system, or voluntary exposure to dissonance increasing views. For example, a man may believe
very strongly that all is well with the world, that a benevolent deity
rules over it and protects his personal servants. Such a belief may
make sense of his life and explain the order he sees in the world
around him. However if one day disasters strike his life, kill his
family and destroy his property (cf. Job 1, 2) then his cognitive
views about the world will take a severe shaking. Over that sort of
dissonance-producing occurrence nobody can have any control –
hence the sensible believer's prayer 'do not put us to the test'.[13]
Being social creatures people generally have to interact with other
people, both in the community and at work. Such exposure to other
people, whose cognitive systems can be very different, may also
introduce dissonance-arousing factors into people's lives. This kind
of exposure can be partly avoided by choices exercised (cf. closed
shop type of community) but inevitably entails a fair degree of
exposure to possible conflict.

Steps can be taken to modify all occasions that might produce
dissonance and provided a person or group do not encounter acci-
dents of a tragic nature it may be possible to create an environment
relatively free from dissonance arousal. The creation of such envi-
ronments is essentially a group concern so the existence of clubs,
communities, organizations, parties, churches and sects provide the
most potentially effective means of dissonance avoidance.

Social support. The group is both the main source of cognitive
dissonance for the individual and the major vehicle for reducing or
eliminating dissonance. What the individual hears from or encounters with other people may be the cause of the dissonant experience,
but by seeking out other people who share the same opinions the
individual may resolve or safely ignore the original cause of conflict.
By discarding one set of cognitive elements in favour of another the
individual may find a group whose cognitive holdings constitute a
dissonance-free environment. This feature of group support is well
known in religious and political systems where conversion and
commitment to specific programmes of belief are so important. The
group provides the context of a rationally organized system of

cognitive elements, including a well tried arsenal of propaganda and polemic both on behalf of the group and against alternative groups, and a ready ability to explain most major problems in terms consonant with the cognitive system. Here both group support and explanatory power are linked together.

The majority of methods for reducing dissonance are to be found in this category of social support. If the main point in dissonance resolution is to reduce the force of the dissonant cognitions this may be achieved by the group. In the first place the existence of the group provides social validation for its beliefs – it is a confirming instance of the group's holdings. Additional cognitive elements, i.e. more people joining the group, may be added to the group thereby increasing the power base of its cognitions. If more and more people come to share the group's cognitive beliefs then (it is argued) there must be something right or influential about those beliefs.[14] Commitment to a group followed by schemes for converting others to that group are probably the most effective social methods of resolving dissonance. Such conversionistic techniques are analogous to changing one's environment and thereby reduce dissonance.

Groups devoted to the maintenance of certain views about the world and the preservation of the group's equilibrium are ideal contexts for dissonance avoidance. Where such groups have a long history, i.e. a rich tradition, then they provide admirable protection against dissonant cognitions by supplying explanations which rob the dissonance producing elements of their force or supply alternative accounts of the data which show that no dissonance need be experienced. These groups not only provide a worldview they also provide an environment for the individual. In these ways the major religions of mankind have continued to be sources of support for groups and individuals. Such provisions tend to relate to the more serious areas of life where dissonance may arise in relation to pressing problems and conflicts of life. At lower and simpler levels groups such as fan clubs simply exist to maintain the interests of individuals in the common focus, though they obviously provide a dissonance-free context in relation to that centre.

One of the major ways in which dissonance may be reduced is for a group committed to a certain set of cognitive beliefs to engage in proselytizing activities. This is an alternative method of adding new cognitive elements to the group. Each new convert is one more person who thinks in a similar way. This can be an effective means of reducing dissonance when explanatory schemes no longer deal effectively with dissonance caused by events or experiences impinging on the belief system. Festinger argues that more elements of cognition can be added 'by persuading more and more persons that the belief system is true, that is, by proselyting and obtaining converts'.[15] As more and more believers join the group the strength of the dissonance producing event is steadily eroded and becomes less and less a source of significant cognitive dissonance. The force of this approach may be seen in the standard advertising ploy of commending a product on the grounds that more and more people are turning to it. The implication being that it must be good if so many people are changing from their normal habits to this new product. The same implication can be used in campaigns for mass conversion where '*x* number of people cannot be wrong' type of slogans attempt to provide a social validation for the group's beliefs.

Explanatory schemes. Explanations designed to rationalize the source of dissonance are the normal means of dissonance reduction or resolution. These may take the form of modifications of the offending cognitions or interpretative shifts in the subject's cognitions. Such moves are available to both individual and group. The group provides a stronger source for such responses to dissonance because it is part of the intellectual equipment of any group to be able to provide very strong arguments for its own position and very clever polemics against other viewpoints. Where religion, philosophy and politics are involved there are long traditions of such defensive and polemical stock-in-trades. That the individual can also modify dissonance by disputing the truth of the disturbing cognitions or shifting ground on other cognitions should be clear from the four cases considered above. There is an endless supply of possible reinterpretations or rationalizations available for neutralizing dissonance. In religious contexts one of the standard methods of treating the dissonance caused by encountering people with different belief structures, whose morality appears to be so impeccable that they qualify as 'righteous', is to call them 'self-righteous', or even 'righteous in their own eyes'.[16] Here reinterpretation of the disparate cognition by means of disparagement and shifting of terms is a technique of rationalization which reaffirms the

threatened belief system and effectively blocks any dissonance arising from other belief structures. It has to be noted that because
religious, philosophical, and political systems are so deeply
entrenched in society it is often the case that the dissonance liable to
be caused by encountering other cognitive systems does not arise in
the first place at all. This social phenomenon indicates the dissonance avoidance function of belief systems in that they provide a
place for everything in the world and have explanations of all
phenomena, events and experiences so that it is very difficult for
different or newer cognitive elements to penetrate such systems.

In tests where prejudiced people have been exposed to anti-
prejudice propaganda it has been shown that prejudiced persons
quickly set up defensive systems that vitiate the propaganda. These
defensive processes may involve rejecting the propaganda as not
applying to themselves personally, dismissing as incorrect the presentation of the life situations of the group under criticism or
imposing their own frame of reference on the information provided
they can frustrate the thrust of the propaganda.[17] A standard reaction to criticism by an alternative cognitive system is to complain
that the account given by that system of the criticized structure is a
caricature. It can be very difficult, if not impossible, to provide an
account that will satisfy the adherents of the system and thus there
will always be a very effective block to the possibility of dissonance
being aroused. However when dissonance arousing circumstances
cannot be avoided it remains possible to provide defences against
them by subtle forms of response to the data which may effectively
eliminate dissonance.

I have outlined at some length three paradigms of dissonance
response which I consider to be the main ways of handling dissonance because they have direct bearing on the subsequent analysis
of prophecy. It has to be kept in mind, of course, that dissonance
may be so strong that the individual or group is forced to concede to
it and either give up the older cognition altogether or convert to the
dissonance-producing cognition. This is what normally happens in
conversion experiences, whether religious, philosophical, political
or whatever. For example, Christian in *The Pilgrim's Progress*
resolves the terrible dissonance caused by his becoming aware of his
condition of sinfulness and the doom awaiting the people of his
territory (through reading the book) by changing his cognitive

holdings completely (achieved when his burden falls from his back at the cross). Despite this possible response to serious dissonance the relevant responses for this discussion are those related to reducing or resolving dissonance. To consider the theory of cognitive dissonance as it directly bears on biblical prophecy it is necessary to include in the examination Festinger's treatment of predicted expectations.

Dissonance theory and prediction

In *When Prophecy Fails* Festinger and his colleagues provide a study of a group who predicted the destruction of the world and lived to contemplate the failure of that prediction.[18] The focus of the study was a Mrs Keech who in the 1950s began to receive messages from outer space predicting the destruction of her city by flood on 21 December. The announcement of this approaching catastrophe appeared in the local newspaper three months before the day of doom and so the investigators were able to visit Mrs Keech and spend the next three months observing and reporting on the group involved in the predictions. It was an ideal opportunity to test the general hypothesis about dissonance because it allowed for observations to be made before, during and after a predicted event.

In the days immediately before the great flood the group of believers, who called themselves the Seekers, expected to be rescued by intervention from outer space and so made preparations accordingly.[19] However a series of disconfirmations occurred from 17 December to 21 December which required various explanations by Mrs Keech. These were failures of expectations of the death and resurrection of Mr Keech and the arrival of a flying saucer to rescue the group. The non-appearance of the flood meant that their central expectation also had failed. Given the force of these disconfirmations the group ought to have disintegrated but, on the contrary, further messages were received which explained to the satisfaction of most members of the Seekers the reasons for the failure of the predictions. Apparently God had been so impressed by the light spread by the small group that he had saved the world from destruction.[20] In the days before the expected catastrophe the group had isolated itself from the world and avoided all publicity, but after the set date the group began to spread the word and sought publicity.

They continued to seek confirming evidence of the approaching catastrophe and found such in reports of earthquakes. There was some reinterpretation of the original message which suggested that the first date was only intended to be a warning to give people time to be prepared. Further expectation of being picked up by flying saucer on 24 December also failed to be realized. The subsequent weeks after the destruction and rescue should have taken place were occupied by a persistent, frustrating search for orders from anybody the group imagined to be a spaceman. Eventually external forces broke up the group.

So Festinger and colleagues had sufficient data to construct an account of reactions to the disconfirmation of prophecies.[21] By observing the various members of the group they could plot the way each individual reacted to the succeeding series of disconfirmations and their responses to the rationalizations of them by the group leader. The two leaders, Mrs Keech and Dr Armstrong, appear never to have wavered in their faith at all. Months after the group broke up they were still receiving messages from outer space and Dr Armstrong was heavily involved in preaching his new faith (and still expecting to be picked up by flying saucer). Some of the group remained faithful to the vision created by the prophecies and their faith persisted after the disintegration of the group. Others, who had wavered in their beliefs as the 21st approached, became enthusiastic supporters and purveyors of the group's beliefs after disconfirmation.[22] Still others became confused and disillusioned. The general analysis of responses is summarized as yielding the evidence that those who were heavily committed to the beliefs survived the disconfirmation well but that those who were lightly attached to the group completely gave up their belief. The difference between those whose beliefs were unshaken and those whose beliefs were shaken would appear to have been related to having had to face the disconfirmation in a situation of isolation away from the group.[23]

One important aspect of Festinger's study concerns the proselytizing behaviour of the group. Apart from a brief period of such activity at the beginning of the group's existence (mainly by the one person), the group became very secretive until the final disconfirmation. After that setback most members of the group became involved in proselytizing; as Festinger notes 'proselytizing increased meteorically following disconfirmation'.[24] This public activity appears to have been an attempt to gain converts and thereby provide social validation for the belief system. The researchers also noted the persistence of prediction whereby the group sought desperately for confirmation of their expectations. This usually took the form of designating visitors as the expected spacemen. Such designations were attempts to confirm predictions.

When Prophecy Fails is an immensely fascinating account of a phenomenon characteristic of postwar Western civilization but its main relevance for the present study is its theoretical analysis of the nature of responses to unfulfilled prophecies. In the opening and concluding chapters of the book Festinger sets out conditions which must be operative if expectations and reactions to their disconfirmation are to be properly tested.[25] He also discusses some of the historical occasions where expectations and apparent disconfirmations have occurred. These include the second coming of Jesus, the Sabbatai Zevi movement and the nineteenth-century Millerites. Because these movements provide expectations they should also afford opportunities to examine responses to disconfirmations. However ambiguities and lack of sufficiently clear data make them less than ideal subjects for analysis. It is in such a context that Festinger introduces his study of the group of Seekers which, in comparison, proved to be an easier prospect for study.

Recently there has been increased interest in the movement centred on Sabbatai Zevi in the seventeenth century.[26] The essential facts about the movement are set against a background of belief among the Jews of the period that messiah would come in 1648. Sabbatai Zevi proclaimed himself as messiah to his small band of disciples in that year but it passed without the expected deliverance taking place. This disconfirmation does not appear to have greatly disturbed the group. After banishment from the Jewish community in Smyrna he seems to have accepted the general Christian expectation of the second coming in 1666. He moved about acquiring disciples until in 1665 he returned to Smyrna and proclaimed himself messiah. Soon he was heralded everywhere as the messiah and many Jews in distant Europe sold their possessions and prepared for the return to Jerusalem. Sabbatai Zevi and his followers set out for Constantinople in early 1666 in order to depose the sultan as a preliminary act in the return of the Jews to the Holy Land. However he was arrested there and imprisoned. Instead of the movement collapsing at this setback it thrived and more Jews flocked to the prison where Sabbatai Zevi held court. Eventually the sultan converted him to Islam. Some Jews followed his example by becoming Muslims and others continued to proselytize on his behalf. However soon after that the movement collapsed as the European Jews were unable to absorb his conversion to Islam. The movement dwindled and now very few Sabbataeans exist in the Near East.

The main interest in this movement for Festinger is the fact that when people are committed to a belief and a course of action, clear disconfirming evidence may simply result in deepened conviction and increased proselytizing. Of course a point is eventually reached when the amount of disconfirming evidence becomes too great for most of the believers to be able to maintain their belief structure.[27] In such a context Festinger introduces the notions of consonance and dissonance. The dissonance caused by disconfirmation of expectations can be modified by seeking reasonable, or even ingenious, explanations, e.g. the fact that Sabbatai Zevi was still alive in jail rather than dead was certain proof of his being the messiah. For such rationalizations to be effective they require strong social support. If the social support can be increased by gaining converts then the dissonance will be further reduced. In the decades following the apostasy of Sabbatai Zevi much thought was given to accounting for what had and had not happened. Scholem summarizes the essence of the Sabbataeans' conviction in one sentence: 'It is inconceivable that all of God's people should inwardly err, and so, if their vital experience is contradicted by the facts, *it is the facts that stand in need of explanation.*'[28] Rationalization as response to dissonance could hardly be stated better. In fact the Sabbataeans decided that the deception of the followers of Sabbatai Zevi was part of the divine plan. In this they were (consciously or otherwise) following precedence set by the earlier biblical tradents on the subject of prophets deceiving their hearers (cf. I Kings 22.19–23; Jer. 4.10; Ezek. 14.9).

For my purposes the most important aspect of Festinger's analysis is his statement of the conditions which determine whether there is sufficient data available to indicate increased activity after disconfirmation or not.

1. A belief must be held with deep conviction and it must have

some relevance to action, that is, to what the believer does or how he behaves.

2. The person holding the belief must have committed himself to it; that is, for the sake of his belief, he must have taken some important action that is difficult to undo. In general, the more important such actions are, and the more difficult they are to undo, the greater is the individual's commitment to the belief.
3. The belief must be sufficiently specific and sufficiently concerned with the real world so that events may unequivocally refute the belief.
4. Such undeniable disconfirmatory evidence must occur and must be recognized by the individual holding the belief.
5. The individual believer must have social support. It is unlikely that one isolated believer could withstand the kind of disconfirming evidence we have specified. If, however, the believer is a member of a group of convinced persons who can support one another, we would expect the belief to be maintained and the believers to attempt to proselytize or to persuade nonmembers that the belief is correct.[29]

So the expectation must be deeply held, i.e. it must not be a trivial view, and have direct consequences on behaviour. Commitment to it must be of the kind that involves decisions that are difficult to go back on, e.g. giving up of house, job, property, family or way of life. The belief must be specific enough to be capable of confirmation or otherwise by events in the real world, i.e. it must in some sense be public. Such a disconfirmation must have occurred and have been recognized by the believer as such. Conditions 1 and 2 specify the circumstances that will make a belief resistant to change, conditions 3 and 4 indicate factors that will exert pressure on the believer to discard belief, and condition 5 draws attention to circumstances under which the believer will be able to maintain the belief.

It was as a test of such a theory that Festinger and company studied the Seekers and to a great extent confirmed their diagnosis of dissonance response. However as they admit it is far more difficult to produce confirming evidence for the theory in relation to the more famous cases of disconfirmation in history, e.g. the second coming, the failure of Sabbatai Zevi and the Millerites' expectation of the second coming in 1843. It is highly unlikely that the early Christians set about converting people because the second coming had not happened, though they might well have begun their missionary activities as an attempt to reduce the dissonance caused by the death of Jesus.[30] Yet in circles that still maintain a belief in some form of literal return of Jesus there is a remarkable coincidence of rationalizations devoted to explaining the delay of the parousia and vigorous preaching campaigns designed to gain converts. However lack of unequivocal evidence makes it difficult to provide a convincing account of such movements as dissonance response structured. The theory can only be properly tested against cases that are unequivocal, such as are available in modern society. Examples drawn from the major religious systems of belief are further complicated by their possession of complex hermeneutic systems allied to transcendental concepts which already provide for the reduction or resolution of dissonance. Such factors underline the difference between a small modern group of urban dwellers hoping for flying saucers from outer space and the more deeply structured movements of religious traditions. This difference should be kept in mind when analysing the prophetic traditions in the light of the theory of cognitive dissonance.

Critique of dissonance theory

The advocates of the theory of cognitive dissonance tend to praise the theory for its functional value in generating research. In so far as there is a consensus among social psychologists on the theory it relates to this ability to launch research programmes. Thus it is claimed that 'Dissonance theory is helpful, not so much as an explanation of events, but rather as a way to think about problems.'[31] 'The theory of cognitive dissonance is not a theory in the strictly formal sense of the word. Rather, its contribution is best appreciated if we regard it primarily as a heuristic device, whose major purpose (and actual consequence) is the stimulation of research.'[32] 'Undoubtedly Festinger would rather be stimulating than right. This attitude is entirely sensible. In the present stage of development of social psychology, no one is ever "right" for very long. The life span of any theory is short. By its very provocativeness and bold generalization, Festinger's work stimulates the research which will create new ideas, some of which constitute a more systematic development of ideas that he first brought to life.'[33]

These claims are, no doubt, true and it will be as a heuristic device that the concept of dissonance and its resolution will be used in this analysis of prophecy. However criticisms of a general and a specific nature have been made of the theory and some of them are worth looking at briefly.

In general terms the theory states that when two cognitions are in conflict there will be a drive to resolve the conflict. To a certain extent this may be true but it can easily ignore the fact that most people live with conflicting cognitive elements and do so without attempting to resolve any dissonance experienced. Because such tensions and conflicts can have great utility it is often the case that people learn from their experience of dissonance and therefore attempts to reduce or resolve it would entail the loss of such learning potential. Where utility is stronger than dissonance then people will prefer dissonance-arousing information, but where dissonance is stronger than utility then dissonance-reducing behaviour will be manifested.[34] Tolerance of dissonance should be seen as part of what John Keats called 'negative capability', what he defined as 'when man is capable of being in uncertainties, Mysteries, doubts, without any irritable reaching after fact and reason'.[35] In place of dissonance reduction Paul Halmos would put 'dissonance equilibration', i.e. an oscillation of preference which tries to maintain a state of equilibrium between opposites rather than seeking to obliterate the problem.[36] Such possibilities as negative capability and dissonance equilibration entail the modification of the theory's claim that there is a drive to reduce dissonance as well as the treatment of dissonance as a noxious state.

Many psychologists have been critical about the loose use of the term 'cognition' to mean knowledge, belief, opinion, attitude, or practice. If the term used is so broad that more and more elements are subsumed under the theory then it becomes less effective in explanatory power. Brown notes that the definitions of elements used in dissonance representation are 'imprecise hodgepodges of logic, grammar, and common sense cognitive psychology'.[37] Furthermore cognitions held by people may not be so incompatible that they are recognized as such – the point about man being a rationalizing animal is that his ability to rationalize is such as to prevent him seeing incompatibilities in the first place. Many cognitions may be contraries rather than contradictions so there will be fewer occasions than expected when dissonance will of necessity be experienced. So how a man reconciles two apparently contradictory cognitions may be explained on the grounds that he sees no need to do so because for him they are not contradictory (e.g. the writings of Paul and James in the New Testament).

Further vacuity of terminology may be seen in the use of the term 'drive' to describe the human need to reduce or resolve dissonance. Such a need can hardly be said to be a drive in the normal sense of that word. Drive is a biological term relating to basic needs which must be satisfied or the organism will die. Thus oxygen, food and water, sleep meet the basic drives of man for survival, and reproductive sexuality is a drive for sustaining the survival of the species. However a drive to reduce the discomfitting experience of dissonance and arrive at a homoeostasis of consistency in conceptuality is either reductionistic of psychology to biology or simply an analogous way of talking. Festinger posits a drive (it is an axiom of his theory) but offers no explanation for it.

There are further weaknesses in the theory. It is very difficult to construct the conditions for determining that disconfirmation of an expectation has both taken place and resulted in a concomitant experience of dissonance. Any group may explain the supposed disconfirmation in terms of its faulty understanding of the original prediction and therefore maintain that the expectation has not yet been disconfirmed. This normative move may be taken as dissonance response but it is difficult to see how natural misunderstanding of a prediction is to be separated from dissonance reduction forms of explanation. A group may well have misunderstood the import of the original prediction and its failure to materialize may be the first step in the group's recognition of their misunderstanding (a kind of disclosure situation). Without being able to distinguish clearly between these two possibilities the theory lacks precision. In confining itself to what can be clearly established the theory limits itself to the trivial. Brown makes a similar point in noting that the logic used by the Seekers after the disconfirmation of their flood expectation is very similar to that used in the story of Abraham's would-be sacrifice of Isaac.[38]

This comparison with the Genesis 22 story raises an important critical question: is this test of faith explanation predictable by dissonance theory? Supposing the group were wrong to believe that a certain prediction should be understood in a literal sense how would they recognize their mistake? Here dissonance theory can only account for one possibility provided that the prediction is to be taken literally. Yet it cannot rule out the alternative explanation on *a priori* grounds even though it looks like a classical response to dissonance. Thus there is an alternative account of the matter relating to an increased understanding of the nature of the expectation to that of dissonance resolution. Which explanation is the better one then depends upon a careful exegesis of all the relevant details of the case. This possibility indicates the imprecision of the theory of cognitive dissonance in that it is equally as useful to argue that unconfirmed expectations point to misunderstood expectations as it is to insist that such explanations are necessarily attempts to reduce dissonance caused by disconfirmation. If dissonance gives rise to hermeneutic, i.e. interpretative explanations, it is also true to say that hermeneutic may be an alternative to dissonance in the first place. Indeed it could be argued that in some cases the arousal of dissonance is a prerequisite for indicating the true nature of the expectation under discussion.

Many of the experiments designed to test the theory are about what Festinger calls 'forced compliance'.[39] This involves 'public compliance without private acceptance' type experiments whereby a student is hired for a sum of money in order to take part in an experiment which yields the predicted result that the larger the reward sum the smaller the dissonance experienced in the test. These tests are designed to relate expectations to experiences and to check for dissonance response substantiation. The tests have been severely criticized for being confused and unnecessarily elaborate.[40] To a great extent the appeal of the theory is in its simplicity of formulation and application but it is a deceptive simplicity often cloaking a number of concealed variables. As the theory tends to work with two simple cognitions said to be in a dissonant relationship to one another experiments may be set up with great ease. However the simplicity of dissonance theory may well be a self-defeating limitation as it is seldom possible to reduce the essentials of a complex social situation to just two opposing cognitions.[41]

The thrust of many of the criticisms of dissonance theory may be brushed aside by admitting to methodological naïveté in the early years but claiming a growing methodological sophistication as the theory developed and was expanded or modified by researches. The elimination of alternative explanations through the purification of operations afforded by conceptual replications increased the validity of the theory in spite of its simplicity and inelegance as a conceptual statement.[42] It is certainly the case that the prodigious amount of research generated by the theory has led to important modifications of the theory which have made it a more useful tool for the analysis of attitude change and dissonance arising out of post-decisional conflict. Two specific points only will be mentioned here in relation to this streamlining of the theory.

The general theory predicts that where there is sufficient social support following an unequivocal disconfirmation of an expectation of a serious nature the response to the dissonance so aroused will be an attempt to seek converts from the outside world. This prediction needs to be modified to take into account whether the environment of the group is hostile or friendly. In an experiment designed to replicate the theory's predictions Hardyck and Braden found that they only held for groups that had minimal social support and were subject to ridicule by outsiders.[43] Where there was solid social support and a friendly environment there was little evidence of any conversionist programme. As the function in dissonance theory of conversion is to reduce dissonance by increasing cognitive elements within the group there is obviously less need for such an operation if the public is not overtly hostile. For such hostility forces awareness of dissonance on the group and challenges the group to resolve it. Where it cannot be resolved the group must either attempt to convert its opposition or move away from its environment so as to live quietly without hostile forces keeping awareness of dissonance aroused.

The researches of Brehm and Cohen have stressed the importance of commitment as a necessary condition for the arousal of dissonance.[44] The notion of commitment facilitates the specification of what is consonant and what is dissonant. It also increases the resistance to change of an individual or a group and so affects the kinds of attempts to reduce dissonance. So in order to analyse a situation for evidence of dissonance response it is necessary to examine the part commitment contributes to the expectation and the motivation it provides for reducing or resolving the dissonance.

In concluding this critique of dissonance theory it is worth noting briefly a major rival theory which provides an alternative account of attitudes. Daryl Bem's theory of self-perception asserts that generally people are not aware of their own cognitions, let alone inconsistencies among them.[45] Therefore they are unable to experience dissonance. They tend to infer their attitudes from their behaviour, e.g. if I am always doing *that* then I must indeed have such an attitude. The debate between the approaches of dissonance theory and self-perception theory centres on whether people were aware of their attitudes or not when confronted with specific tests. However Bem found in experiments that although support was provided for his theory it was not possible to provide conclusive evidence against dissonance theory. One particular experiment found that subjects tended not to remember their initial attitudes and therefore recalled their initial attitudes as being more consistent with the attitudes taken by them in the experiments than actually had been the case. Bem admitted that this forgetting of initial attitudes could be evidence for dissonance theory's assertion that forgetting earlier conflict is itself a mode of dissonance reduction.

The inconclusive nature of the results of various tests in favour of self-perception theory or dissonance theory, depending upon who conducted them and for what purpose, indicates that tests may only show what they are designed to show and that opposing parties are less likely to be impressed by their opponents' results. It is unlikely that sufficiently complex and precise tests could be constructed which would satisfactorily answer the basic contentions of both parties to the point where one theory would be shown to be more accurate in its predictions than the other. This inconclusiveness may be taken as an indicator of the large area of ill-defined concepts and factors involved in the basic questions posed by the two theories. Cognitive dissonance poses the question: 'how am I to maintain my belief in the light of this obviously disconfirming occurrence?' Self-perception theory asks the question: 'what must my attitude be if I was willing to behave in this fashion in this situation?'

The strength of self-perception theory seems to be in the area where there is no dissonance arousal. There it can be tested to show that the more a person is paid for stating a belief, the less certain that person can be of really believing it. That is, he can never be sure that his advocacy of that belief is due to his actually believing it or to his being paid to believe it. In assessing dissonance theory with reference to self-perception theory it is very difficult to demonstrate that one is wrong and the other right. There are doubtless many occasions when people are not aware of their attitudes and would have to infer from their practice what those attitudes might be. Yet it can hardly be denied that people do possess some awareness of attitudes and actions. Therefore self-perception theory may be a good functional analysis of situations where people learn what their attitudes are by attending to their practices. However where awareness is shown of beliefs and attitudes then inconsistencies between them and behaviour may be related to dissonance theory. People aware of their beliefs and also aware that certain counter-beliefs or events militate seriously against those beliefs will be strongly motivated to change either their beliefs and attitudes or their understanding of the counter-indicative facts. Dissonance theory should certainly apply where expectations based on predictions are involved and where there is evidence to suggest that the predicted events have not occurred. Within such prophetically inspired communities it should be possible to detect dissonance response where there are grounds for believing that disconfirmation has been experienced. However neither theory should be seen as exhausting the limits of the possible range of explanations and analyses of human beliefs and practices.

The concept of dissonance for biblical studies

This chapter has been concerned with providing an account of the theory of cognitive dissonance for the general reader. My aim in doing so is to be able to use the term dissonance with reference to biblical prophecy and to explore the prophetic traditions by means of dissonance resolution models. Such an exploratory analysis will be in itself only a preliminary investigation of the hermeneutic of prophecy.

The main relevance of dissonance theory for biblical studies is its handling of ways in which people respond to disconfirming information. Where there are expectations of a specific nature and where such expectations remain unfulfilled or are refuted by experience there dissonance is said to exist. Here dissonance means the gap between expectation (belief) and reality. If the belief is a very important one affecting behaviour and worldview then there will be some movement towards an effective explanation whereby the conflict can be resolved. So throughout this study dissonance will be used to indicate problems of prediction and fulfilment in prophecy.

To assist the analysis of prophetic texts for evidence of dissonance response the three categories of dissonance resolution outlined above will be used. The fundamental activity of social support or social validation has obvious links with the existence of prophetic groups, followers of the prophets and groups of tradents maintaining the traditions. Where it is not possible to achieve empirical verification of a belief group support becomes a way of verifying belief. Thus social support has a cognitive value as well as providing an environment for belief. Where groups could live in isolation from opposing views or under exclusivist regimes the avoidance of dissonant information was facilitated. In a context of faithful disciples it is unlikely that a prophet would have been bothered by information that appeared to militate against his predictions. Explanatory schemes designed to change the original cognitive holdings or to rationalize dissonant cognitions may have constituted the reinterpretative processes present in the texts. Here the texts have to be analysed to see if their reinterpretation within the traditions points to dissonance response. The important principle for this study is *dissonance gives rise to hermeneutic*. That is, the experience of dissonance forced individuals or groups to reinterpret their basic material or the contemporary events so as to avoid dissonance.

Two things need to be remembered in this analysis. Prophecy was only a small part of a larger cultural movement and therefore dissonance experienced among prophetic groups did not affect the larger religious structure. Theological factors in that structure could provide a very sophisticated hermeneutic system for dealing with such problems and these factors are hardly susceptible to analysis by dissonance theory. In the second place dissonance theory is essentially a heuristic device which permits understanding and uncovers many nonobvious sources of tension.[46]

·⇒‖ 3 ‖⇐·

Dissonance Theory and the Prophetic Traditions

I have chosen the theory of cognitive dissonance as a method of analysing the prophetic traditions because it is concerned mainly with problems similar to those involved in the interpretation of prophecy. There can hardly be a straightforward transference of research material from the field of social psychology to that of biblical studies so in this chapter I want to examine some of the ways in which the concepts of one discipline may be suitably modified and then applied in another field of study. This cross-disciplinary approach to biblical prophecy must then be judged to see whether it renders any of the material so studied more comprehensible. In using the techniques of dissonance resolution as analytical and descriptive ways of handling the biblical traditions I am not trans-ferring the whole range of experiments, tests and paradigms associ-ated with attitude changes and post-decisional problems in modern psychology to the more traditional systems of biblical interpreta-tion. However I am adapting some specific aspects of modern theory as analytical tools and heuristic approaches in order to restate the biblical material along lines which I think can be illuminating. I must stress that the application of dissonance theory to biblical prophecy is intended to be only *one* method of interpret-ing prophecy, in particular the predictive aspect of it. This limitation to the predictive aspect is because predictions set up expectations which allow success or failure, reactions to failure lead on to expla-nations which incorporate the failure into the community's network of existent beliefs and the group's survival is probably to be linked to its ability to assimilate such failures into its belief system. The predictive aspects of prophecy appear to offer good research material for analysis using the insights of dissonance theory.[1]

The prediction-fulfilment problem

The essential problem here is 'what constitutes the fulfilment of a specific prediction?'. This question depends on a prior question about the content of a prediction. Where the terms of the prediction are clear then what would count as its fulfilment should be fairly clear. Thus the prediction that it will rain tomorrow is capable of being verified or falsified. However, many predictions are of a more complex nature and therefore entail much more dispute about possible fulfilment or failure. For example, government predictions about the level of inflation by the end of the year: no government seems prepared to admit to being wrong so complex explanations are provided to show how the failure of the prediction is in fact evidence of its verification! The interpretation of biblical prophecy has historically been of this kind of explanation. Both sets of interpretations may be considered in terms of the following paradigm. A punter dreams that Red Swallow will win the 2.30 at Leopardstown on Saturday and announces this dream to all who will listen to him. The horse does not win and he is ridiculed by his friends and those who heard him. However on Wednesday Green Eagle wins the 3.30 at the Curragh and the punter announces that this was what he had really been dreaming about. He explains away the mere differences of detail so that his premonition consisted of a horse with the name of a coloured bird winning a race that started on the half-hour. In horse racing terms this ludicrous explanation would be dismissed instantly and no bookmaker would entertain it for a moment. However the history of theological and political explanations of predictions is full of this type of reinterpretative adjustment of expectations to facts so it is necessary to recognize that predictive prophecy should not be always taken at its face value.

The one to one correspondence between prediction and fulfilment is the type of prophecy favoured by the deuteronomistic editors of the history of Israel and Judah. However much of the prophetic traditions contain the type of prediction that has had no one to one correspondence between expectation and event. Various ways of interpreting this material have been discussed already and the possibility that the later tradents misunderstood the prophets has to be allowed for. Furthermore the distinction between the failure of predictions and how the tradents and later communities understood the traditions has to be maintained. This difference allows two levels to be distinguished: a first order level that had no correspondence between expectation and fulfilment and a second order level whereby groups maintained a belief in the first order level and edited the traditions along such lines. The second order level is the one of primary concern for this study. On the first level it has to be granted that prophetic expectation for a glorious future presided over by the house of David was a complete failure. Yet it has to be recognized also that the traditions about such beliefs were maintained and did become significant in subsequent centuries. The editing of the prophetic oracles in order to maintain the dialectical relationship between threat-destruction and promise-salvation indicates that the prophets were taken much more seriously than simply as mispractitioners of the art of proclaiming future salvation. Hence we must see in the failure of prophecy the opportunity of prophecy to become a living tradition rather than a record of past successful predictions. It became necessary to reinterpret and maintain a transformation of tradition to rescue prophecy from that failure. In this sense the subsequent creation of the prophetic tradition was the response of the post-exilic communities to the dissonance caused by the failure of the prophetic expectations for that period.

Ian Ramsey argues that if prophecy be fulfilled in a literal sense, rather like a weather forecast or scientific prediction, then it would lack a distinctive religious point.[2] For it to achieve this more important significance it must bring about a disclosure. This disclosure comes about when the language of the original disclosure is used in relation to other facts for a second disclosure. 'Fulfilment of prophecy relates to what might thus be called, a disclosure beyond a disclosure; a second order disclosure.'[3] Ramsey offers as an example Isa. 7.14–16 with its original disclosure to Ahaz in the eighth century and its second order disclosure in Matt. 1.22. A complete match between prediction and fulfilment would leave no room for the second disclosure, so there has to be a gap. The example he uses is unfortunate in that its original context does not require either a gap or a second order disclosure to make sense of it.

That some early Christians used it to link prophecy with the birth of Jesus was due to their interest in biblical prophecy but the prediction itself does not require such a handling to be either coherent or meaningful. To produce a second order disclosure it is necessary for there to be a set of circumstances available for the reinterpretation of the first order disclosure. In this sense the failure or success of the first order prediction is immaterial. Only its existence is necessary and its incorporation into another system of thought will provide the disclosure. To a certain extent this may have happened in the transmission and maintenance of the prophetic traditions throughout the centuries from the fall of Jerusalem to the revolt led by Bar Kokba. The practice of identifying current events with statements in the prophetic traditions can be found in the Qumran community (e.g. the Habakkuk *pesher* commentary) and among early Christian communities (e.g. biblical quotations in the synoptic gospels). In such ways did different communities provide an account of the fulfilment of prophecy and thus avoided the dissonance of unfulfilled predictions arising in the first place. However such dramatic events or circumstances were not always available to provide the means of new disclosures and in such cases dissonance may well have been a problem.

Ways of interpreting the language of prophetic predictions have been discussed in order to show how complex is the matter of understanding prophetic language. The prophets can be protected from a good deal of error if their language was originally conditional, symbolic or even performative. Some modern philosophers, particularly neo-Wittgensteinians, have interpreted religion as using a mode of language which constitutes a form of life but which must not be confused with empirical realities.[4] If such an interpretation of religious language could be sustained it might point to an aspirational level for prophecy. Prophecy certainly functioned as an attempt to change social consciousness in various ways and to shape the community's future but it failed to achieve its ends. Such a failure is quite different from that entailed by predictions not being fulfilled. Unfortunately a rational account of prophecy conflicts with the account given by the deuteronomistic editors and the subsequent handling of the prophetic traditions in the later communities. To have failed to change society was an aspect of prophecy not considered that important for the preservation of prophecy but the element of vision for the future was. Such expectations of salvation were maintained in terms of a literal hope by many groups and in such a sense they were effective in constructing expectations of an empirical nature. The account of religious language as being non-empirical might make sense of prophecy in its own right but not of the subsequent traditions generated by it nor of the communities holding such beliefs. Such being the case it must have become apparent during the Persian, Greek or Roman empires that the expectations had never been realized. If that awareness of failure was felt sufficiently strongly it may be possible to detect it in the editing and transmission of the traditions.

It is a primary feature of Festinger's theory that in order for there to be any attempt to reduce or resolve dissonance there must first be an awareness of dissonance. The practical problem for studying biblical prophecy occurs at this point: what would have constituted awareness of disconfirmation? The transcendental aspects of the prophetic message must have strongly militated against any belief that expectations would not have been realized. Commitment to the community's way of life allied to faith in Yahweh may have prevented any such awareness arising in the first place. The lament psalms provide the clearest evidence of dissonance experience but they are outside the sphere of prophecy and pose major problems of interpretation. The nature of hope for the future is such that it can hardly be falsified by any amount of apparent disconfirmation. If the prophetic traditions provided hope for elements in the community that hope could have been maintained under circumstances of the gravest difficulty without collapsing (cf. the messianic hope in Judaism). Aspects of that hope may have been damaged by the passage of time (e.g. the Davidic dynasty) but hope itself is a far more resilient force and will have provided a constant resource for overcoming temporary setbacks.

Establishing awareness of dissonance as the prerequisite for dissonance reduction response is only one problem entailed by this approach. A further problem is showing that the communities which cherished prophetic traditions were such as to be disturbed by the failure of their expectations. Each disastrous occasion simply identified itself as not being the expected time therefore the oracles referred to yet another period in the future. If hope renders all disappointments bearable how much more does hope functioning within a theological outlook protect the community. There are many examples in history of movements of hope where a series of disconfirmations or apparent failures of expectations have simply deepened the expectations of the groups concerned (e.g. the Sabbataeans). To this day there are many Christian groups who still have a lively faith in the second coming of Jesus in spite of the passage of nearly two thousand years; hasidic Jews still expect messiah to come and inaugurate the state of Israel and Jehovah's Witnesses thrive on proclaiming the imminent establishment of the kingdom. All these groups may be wrong to have such faith and their understanding of biblical language may be false but nothing is regarded as counting against their beliefs. Such capacity to explain away all contrary evidence provides the impetus for dissonance resolution yet is indistinguishable from a position that denies the possibility of dissonance ever arising.

The unsatisfactory nature of this analysis is due to the way religious language is said to operate. However, similar defects can be seen in political structures where predictions also play an important role. The eminent Marxian literary critic Georg Lukacs put the case in this way: 'Let us assume for the sake of argument that recent research had disproved once and for all every one of Marx's individual theses. Even if this were to be proved, every serious "orthodox" Marxist would still be able to accept all such modern findings without reservation and hence dismiss all of Marx's theses *in toto* – without having to renounce his orthodoxy for a single moment. Orthodox Marxism, therefore, does not imply the uncritical acceptance of the results of Marx's investigations. It is not the "belief" in this or that thesis, nor the exegesis of a "sacred" book. On the contrary, orthodoxy refers exclusively to *method*.'[5] Lukacs may be right about Marxian thought being a method but that is not how it has developed nor was his point accepted by the orthodox of his day. If everything produced by the method can be shown to be wrong and yet the method retains its place as the basis of orthodoxy then one is forced to ask questions about what constitutes rationality and meaning. Similarly if nothing falsifies a prediction and if anything or everything may be its fulfilment how can one distinguish between a fulfilled and an unfulfilled prediction? This epistemological question directed at the tradition is part of the positive contribution of the analysis of the prophetic traditions in terms of cognitive dissonance theory. For the theory raises questions about issues that need to be clarified in order to apply it properly. By asking how a prediction might be falsified or confirmed one is on the track of discovering how prophecy was understood in its own time and how it functioned in the traditions.

A final point about the prediction-fulfilment problem relates to the period when the predictions were made and the subsequent period of the collection and transmission of the traditions. In the early period there would have been little awareness of disconfirmation or even of the possibility of failure of expectation so no traces of dissonance response can be expected in the major oracles. Furthermore the experience of dissonance will have related to the communities holding prophetic beliefs and seeking the fulfilment of expectations and this need not have involved any changes being made in the written record of the traditions. Explanations in response to problems arising from the traditions would have been provided within the group orally and again may never have been incorporated into the texts. For written traditions were only the iceberg tip of prophetic communities; the other nine tenths of the iceberg were constituted by the community and its various activities. So we cannot judge reality from the texts though only they provide us with any data for reconstructing that reality in any way. How texts are read and explained depends entirely upon the hermeneutic system employed by the community and it may be surmised that the prophetic traditions were maintained by communities devoted to the exposition of prophecy in terms of its potential fulfilment rather than its actual failure. Such a consideration means that even if there had been substantial dissonance response it may not have been incorporated into the written traditions.

Transposition of terms

The detailed questionnaires and tests associated with post-decisional problems and attitude changes in modern society will have little significance for ancient literary traditions but the application of dissonance theory to predictions associated with failed messiahs and groups committed to future expectations shows that the theory can be made to yield a valuable analysis of the material. The main responses to problems caused by dissonant experiences, i.e.

techniques of avoidance, social validation by group support and re-evaluation of cognitive holdings, can be shown to have applicability to the biblical traditions. Perhaps it would be as well to transpose these categories into terms more familiar to biblical scholarship. Avoidance techniques could be associated with movements towards exclusivity of grouping and the avoidance of various cultural practices common to other groups. Social validation by group support is transferable to community life and the existence of smaller groups within the larger community. Explanatory schemes or rationalization processes may be subsumed under the general heading of hermeneutic. From post-exilic times at least these three categories of activity were important features of the Jewish community gathered around Jerusalem. The categories are by no means so discrete that they cannot have existed together as responses to disappointed hopes and frustrated beliefs.

The focal point for dissonance resolution is the group which provides identity and protection for the individual. The group may be as small as a cell of believers reaffirming each other's beliefs or as large as a community geophysically located and providing an environment for living. Within the life of the group the individual can avoid the strains caused by exposure to dissonance arousing ideas, events or experiences. Never to see, hear or contemplate anything contrary to the belief system is the most effective way of preventing dissonance arising in the first instance. It is not known to what extent prophetic groups were exclusive movements in Israelite society. Apart from the Rechabites, a group opposed to urban civilization (Jer. 35; cf. II Kings 10.15–17), there is no evidence for exclusivist movements among the prophets; though it could be argued that the communities of prophets tended to keep themselves away from the cities. After the exile the emergence of the Aaronite priestly power group and the administrations of Ezra and Nehemiah helped to develop an exclusivization process among Judaeans that later became Judaism. However such a process was designed to create and maintain purity of religion by protecting it from assimilation to other religious structures. The exclusivizing tendencies made a formidable contribution to the creation and survival of a distinctive identity for the community.[6] Yet I would not want to argue at this stage that such movements towards exclusivity should be treated as dissonance response, even though they would have provided admirable protection from problems aroused by contact with discrete religious groups.

The conjunction of avoidance techniques as one series of responses to the experience of dissonance with proselytizing activities as another series of responses indicates a paradoxical element in the role of the group for dissonance theory. The two types of response need not be incompatible in that a group may avoid contact with other groups in terms of being influenced by them yet make contact with them in order to convert them (cf. regular demands by churchmen that 'the church is called to monologue (preach), not dialogue'). Transposition of terminology would yield mission for proselytizing, though mission does not carry the nuance of response to dissonance structured by a hostile environment that dissonance theory posits of proselytizing activities. There can be little doubt that the social context of prophecy involved a good deal of hostility, especially in the later period of prophecy (cf. Jer. 23.33–40; Zech. 13.2–6). Furthermore prophecy was, almost by definition, preaching or proclamation though it may not have been intended to gain converts so much as to influence the behaviour and destiny of the community as a whole. Whether a prophet went on preaching all the more because his expectations were not realized is difficult to determine because the available data are not sufficiently informative to indicate what may have been the case. The persistence of a Jeremiah might have been due to some such motivation but the evidence is too ambiguous to be read off simply as dissonance response. The proclamations of Second Isaiah could conceivably be treated as response to the failure of his grandiose expectations associated with Cyrus but again the matter is ambiguous because his preaching could also have been anticipatory or cultic in nature.

A reading of Second Isaiah's oracles could produce the following scenario: the small group of exiles will not only be redeemed and triumphantly returned to their land, but they will become missionaries to the nations and convert them to Yahweh.[7] Set against a background of little response to the prophet and a meagre return to Palestine the notion of mission to the pagans (cf. 49.7, 8; 51.4, 5) could have been a normative response to failure of expectation. Such a scenario is a tempting way to read Second Isaiah because it would provide evidence of dissonance response in the prophetic

traditions but I hesitate in putting it forward because the existence
of a missionary motif in Second Isaiah is a highly questionable
reading of the text.[8] The idea of a mission to the nations would
certainly fit in well with dissonance theory analysis but must remain
not proven with reference to Second Isaiah's oracles.

The prophet could be associated with a group of followers, e.g.
Isaiah (cf. 8.16–18), or have powerful supporters e.g. Jeremiah (cf.
Jer. 26.24; 36.25), and such contexts may have provided opportunities for the prophet to have explained, modified or expanded his
oracles. The details of such activities are beyond our knowledge
though not beyond our fertile imagination but, at least, they provide
a setting in which delay or failure of expectation could be explained.
Such explanatory processes are the mainstay of dissonance resolution and offer the most promising approach to prophecy in terms of
dissonance theory. The presence of hermeneutic activity in the
prophetic traditions is very conspicuous and indicates that prophecy
had the means for dealing with dissonance whenever it occurred.
The prophet interpreted the community's traditions so as to put
across his message and often this involved the inversion and transformation of popular beliefs, e.g. the preaching of Amos. By reinterpreting older beliefs the prophet made clear his analysis of society and set up a dialectical relationship between the community's
cognitive holdings and his own critique. As the prophetic traditions
were developed this reinterpretative process was extended to
include the prophetic oracles so that their significance was also
contemporized and the hermeneutic activity became the means of
preserving prophecy. It could also meet the exigencies of dissonance arousal by adjusting one set of cognitive holdings to meet
changing reality or the dissonance arousing set of holdings could be
explained in such a way that it ceased to pose intractable problems.
The scope for hermeneutic activity in this context is very great as
may be confirmed by examining the explanations provided by any
millennial cult for the non-occurrence of their version of the ending
of the world. Whether it also operated in the circles that preserved and explained the prophetic traditions is for the analysis
of part three to determine. As such hermeneutic activity leaves
the most traces in documents and so can be explored by the
exegete more satisfactorily than the other response to dissonance
categories.

Limits of dissonance theory as an analytical method

The types of expectation orientated groups and forced compliance tests analysed by the theory of cognitive dissonance are quite different from the communities that produced the biblical traditions and this distinction limits the effectiveness of the theory for analysing those traditions. A few of the limiting factors will be considered here in order to bring out the implications of this difference and also to provide a fuller account of prophecy in its Israelite setting.

The first limiting factor must be the general principle of *transcendence*. By transcendence is to be understood the belief in the sovereignty of Yahweh as the lord of Israel, the world and creation. This sovereignty meant that Yahweh's will was the only effective will operating in the world – he did what he wanted to do and nobody could prevent him or question his actions (cf. Isa. 10.15; 40.12–17; Dan. 4.34, 35 (Aram. 4.31, 32)). Thus the history and religion of Israel were seen as products of the divine will and are so presented in the biblical traditions.[9] Of this deity the formulations of Torah posited a number of negative and positive features. Negatively he was that which could not be named, represented by images, manipulated by magical or verbal means, or controlled by man (cf. Ex. 20.3–7; Deut. 5.7–11). He was the incomparable one among the gods, the one whose like was inconceivable (cf. Jer. 10.6, 7, 12–16; Isa. 40.12–20; 44.6–8; 45.20, 21; Ps. 115; 135). Positively he was the one who revealed himself to Moses in the desert and the people at Sinai. He was the encountered presence in the experience of Israel. Such a theology constituted part of the worldview of Israel by exilic times and it must be incorporated into any analysis of prophecy. It entails recognizing that prophecy functioned within a conceptual framework of the transcendence of Yahweh and that therefore comparisons between such a system of belief and modern viewpoints constructed around flying saucers and car model choices have severe limitations. It also means that there must have been a strong motivation among prophetic groups to explain why expectations had not been realized and therefore a concomitant exposure to serious dissonance arousal.

The second limiting factor is Torah *as the context for the post-exilic community*. Too much stress on the prophetic tradition can give the impression that it was something independent in ancient

Israel but it was always only a part of the community. Only the preservation and survival of a series of texts gives the impression that it was somehow a major, independent movement. In post-exilic times it was even more subservient to other social forces because the prophets to a great extent had disappeared and only collections of their oracles had survived. The dominating ideology, or theology if that is a preferable term, in that period was Torah as it came to be under the aegis of Ezra and subsequent theologically minded people in Judah. Torah became the community's centre and identity and therefore we need to adjust our assessment of prophecy in order to make allowance for its secondary role in relation to Torah. By that time many of the great prophetic expectations had languished unfulfilled too long to be of major importance to most of the community, though there must have been some elements who still maintained them in the hope that they might yet be realized. In stressing the importance and centrality of Torah as that which constructed the worldview of the community and which became its way of life there is provided an indication of how questions relating to prophetic expectations might have been answered. That is, there may have been some awareness of dissonance among prophetic circles but for the average Judaean citizen such esoteric matters were relatively unimportant because keeping the regulations (*mišpāṭîm*) of Torah was the focus of life.

The contextualization of prophecy within the life of the post-exilic community in these terms provides the right perspective for considering response to dissonance. Most people were not troubled by such problems because they were not orientated towards prophecy. Among those who were involved in circles devoted to maintaining the prophetic traditions dissonance must have raised serious questions, though it was always possible to give up such expectations without losing religious identity because the larger community provided that. A combination of the New Testament and Reformation mythology has tended to produce the view that the prophets were the high point of Israelite religion, its flower. Whatever may have been the case before the exile when temple and popular religion were the centres of religious life, after the exile Torah gradually emerged as the community's centre. At no stage in Israelite society did prophecy have a dominant status and this fact should be stressed so as to provide a balanced picture of the matter.

In much later Jewish life prophecy came to be seen as commentary on Torah, i.e. *haftora*.[10] Reflection on this relation between Torah and prophecy will show that it emphasizes the centrality of Torah and stresses the ethical and interpretative features of prophecy. The predictive element was not important in this relationship but that was inevitable in view of the paucity of prophecy-type expectations in Torah (cf. Gen. 49.10; Num. 24.15–24; Deut. 18.15).

It was not prophecy but Torah and wisdom (*ḥokmā*) which provided the context and constructs for Judaean life in the centuries following the Babylonian exile and particularly in the centuries after the Bar Kokba revolt when Jews were scattered throughout the Roman world. Prophecy did not completely disappear nor were the traditions uninfluential from time to time, especially during periods of persecution (e.g. the rise of apocalyptic literature during the Maccabaean and Roman periods). In times of such opposition the older prophetic expectations appear to have flourished once more and therefore must have been kept alive in various ways through the periods when little hostility existed. For opposition can be a fine sustainer of belief and many a man has been readier to die for his beliefs than to defend them logically to others. However the limiting factor of Torah means that the popularity of prophecy as a social movement has to be modified to a minor group commitment whose depressing experience of dissonance would have had little effect on the community at large. That community may have maintained the prophetic traditions for more practical purposes than their futuristic hopes would have provided.

The third limiting factor arises out of the first two and relates to *complex social structures*. Ancient Israelite religion is an example of such a complex system. Prophecy was an element embedded in an already existent belief structure of considerable sophistication. Explaining how one's view of God and the world interact within one's belief system is a far more complex process of human understanding than post-decisional conflicts about the colour and performance of a recently purchased car. Beliefs about transcendence and ethics belong to complex structures and provide very sophisticated forms of argument for choices, actions and decision making which also contribute explanatory schemes for dealing with the types of problem analysed by dissonance theory. The impact of transcendence on expectation yields a permanent explanation for the failure of that expectation: the deity has changed his mind or has a different purpose in view (Barthians would call this 'preserving God's freedom'). Now such an explanation might well be a classic instance of dissonance resolution (i.e. shift of cognitive ground) but it is also entailed by the original theological system irrespective of expectation failure or not. Thus there can be no clear demonstration that a certain type of religious explanation is a response to dissonance rather than a normative exposition of the complex structure. The theory functions better with simple systems that contain few variables and no complex hermeneutic system built into them. In complex structures there are too many variables and a deep hermeneutic structure which render any attempt to produce unequivocal evidence of dissonance response ineffective. Furthermore ways of life are always less vulnerable to refutation than expectations of a predictive nature so communities orientated around *Torah* as the way of life provided a larger context for small groups of tradents devoted to prophecy to live in and to utilize some of the available hermeneutic techniques as responses to dissonance. Hence a distinction must be made between expectations held by a group with its roots in a larger community and an isolated group without such resources. Vulnerability to dissonance would then depend upon access to complex systems or the lack of such access. The survival of prophecy in spite of the failure of its salvationistic elements was due to its incorporation into the larger hermeneutic system of postexilic Judaism and its maintenance by later Pharasaical Judaism. Such incorporation greatly complicates the analysis of prophecy using the techniques of dissonance theory.

Dissonance gives rise to hermeneutic

The core of my thesis is that some of the hermeneutic processes evident in the prophetic traditions are indications of dissonance response, hence the stress on the principle *dissonance gives rise to hermeneutic*. As editors worked with the texts they occasionally provided explanations that reduced some of the problems associated with the expectations in the traditions. Normally such explanatory schemes would have been given orally but the maintenance and transmission of the traditions provided opportunities to incorporate some of the responses into the text. Notes indicating the way the texts were to be read also made available a hermeneutic for resolving difficulties. In this final section before the actual interpretation of the prophetic traditions as evidence for this contention it is important to realize some of the ways in which texts may be controlled by hermeneutic techniques so as to resolve effectively the experience of dissonance.

Traditions are produced and controlled by small groups within the community and are passed on to larger groups by means of oral teaching which provides a simplified presentation of the main thrusts of the traditions. The ancient and medieval world did not afford common access to manuscripts so the preservation of recorded traditions was controlled by a few tradents. This arrangement entailed that few of the problematic texts were accessible to any but the inner core of the group maintaining the teaching. Where there were problems they related to the general expectations of a glorious future when the community's enemies would be crushed and it would rule in a golden age. We do not know how such problems were explained to the satisfaction of those who realized that there were real problems, but it may have been the case that only those who were prepared to live with such problems would have been interested in the traditions in the first place. However leading individuals or competent teachers within the traditional outlook could have provided sufficient explanations of either the texts or the problematic occurrences that raised difficulties for the group. The New Testament provides a classic instance of such a resolution of dissonance aroused by failure of expectations.

The story of the two disciples meeting with Jesus on the road to Emmaus on resurrection day is a paradigm case of dissonance resolved by hermeneutic (Luke 24.13–35). The weekend in Jerusalem had been rather disappointing to say the least and the two disciples travelled to Emmaus discussing what had happened and how it had not measured up to their expectations. Apparently they had believed Jesus to have been the redeemer of Israel but he had been executed by the Romans so that hope was dead. They told their sad, perplexed story to Jesus and the text provides the following reply: 'And he said to them, "Oh foolish men, and slow of heart to believe *all that the prophets have spoken*! Was it not necessary that the Christ should suffer these things and enter into his glory?" And beginning with Moses and *all the prophets, he interpreted* (*diermēneusen*) to them in all the scriptures the things concerning himself' (verses 25–27). The weekend events had destroyed their expectations so they were suffering from severe dissonance caused by the brutal collapse of their hopes. This dissonance was resolved by a hermeneutic approach to the scriptures which provided a reading of the traditions that made sense both of their expectations and the tragic execution of Jesus. The hermeneutic consisted of showing that the disconfirming event was not disconfirmation but actually *confirmation* of their expectations. The dissonance had arisen in the first place because they did not know how to read the scriptures properly – they lacked the right hermeneutic for coping with the problem of dissonance.

The text only provided part of the tradition and without the accompanying hermeneutic the text was meaningless. The point is well made in Acts 8.26–39 where the Ethiopian eunuch failed to understand the meaning of Isa. 53.7, 8 without the assistance of Philip who already possessed a hermeneutic capable of reading and making sense of that difficult passage. 'So Philip ran to him, and heard him reading Isaiah the prophet, and asked, "Do you understand what you are reading?" And he said, "How can I, unless some one guides me?"' (verses 30, 31). Without the controlling hermeneutic the text made no sense to the reader and only the control of the text by a specifically Christian hermeneutic made it yield the meaning Philip offered the Ethiopian. In this way the early Christian communities were able to show that the prophetic expectations had been fulfilled in their experience (e.g. Luke 4.16–21 of Isa. 61.1, 2; Acts 2.16–21 of Joel 2.28–32). The technique of referring prophecy to one's own time forestalled problems of unfulfilment. This technique can also be seen in the writings of the community that lived in the Judaean desert by the wadi Qumran, especially in their *pesher* commentary on Habakkuk.

The hermeneutic for reading a text was provided by the larger religious structure. This structure may be called the 'resultant system', so named by James Barr because 'There are two systems or levels at work: the first is the text, the second is the system into which the interpretation runs out.'[11] The importance of this resultant system is that it determines how texts will be read. So a particular resultant system might not see any problems in the texts because its hermeneutic was concerned with certain features of those traditions and disregarded other elements as irrelevant (cf. I Cor. 9.9, 10). Different resultant systems will have provided different accounts and interpretations of the same texts, e.g. Qumran, Samaritan, Pharisaical and Christian readings of the prophetic traditions will have been quite distinctive.

As well as the hermeneutic of resultant systems which provided commentaries on texts and ways to read them we should also note that the hermeneutic used by translators of texts could contribute much to the understanding of the texts. Translation is a very important aspect of the hermeneutic process and the necessity for translating biblical traditions into various languages afforded many opportunities for building certain interpretations into the translated text because it is impossible to translate without interpreting.[12] A byproduct (if not an intention) of changes in the text caused by the translators not sharing the same worldview or cultural outlook of the original producers of the text can be changes in the meaning of texts which resolve some of the problems associated with those texts. If the Hebrew, Greek and Aramaic versions of Isa. 19.24, 25 are compared this point will become clearer.

The Hebrew text may be translated as follows: 'In that day Israel will be the third with Egypt and Assyria, a blessing in the midst of the earth, whom Yahweh of hosts has blessed, saying, "Blessed be Egypt my people, and Assyria the work of my hands, and Israel my heritage."' It would be difficult to find a better example in the prophetic traditions of a prediction that failed. The Greek has: 'In that day Israel will be the third with Egypt and Assyria, a blessing in the midst of the earth, whom the Lord has blessed saying, "Blessed be my people *who are in* (*ho en*) Egypt and *who are in* (*ho en*) Assyria and my heritage Israel."' The Targum (Aramaic) provides: 'At that time Israel shall be the third with the Egyptians and with the Assyrians, a blessing in the midst of the earth: whom Yhwh of hosts has blessed, saying, Blessed be my people whom I brought forth out of Egypt. Because they sinned before me I carried them into exile to Assyria, but now that they have repented, they shall be called, My people and my inheritance, even Israel.'[13]

The unfulfilled prediction of verse 24 remains constant in all three texts, though one problematic aspect could be resolved by referring the names to the territories rather than the nations: in a future time the land of Israel will be on a par with that of Egypt and

Assyria. In verse 25 the Greek adds 'who are in' as prefixes to Egypt and Assyria. The addition may be equivalent to the Hebrew or it may represent a slight modification of the original so as to deny the designation 'my people' to Egypt and Assyria. The Targum avoids the universalism of the text by expunging the references to Egypt and Assyria as peoples of Yahweh and reading them as trigger words for exodus and exile. The pietistic paraphrase then indicates the turning of the exiles to Yahweh and their restoration as the people of Yahweh. It is not clear whether the targumists made this change because their theology did not envisage Egypt and Assyria as also the people of Yahweh (cf. verses 21, 22) or simply took Egypt and Assyria to be shorthand for the great events of exodus and exile associated with those countries. Their tendency to use pious paraphrase and explanatory expansions (cf. 6.13; 8.18–20; 20.2, 3) may have made them read the verse as yet another reference to sin and repentance. However it is clear that the hermeneutic of the targumists has contributed to their translation of the Hebrew in such a way that they may have resolved the problems of Egypt and Assyria becoming the peoples of Yahweh by an entirely different understanding of the text.

The *art* of hermeneutic is an essential part of understanding the traditions which were produced by various hermeneutic processes and is also necessary for analysing them for evidence of dissonance response. Hermeneutic is not inevitably a response to dissonance but in structures vulnerable to dissonance its presence provides powerful support for reducing dissonance. The biblical traditions are sufficiently complex and hermeneutically deep to permit yet another analytical probe, even if its origins belong to social psychology rather than a field more closely related to biblical studies. If dissonance theory can make old data in social psychology suddenly become clearer then perhaps it can also clarify and tease out some of the more problematic aspects of predictive prophecy.[14]

PART III

Hermeneutic of the Traditions

ᴈ 4 ᴈ

Text and Interpretation I

The analysis of the prophetic traditions for evidence of experience of and response to dissonance is a mammoth task and therefore in order to keep it within reasonable boundaries this investigation will be limited to a number of areas where prophecy may be illuminated by this approach. The interpretation of prophecy is a very complex process of uncovering layers of meaning in various oracles and relating them to the whole work of the individual prophet, at the same time it is necessary to isolate editorial work and interpretative glosses so as to see how they contribute to the construction of the individual tradition. To this difficult hermeneutical task my analysis of prophecy in terms of dissonance theory is intended to contribute a further interpretative level. The focus of the analysis will be those prophetic traditions enhanced by secondary material, in particular the book of Isaiah. However the enquiry is necessarily limited to those aspects of prophecy which deal with future hopes of wellbeing because they constitute the problematical features of prophecy relevant for dissonance theory examination. As so much of the prophetic traditions relates to oracles of doom, oracles bound to be accurate reflections of a period of turmoil and foreign invasion, this investigation is bound to be concerned with limited elements in the traditions and to be curtailed by a serious lack of knowledge of how certain events and expectations were dealt with by those exposed to the possible disappointment of their hopes.

The Isaiah traditions

Among the scrolls found in the caves at Qumran were two copies of

Isaiah and, given the nature of the community that had cultivated such isolation from other Jews in order to seek salvation when messiah came, it is not surprising that Isaiah should have been so important for such a group. Over a long period the oracles of Isaiah had been built up, by the addition of substantial collections of prophetic material and editorial work, into the largest of the individual prophetic traditions. The thrust of the bulk of the additional material had been related to the motif of salvation, so a salvation seeking community such as Qumran would have inevitably concentrated on the exposition of the enlarged Isaianic vision. No other tradition has such a concentration of salvationistic material or has been expanded along such lines among all the prophetic traditions. This identification of Isaiah with future salvation expectations made it the core for the accretion of blocks of oracular and editorial material relating to the restoration of Jerusalem and the wellbeing of the community. Whatever the sources of such expectations may have been their products came to be associated with the earlier oracles of Isaiah of Jerusalem so that the book of Isaiah as it now stands is a great palimpsest of interpretations of the ongoing experiences of the city in the light of future expectations. Thus on the surface the book of Isaiah looks like ideal material for showing that the reinterpretative (hermeneutic) response to dissonance was an important feature of the *earliest* interpretations of prophecy.

The major problem confronting the interpreter of Isaiah is that of determining which sections are to be attributed to Isaiah and which should be treated as secondary. This problem underlines the nature of the transmission of prophecy as well as indicating the difficulty of separating prophetic oracle (i.e. prophet) from interpretative response or editorial placement (i.e. follower). The differentiation of word from interpretation in the tradition does not materially affect the presentation of prophecy in terms of dissonance theory because the issue of reinterpreting predictive elements remains essentially the same whether that reinterpretation was carried out by editors responding to original oracles or by the creators of the oracles responding to subsequent disconfirming events. However it does emphasize that the prophetic traditions are very complex collections of material that have been reworked over and over by generations devoted to understanding the prophetic vision. We may not be able to determine all the complex factors that created the rich network of oracles plus interpretative editing but we must avoid any simplistic approaches which fail to appreciate the layers and depths of material present in the Isaiah traditions.[1]

The relevant elements of the Isaiah traditions for this analysis are (1) the core of Isaiah of Jerusalem's oracles, particularly the material in chapters 6–9; (2) the reinterpretative elements to be found scattered throughout Isa. 10–39; and (3) the salvation oracles of Second Isaiah (40–55) and the responses to his vision of his circle of followers in 56–66. The concentration is necessarily on any material that appears to be a response to prior statements or a reflective reassessment of such material. This is because dissonance theory depends for its analysis on responses to problems aroused by conflict between sets of events, experiences or beliefs. The types of oracles found in Amos hardly permit any analysis for the possibility of dissonance response due to the lack of substantial additional material interpreting them and the essentially negative character of the preaching. Such factors severely limit the amount of data available for dissonance response analysis in the prophetic traditions. However the Isaiah traditions are rich in accumulative reinterpretations and major transformations which make them the most likely area of research for dissonance response.

Isaiah of Jerusalem

There are formidable problems awaiting the scholar who would disentangle primary from secondary material in Isa. 1–39, so to avoid a long and inconclusive detour I will confine my analysis to the autobiographical section 6.1–9.7 (Heb. 9.6), with some remarks on the Assyrian crisis problem. Only where a prophet, or his followers, editors or other interested parties, reflect upon what has been said in the light of further statements, experiences or events is it possible to provide any analysis for the experience of dissonance. So the data gathered together in the ostensibly autobiographical section afford a good probability of indicating either the prophet's reflections on some of his work or the editors' assessment of what the prophet was doing.

Isaiah 6.1—9.6. The structure of this section is very interesting. It contains a number of first person accounts relating to Isaiah's activities and preaching (6.1–8.18) to which have been appended a few supplementary fragments and an oracle about kingship (8.19–9.7). This arrangement of the material means that the section begins with the death of the old king (6.1) and ends with the accession of the new king (in vision at least 9.6, 7). The opening vision takes place in the temple and in the closing hymn the new king occupies the throne. Thus the twin foci of Isaiah's preaching, the temple city of Zion and the Davidic king, encapsulate the whole section. Themes of kingship dominate it, from the dead king through the kingship of Yahweh (6.5), the activities of kings Rezin and Pekah, the plot to make Tabeel king, king Ahaz's refusal to trust Yahweh, (interpolated glosses about the king of Assyria), the king of Assyria (8.7), the cursing of the king (8.21), to the establishment of justice by the new occupant of the throne (9.6, 7). There is a progression of disintegration in kingship until the closing hymn transforms the gloom that has befallen Judah. It is a very neatly structured work and its thematic portrayal of kingship suggests that a fair amount of editorial activity has gone into shaping it. If we allow that nevertheless it contains genuine Isaianic material we have then the prophet's negative evaluation of the kingship current in his time with possibly his firm commitment to the Davidic house as the nation's future hope. So the prophetic dialectic in Isaiah here constitutes a no to current kingship and a yes to the future king.

To what extent, if any, should this material be attributed to Isaiah of Jerusalem? It is not, with the exception of the oracles in 6.9–13; 7.7–9; 10–16 (?); 8.9, 10, made up of the usual prophetic oracles but is a series of prose passages of a quasi-(auto)biographical nature. Usually such arrangements are the creation of editors. So we may have here an editorial construct incorporating oracular material which set out to depict the prophet in action in relation to king and temple. Yet how much of it is genuine Isaiah? Kaiser, for example, regards all of 6.1–9.7 as non-Isaianic and considers the possibility of getting behind the exilic collection of Isaiah's sayings unlikely.[2] This is a view likely to be disputed by many scholars inclined to be less sceptical about establishing genuine Isaianic material in the section. However the problem of determining primary from secondary material, especially in prose sections and salvationistic oracles, is a complex issue for biblical literary criticism and a fully worked out criteriology has yet to be produced for it. Part of the difficulty is entailed by the problem of the relation between sayings of doom and oracles of wellbeing. Even Hebrew prophets must have been able to recognize contradictions in thought and so should not be interpreted as happily allowing such logical mistakes in their preaching. A further part of the difficulty is the survival of their traditions; such a survival presupposes the existence of individuals or groups who preserved their work. Therefore there was always a context of others handling and passing on the tradition. This context was not simply passive but had a creative role to play in the presentation, interpretation and possibly extension of the prophetic traditions. How creative it was is the crux of the matter for this debate. However, as important as the question is, it only marginally touches my thesis about prophecy and dissonance and should not be allowed to distract unnecessarily from the exegesis of the texts.

Isaiah 6.9—13. This oracle is presented as the reply to Isaiah's response to the divine voice and gives the substance of his preaching to the nation. It poses two interpretative problems, one of which is important for the thesis of dissonance response. The prophet is commissioned to proclaim a message that will close the minds of the people to the possibility of turning from evil: 'Go, and say to this people: "Hear and hear, but do not understand; see and see, but do not perceive." *Make* the heart of this people *fat*, and their ears *heavy*, and *shut* their eyes; *lest they see* with their eyes, and *hear* with their ears, and *turn* and *be healed*' (verses 9, 10). The Hebrew causatives show clearly that this process is to be created by the prophet himself. He is to preach in such a way that the people will become incapable of response and therefore will not turn from evil and be healed. The starkness of the activity envisaged is difficult to comprehend but in itself the commission is coherent and meaningful. However it poses a major hermeneutic problem for two reasons: (1) the general view that repentance was a fundamental element in the prophetic proclamation is obviously countered by this activity aimed at preventing the people from repenting; (2) it is impossible to reconcile this prevention of turning with the elements elsewhere in Isaiah's preaching where he posits the possibility of changing (cf. 1.16, 17; 30.15). The challenge to the community to 'wash yourselves; make yourselves clean; remove the evil of your doings from before my eyes; *cease to do evil, learn to do good*; seek justice, correct oppression; defend the fatherless, plead for the widow' (1.16, 17) is so clearly a call to turn that either it must be rejected as an authentic Isaiah saying or the statement in 6.9, 10 must be understood in another way.

The harshness of the Hebrew causatives was recognized by the Greek translators who modified them and simply indicted the people for having become incapable of perceiving the prophetic word and therefore of being unable to turn from evil – 'Go, and say to this people, "You shall hear indeed, but you shall not understand; and you shall see indeed, but you shall not perceive." For the heart of this people has become fat, and their ears heavy of hearing, and their eyes they have closed; lest they should see with their eyes, and hear with their ears, and understand with their heart, and be converted, and I should heal them.' The Greek translation of Isaiah is of very mixed quality so perhaps it is an open question whether they misunderstood the Hebrew causatives or attempted to produce a rational translation by modifying them. Our concern is necessarily with the Hebrew version, though the Greek translation does illustrate the point about translation having an important hermeneutic role to play. The question that arises from the difficult text of 6.9, 10 is 'did Isaiah understand his life's work to be the denying of the possibility of the people of Israel turning to Yahweh?' or must another explanation be sought for it?

Two approaches to resolving the problem may be considered before treating it as an example of dissonance response. Jacob Milgrom has argued that the references to repentance in 1.16–20; 2.5 are genuine and should be dated to the earliest period of Isaiah's preaching, i.e. during Uzziah's reign.[3] This call to repentance was rejected and so after the king's death Isaiah was commissioned with a different message, one that reflected the earlier rejection and which now declared the inevitability of devastation for the whole people from which there was no escape. In this way there is no conflict between 1.16, 17 and 6.9, 10. Milgrom attributes 1.10–6.13 to the earliest period of Isaiah's activity and regards chapter 6 as the culmination of that period. Thus it cannot be considered Isaiah's inaugural vision but should be seen as a sequential vision to the earlier activities. He finds a parallel between Amos and Isaiah in that both prophets' mission of repentance ended in a temple vision of final destruction (cf. Amos 9.1–4).

Another way of treating the problem is to reject all references to repentance as inauthentic on the grounds that 'The historical prophet Isaiah was neither a preacher of repentance nor a man who one day proclaimed the deliverance and the next day the ruin of his nation, but consistently announced the coming disaster as an unalterable act of punishment by Yahweh (cf. e.g. 5.1ff. with 22.1–4, 12–14).'[4] The 'hardening of the heart' motif in 6.9, 10 then belongs to the exilic or post-exilic editorial reflection on why the hortatory preaching of the prophet did not turn the people from disaster. This approach resolves all the difficulties by making them the creation of the editors in the first place but provides no account of why Isaiah came to be associated with such a dominant theme of salvation.

A third approach to the difficulty is to see 6.9–13 as the prophet's mature reflection on his call seen through the years of bitter struggle to persuade the people to turn from evil. Having failed to achieve that aim the prophet came to see that this failure was intended to be part of his mission. This retrospective judgment fitted in with the prophet's basic theological outlook that the source of real activity in the world was Yahweh himself – not the people but Yahweh was the real actor in what happened in society and politics (cf. 3.1–5; 10.5, 6, 15; 29.9, 10). If the nation failed to turn to Yahweh it was because Yahweh so intended it and it was the prophet's duty to enforce that intention. It was perhaps a counsel of despair but all Isaiah's attempts to make the people turn had failed so he made a virtue out of necessity and reinterpreted his mission accordingly.[5] Whether that failure was achieved by popular obduracy or prophetic antagonizing of the nation is a moot point. In the light of years of such lack of success, the disappointment of Ahaz's rejection of his salvation strategy, and the eventual incursion of the Assyrian forces into Judaean territory Isaiah concluded that he was meant to fail. Such an interpretation of 6.9, 10 takes an intermediate position between Milgrom's schematic organization of material into pre- and post-Uzziah activity and Kaiser's sceptical reconstruction of the tradition as dominantly exilic or later in content. It also sees the element of repentance as a possibility posed by the oracles which announced destruction in an attempt to make the people react and turn from such a prospect.[6]

Such an explanation of 6.9, 10 would make it a classic example of response to failure by reinterpretation of original cognition. It infers from the text and other references (e.g. 8.17) that Isaiah experienced dissonance caused by the rejection of his preaching, particularly on the occasion of Ahaz's scorning of his offer (7.12), and that he tried to resolve that dissonance by reinterpreting his commission in such negative terms that it coincided with his experiences. Yahweh might well be salvation, as Isaiah's name clearly affirmed, but not for this people and not in this time or place! So might a prophet explain the failure of his salvationist expectations. The explanation provided by the reinterpretation was to provide the early Christians with similar dissonance resolution in relation to the failure of their preaching (cf. Isa. 29.10; Matt. 13.10–15; Mark 4.10–12; Luke 8.9, 10; Acts 28.23–28).[7]

A further minor point may be made about 6.9–13, in particular the abstruse phrase at the end of 6.13 'the holy seed is its stump'. Some of the problems of translation and interpretation have been noted already so here I only want to suggest a further interpretation of the phrase in keeping with dissonance theory. The predicted destruction of verses 11–13 provided no problem for prophecy because over the next one hundred and fifty years there were numerous invasions, sieges and destructive campaigns directed against Judaean territory. However no community can thrive on a diet of destruction predicted for the future so at some stage in the transmission of the Isaiah tradition this note appeared at the end of the vision. It is sufficiently ambiguous to provide scholars with evidence for it being a note of further destruction or future hope.[8] Perhaps it was meant to be a note of hope (had not Isaiah himself found purification in spite of being unclean?), a statement of limitation of the extent of the destruction. Though it could also have been a further transformation of a current belief in a remnant as a positive concept into an inclusion of that remnant in the destruction. To be dogmatic about how this brief phrase should be understood in its present context is unwarranted. However it should be noted that its ambiguous brevity is a brilliant defence against failure for there is nothing stated by it that could be refuted by subsequent events. The tradition as it now stands simply asserts that the vast majority of people will be destroyed and that what survives will be the sacred stump (if that is how it is to be translated). Potentially it allows great scope for expansion but actually it says nothing at all! The subsequent editing of the prophetic traditions that put together a more positive remnant motif (cf. Isa. 4.2–6; 10.20–23; 11.11; Hag. 2.2; Zech. 8.6) provided some form of rationalizing process for dealing with destruction and salvation in the traditions by assigning the threat oracles to the nation and the salvation oracles to the remnant. Theoretically the remnant motif provides a resolution of dissonance caused by failure of expectations. In reality it hardly achieved that because at no stage was it possible to identify the survivors of a particular destruction, e.g. the fall of Jerusalem, with the holy, pure remnant under Yahweh's special protection.

As a potential resolution of dissonance the remnant motif may be interpreted as one way in which the community could keep its future open and its expectations operative. Beyond each destructive encounter or event hope survived for a few who might identify themselves with the remnant or, at least, transfer all the future hopes to such a remnant. So potentially the salvation expectations could be maintained whatever happened by being projected on to an actual or metaphorical remnant. As a resolution of dissonance by explanation it has practical value, though it may often have involved explanatory shifts in meaning to distinguish between the survivors of a particular disaster and the future recipients of the salvation expectations. To what extent the remnant motif ever functioned in this way for the communities that preserved the prophetic traditions can only be surmised at this stage of my analysis. Apart from the positive statements about the remnant in the Isaiah traditions the motif is an unimportant one in the biblical documents, particularly in the prophetic traditions.

Isaiah 7. The central prophetic discourse of the biographical section is the Immanuel pericope in chapter 7. The very complex hermeneutical problems involved in the interpretation of that account of sons and the prophet (7.1–17; 8.1–4) only concern this study at one point relating to the editing of the material. The general presentation of Isaiah's conversations with Ahaz (verses 4–9, 10–17) appears to be one of salvation offered to the house of David in a particularly difficult time.[9] Ahaz's rejection of Isaiah's proffered hope (verse 12) was swept aside by the prophet and replaced by his (now famous) Immanuel oracle. The point of that oracle was that the coalition directed against Judah would not survive the infant Immanuel's early years, so Ahaz had nothing to fear from the anti-Assyrian forces. However the final editing of the section has turned that salvation oracle into one of threat because the immediate future for Judah was in fact dominated by the Assyrian monarch (the force of the gloss in 17b). Four further oracles of impending destruction, prefaced by the phrase 'in that day' (18–19, 20, 21–22, 23–25), show how a later age understood the Immanuel oracle. As events developed the defeat of the Syrian-Ephraimite coalition did not entail good days for Judah but introduced the Assyrians into Judaean politics. Whatever Isaiah's original intention may have been with the Immanuel motif subsequent events proved it to have been a word of destruction rather than salvation. The later editing shows that this is how the Immanuel prophecy was to be read.

This editorial transformation of a salvation oracle into a preface to judgment shows how explanatory devices were available for controlling how prophecy was to be interpreted. In this instance the hermeneutic of the editors has been incorporated into the text. Given such an activity it becomes clear that showing how biblical predictions might be falsified is a very difficult task. Either prophetic ambiguity or editorial control indicating how particular prophecies should be understood will militate against charges of unfulfilled predictions. In terms of dissonance analysis such hermeneutic control of the traditions regulates the possibility of dissonance resolution and in the later expositions of the Immanuel pericope it will have been read as a warning of Assyrian inspired destruction.

There is another way of handling the Immanuel oracle which takes it as a salvation oracle but stresses its ambiguity in that it was offered to the king in terms of his own response – 'if you will not believe, surely you shall not be established' (9b). This element of subjectivity introduced into the prophetic situation has the effect of making the outcome of the prophet's prediction dependent upon the king's response to it. Thus the notion of conditionality is reintroduced into prophecy and the predictive element is rendered immune to the normative tests of verification. The sign of Immanuel remains but its import depends upon Ahaz's decision: if he rejects the prophet's offer then Immanuel will be a sign of destruction (which is how the editors take it and accordingly add on the sections in 18–25), if he accepts it then Immanuel will be a sign of salvation. This reading of the oracle is in keeping with Buber's stress on the moral dimension of prophecy but is probably an oversubtle reading of it. It certainly would provide a permanent basis for dissonance resolution in that any unconfirmed prediction could be accounted for on the grounds that the king or the community had not responded to the offer.

This feature of human response structuring the outcome of a prediction seems only to apply to salvation oracles which turn out to be different from their expectations. Given the social and political environment of Judah in the eighth and seventh centuries it was inevitable that it would be dominated by Assyria, either in terms of invasion and conquest or humiliating vassalage. It is hardly surprising that even oracles of hope should be seen as indicative of doom. Those oracles of salvation which were not so transformed by editorial reflections into statements of destruction (e.g. 2.2–4; 4.2–6; 9.2–7; 11.1–9) were used as editorial markers to balance the gloomy pictures of predicted doom, or may have stood as notes of hope in the face of the inevitable (having their origins perhaps in the cult).

Isaiah 8.16–18. The futile struggle to persuade Ahaz to trust Yahweh and the strong antagonism between prophet and people (cf. the transvaluation of 8.11–13) finally led the prophet to retire temporarily from public preaching. This retirement involved retreating into the company of his disciples (*limmudim*) and sealing up among them his teaching (*tōrā*). In a period when the deity had hidden himself from the nation his messenger (6.8) also had to hide himself. The hidden deity meant no further word was available for the community. All that was left was the existence of the prophet and his followers as signs in the community. The (auto) biographical section which began with an assertion of Yahweh's presence in his official residence on Zion now closes with a further affirmation of Zion as the dwelling place of Yahweh.

It has already been emphasized that the social support provided by the group is an important feature of dissonance response. It provides a shelter from hostile criticism and sources of dissonance as well as supplying mutual support. What we have in Isaiah's retirement from public activity is essentially the implementation of such a defence mechanism against dissonance. Turning from a hostile public and a sphere of activity that had proved frustrating and disappointing the prophet now confined his activities to those already convinced of his rightness and therefore sympathetic to his cause. It was not intended to be a permanent retreat from public life but simply an opportunity to rethink policy and determine future tactics (a case of *reculer pour mieux sauter*). By this action he not only avoided further dissonant experiences but in gathering around himself followers he provided himself with a positive context which would reinforce his own convictions and function as a responsive audience.

Some commentators have seen in this move the creation of the remnant by Isaiah: 'his distinction lies less in a *doctrine* of the remnant than in the practical step of creating the remnant in which he believed.'[10] However this reads too much into the reference to his disciples. To treat his retirement among followers as the fulfilment of his son's name (Shear-yasub 'a remnant will return') provides an interesting example of self-fulfilling prophecy (cf. also 7.14 with 8.3) but is unnecessary given the sparseness of information in 8.16–18. Yet the existence of a *tōrā* which might be bound up among followers does raise the question as to what that teaching consisted of in terms of prophetic practice. The answer is necessarily speculative, though presumably it consisted of various oracles preached publicly in the previous years. Were the disciples to be witnesses when the predictions came to pass (cf. 8.1–4; 30.8)? Or should we think more in terms of a positive message of hope that could be entrusted to his followers because they provided the context where subtle variations of interpretation would be ironed out without the same possibilities for misunderstanding that obtained when preaching in public places?[11] Whatever the case may be it is sufficient to note the existence of the type of context that facilitated dissonance reduction.

Isaiah 9.7. Alongside these three points of dissonance reduction by a shift in original cognition (6.9, 10), group reinterpretative editing (7.17–25), and retreat to social support (8.16–18) the final editorial note for the section (9.7) should be noted. In this closing hymn the resolution of Judah's setbacks and territorial invasions is founded upon the accession of yet another Davidic king to the throne (9.2–7). It is a conventional or traditional expression of faith in the Davidic dynasty which was characteristic of Judaean political religion in the time of Isaiah. As Isaiah never attacked the institutions of temple or kingship, though he did criticize practices associated with each, it may not be unconnected with Isaiah's own beliefs about king and city. My concern here however is with the colophon to the vision 'the zeal (*qin 'at*) of Yahweh of hosts will achieve this'. Now this introduces the one note of method in all the visions and hopes about the future. The real problem for the modern interpreter is to work out how the scenes of destruction directed against a corrupt people were to be transformed into the scenes of Davidic controlled prosperity. This problem remains whether the prophet or later editors are responsible for the curious juxtaposition of elements. If the principles of repentance and conditionality are stressed then it has to be accepted that the visions of the prophets about a prosperous future stood a fair chance of never being realized. Because repentance cannot be guaranteed the prosperous future cannot be assured either. To emphasize prophecy as a moral force in ancient Israel is also to recognize that human responsibility is an important feature for the creation of the future. If the community will not turn then hopes for its future must fail. However, the theological dimension of Israelite thought has to be taken into consideration in order to resolve theoretically, at least, this dilemma of a future dependent upon man's decision. For prophecy Yahweh was the all powerful figure operating in the geopolitical sphere. In some sense the future had to be guaranteed by his action or there would be no positive future. This is the force of the note at the end of 9.7. It stresses the transcendental vision and affirms that in spite of human vagaries the future hope for the dynasty would be achieved. Yahweh himself would guarantee it.

Unfortunately this emphasis on the transcendental may have been characteristic of the period or of the cultic view of reality but for the modern interpreter it has a hollow ring because the dynasty was precisely that entity which did not survive the fall of Jerusalem. The note expresses genuine faith in Yahweh but it occurs because there was no other way in which the dynasty could survive. Later traditions also specified the same principle as a guarantee of the redemption of the remnant (cf. Isa.37.32) and others, in a time of distress, appealed to the deity's zeal for help (cf. Isa.63.15). This quality of faith or hope is a characteristically human thing and can provide a very strong defence for the individual or community against the inroads of dissonance, though it is powerless to achieve its own ends if they are unrealistically constructed. To what extent the note in 9.7 was one of hope or of defiance in the face of continued frustration is now impossible to determine but it should be noted as an element of the biblical tradition which will have provided its adherents with a capacity to ignore substantial amounts of dissonance and to go on hoping that one day the expectations would be realized. This phenomenon of human belief means that dissonance theory may not always be able to penetrate the defences of a group prepared to maintain its position in spite of persistent lack of confirmation. For without that belief there is nothing else but abandonment of position. The royal house of David eventually went the way of all flesh and disappeared but not without a protracted struggle to revive it and the survival of a hope that in some sense it would emerge in the future (messianism). Against the attacks of reality the tradents of Isaiah could only hope that Yahweh's zeal would underwrite their expectations.

Loyalty to the house of David persisted in Judah long after the dynasty fell in 587 and elements of that loyalty may have encouraged the Chronicler to produce his account of the history of the Judaean kings. However it is not clear to what extent the prophets shared in such views of the dynasty. Apart from the attempt by Haggai and Zechariah to restore the dynasty under Zerubbabel the prophetic traditions show a remarkable coolness towards the future king. Although there does appear to have been a prophetic expectation about a future ruler from the house of David (cf. Jer. 23.5, 6; Ezek. 34.23, 24) it was a modest one that avoided grandiose expectations about the king's person or achievements. Even the additional material on the subject (cf. Jer. 33.14–16, 17, 19–22, 23–26; Isa. 16.5; 32.1) only stressed his practice of justice and the permanency of his rule. Seldom was the ruler even called king, though it was acknowledged that he would rule as king on David's throne over the kingdom. Such modest hopes may have contrasted with the royal ideology current in their time when the tendency was to think of the king as Yahweh's son, the scourge of the nations. It is difficult to determine whether such a modest belief was also held by Isaiah, i.e. 9.2–7; 11.1–9, or whether he had no outlook on the future of the monarchy after the coming destruction of land and people. It would be strange if he had had no such hope for the future of the dynasty but the period was such a precarious one that he may have had ambivalent views about the prospects facing the dynasty and so have not committed himself to any firm belief. The hopes expressed in 9.6, 7; 11.1–5 belong to the Isaiah traditions but whether they are to be attributed to Isaiah of Jerusalem must remain an open question. The resolution of that question is underdetermined by the available data.

The Assyrian crisis. The political, economic and social background to Isaiah's work was the emergence of Assyria as a world power and its incursions into the territory of Israel and Judah. In typical prophetic fashion Isaiah saw Assyria as the divine instrument for punishing the corrupt Judaean nation (10.5, 6). Yet throughout the oracles of Isaiah there is a strange ambiguity in his attitude to Assyria. The Assyrians would·be a destructive force (cf. 1.4–9; 22.1–14; 28.7–13, 14–22; 29.13, 14; 30.1–5; 31.1–3) on the one hand, but on the other hand there would be a divine deliverance from the Assyrians (cf. 10.5–15; 14.24–27, 28–32; 17.12–14; 18.1–6; 29.1–8; 30.27–33; 31.4–9). These oracles pose many problems of arrangement, authenticity and interpretation and it is far from clear what their precise significance may be for the larger Isaiah tradition.[12] The matter is further complicated by the presence of other material on the Assyrian crisis in the biblical traditions. In II Kings 18, 19 two accounts of the Assyrian invasion of Palestine deal respectively with the occasion of Hezekiah paying tribute to the Assyrians (18.13–16) and the Assyrian response to Hezekiah's rebellion (18.17–19.37). A parallel version of this second account appears in Isa. 36,37. The midrash in II Chron. 32 also provides a version of Hezekiah's response to the Assyrian invasion. Finally a prophetic liturgy in Isa. 33 illustrates how the Assyrian crisis was handled within a cultic framework. The problem posed by all this material is one of how to resolve or reconcile the conflict between the historical defeat of Judah (Isa. 1.4–9) and the miraculous defeat of the Assyrians (185,000 dead).

The difficulties involved in organizing all the material relevant to the Assyrian crisis exemplify the ambiguousness of so much of the prophetic traditions. Isa. 1.4–9 and the Assyrian archival records agree on the nature and extent of Jerusalem's humiliation (cf. Isaiah's simile 'like a lodge in a cucumber field' with Sennacherib's 'like a bird in a cage'). Isaiah's estimate of Judah's survival was that but for the grace of God Judah would have been another Sodom and Gomorrah (1.9). How then are we to make room in that account for the terrifying miracle that destroyed the Assyrians (II Kings 19.35–37)? Apart from suggestions that the Assyrians besieged Jerusalem on two different occasions (Bright), it may have been the case that the survival of Hezekiah as king and Jerusalem as an intact city constituted some sort of negative triumph on the part of the Judaeans. Time and theology produced the later legend of a catastrophic defeat of the Assyrians. However no consistent pattern has emerged from the oracles of Isaiah that would provide a clear account of what Isaiah's view of the crisis was. In his analysis of all the relevant material Childs isolates six distinct genres – the prophetic oracles of Isaiah, the annalistic report of II Kings 18.13–16, a deuteronomistic redaction of historical tradition (II Kings 18.17–19.9a, 36f.// Isa. 36), the legend of the righteous king (II Kings 19.9b–35 // Isa. 37.9b–36), the midrash of the Chronicler, and the prophetic liturgy of Isa. 33. His conclusion is difficult to resist: 'The oracles of Isaiah are far too complex and diversified to allow for a simple formulation of his position on Assyria which could then serve as a criterion for measuring the historical elements in the narrative material. The so-called "Isaiah of legend" is not so easily disentangled from the alleged "historical Isaiah".'[13]

This brief statement of the Assyrian crisis issue is not intended to be a resolution of a vexed problem but is provided in order to make two observations germane to the treatment of Isaiah in terms of dissonance theory. In the first place the intractable nature of the material underlines the insistence on the difficulty of stating clearly what a prophet may have thought about a specific issue. This lack of clarity in the oracles as well as their ambiguousness makes it very difficult to apply dissonance theory. Where the initial cognitive holding is unclear it is not possible to show whether it has been subsequently confirmed or not. So ambiguity in prophetic beliefs renders them less vulnerable to the experience of dissonance. In the second place the belief in Zion's safety probably was an element in Isaiah's thought (cf. 8.18; 28.16, 17) which later contributed to the development of the legend of its miraculous deliverance. If 701 was the collapse of hope for Judah and if the continued Assyrian hegemony appeared to render Isaiah's conviction about a sure foundation stone in Zion false then perhaps the legend of the angel miraculously destroying the Assyrians was an attempt to confirm the prophetic expectation. After the destruction of Judaean territory there had been no subsequent collapse of the Assyrian power – prophecy fails again! However the material in II Kings 18.17–19.9; Isa. 37 represents history as constructed by expectation. I add this possibility to the many that have been put forward as possible explanations for the insoluble difficulties of the biblical traditions on this issue. Dissonance theory provides an excellent explanation for the resolution of the Assyrian crisis in Kings but the data are too confused to show that that actually occurred. Some of the data fit the theory but there are too many tortuous strands to be certain that dissonance was caused by the failure of the prophet's expectations for after the 701 crisis. The belief in the inviolability of Zion may have grown out of this period or it may have constructed the legendary resolution in the first place.[14] That belief was to provide further occasions of dissonance when the Babylonians destroyed Jerusalem a century later (cf. Lam. 4.12). Ironically Isaiah may have contributed to it by his ambivalent attitude towards the Assyrians, an attitude which encouraged his followers to develop and sustain a tradition of salvation expectation associated with their master.

Reinterpretation of Isaiah

A brief consideration of some of the material in Isa. 1–39 clearly shows that Isaiah's oracles underwent substantial editorial activity that produced a number of reinterpretative shifts in his work. These shifts indicate a different thought pattern working with the earlier tradition which tried to relate expectation to experience by commentary on the oracles. Thus the oracle in 7.7–9 was updated by the note in 8b to relate it to events around 670. The explanatory gloss 'the king of Assyria' was added to 7.17, 20 in a period when the material was thought to be too obscure without some such explanation. These additions are really cases of marginalia having been incorporated into manuscripts that reveal an ongoing concern with the meaning of the oracles and their exposition in a specific setting. The variety of additions that expanded the original collection of oracles and sayings is quite considerable so only a few points will be noted here.

Isaiah 10.20–23. This piece was placed after 10.19 due to the occurrence of 'remnant' in both places; a case of word association stressing the fewness of the Assyrian survivors and the comparable fewness of the Israelite survivors of the destruction. The language of 10.20 indicates a significant shift in meaning to that of Isaiah of Jerusalem. In the original prophet's thought the agent of all the attacks on Judah was not the Assyrians but Yahweh (cf. 3.1; 5.5, 6; 9.13 (Heb. 9.12); 10.5; 22.8–12); the Assyrians were merely the instrument of those attacks. The phrase 'him who smote them' (*hammakkēhū*) in 9.13 refers to Yahweh but the same phrase 'him that smote them' (*makkēhō*) in 10.20 refers to Israel's enemy (unnamed but possibly the Assyrians cf. 10.24). The shift in meaning has been caused by the changed worldviews indicative of a different period for the additional oracle. Yahweh is no longer Israel's enemy (cf. Isa. 63.10) so they may return to him. The return of the remnant is a spelling out of the significance of the name Shear-yasub that occurs in 7.3. The complete lack of information provided by the name in 7.3 is made good by this explicit treatment of the phrase. Furthermore the return is not simply an indication of survival or return from deportation but is clearly a positive return to Yahweh (a genuine repentance *be'met*). So the additional oracle provides two reflections on Isaiah's oracles: a transformation of the cause of distress from the deity to the enemy and a transformation of the son's name into a positive message.

Isaiah 10.24–27a. A similar additional oracle intended to reassure the community that the Assyrian threat has a limited time to run. The key element here is verse 25 'for in a very little while (*kî-'ōd m°'aṭ miz'ār*) my indignation will come to an end, and my anger will be directed to their destruction'. The oracle looks like the answer to the standard question 'how long?', an answer assuring the community that the time of trouble is almost over and soon the Assyrians themselves will be destroyed. That note of soon shows an awareness of dissonance caused by the failure of expectations of salvation but reduces the dissonance by emphasizing the shortness of the period before salvation dawns. How to explain the absence of deliverance to the community living under great suffering? Well the answer is *soon*. This approach balances the dialectic of destruction and salvation so well that only a very protracted period of time could disconfirm it. As an element of dissonance reduction it has great potential.

Isaiah 27.2–6. This oracle deliberately reverses the force of Isaiah's song of the vineyard (5.1–7) so that in answer to the threat of the original parable there is this assurance of divine protection.[15] In this way earlier expectations of destruction were replaced with hopes of salvation. Presumably after a period of suffering caused by deportation Isaiah's parable was considered to have been rendered obsolete (27.7–9?) and so its terms were transformed into a hope for the future protection of the community by Yahweh (cf. 4.2–6). The transformation is evidence of an ongoing treatment of Isaiah's work in relation to the developing circumstances of the community centred on Jerusalem. The beleaguered citadel provided a constant context of impending destruction until the exile, then it continued as a partially ruined backwater yet all the time some tradents maintained a vision that the city would flourish in the future. No amount of invasion or destruction could shake that conviction and the oracles of Isaiah provide the matrix for the development of such expectations.

Isaiah 33.17–22. This prophetic liturgy makes an important point about the kingship of Yahweh that should be incorporated into the analysis of Isaiah for dissonance response. The key phrases occur in verse 22 'For Yahweh is our judge, Yahweh is our ruler, Yahweh is our king, he will save us.' The kingship of Yahweh is an important motif in Isaiah (cf. 6.5), though mainly in terms of Yahweh's sovereignty over the nations and his campaign against every lofty pride (2.6–21). In the cult the kingship of Yahweh was celebrated (cf. Ps. 93.1; 97.1; 99.1) so this liturgy sees in that kingship the protection of the city in the future. Whatever the origins of the belief in the kingship of Yahweh may have been (cf. Deut. 33.5) the belief became more important when the Davidic dynasty ceased to exist and hopes relating to kingship had to be either projected into the future or on to the deity. The two levels of kingship in ancient Israel, i.e. divine and human, provided a reinterpretative source for hopes about the dynasty. Evidence of this may be seen in the way the phrase 'mighty god' (*'ēl gibbōr*) is used of the hoped for Davidic figure in 9.6 (Heb. 9.5) but of Yahweh in 10.21. The secondary oracle is from a period when the monarchy no longer existed so the only source of hope was the deity. The expectation of a Davidic occupant of the throne could be reinterpreted to mean faith in Yahweh the king. Apart from 9.6, 7; 11.1; 16.5; 32.1 all the expectations of hope for future wellbeing relate to the deity (cf. 12; 14.1, 2, 32; 17.7, 8; 19.16–25; 24.23; 25.6–9; 26.1–4; 27.2–6, 12, 13; 29.17–24; 30.19–22; 31.4, 5; 32.15–20; 34.16, 17, 35).[16] This substantial collection of oracles is dominated by the thought of Yahweh as the focus of the future community. No other prophetic tradition makes so much of that focus – *this* is the linking feature of all the traditions accumulated in the book of Isaiah. The Davidic hope then is incidental to the Isaiah traditions and its existence there points to the survival of groups of devoted followers of the dynasty. However the tradents of Isaiah were mainly concerned with the future community's focus on Yahweh. Community and city are the two great motifs of the Isaiah traditions. They are given their significance by their place in the vision of Yahweh's future work.

During the existence of the Davidic dynasty it was always possible to entertain the hope that one of the kings would embody the principles of justice and righteousness (cf. 9.5, 6; 11.3–5; 16.5; 32.1–5) but after the collapse of the monarchy that hope became less realistic. It survived in some circles but among the Isaiah tradents it had very little place because their focus was on Yahweh and how he would save community and city in the future. Dissonance caused by the loss of the monarchy could be reduced by transforming hopes about the king into beliefs about the divine king's protection of community and city. Under a righteous king's government it would have been possible to have reversed the blindness created by the initial prophetic proclamation (cf. 6.9, 10 with 32.3, 4) but no such king ever successfully sustained such hopes. So the hopes shifted to the deity and oracle after oracle proclaims the belief that in the future Yahweh will swallow up death, wipe away all tears and display his zeal for his people (25.8; 26.11). However such beliefs may have arisen in the first place (most likely they had some connection with Isaiah) they came to form a dominant strand of prophetic reinterpretation which carried the oracles of Isaiah towards the formation of the major prophetic tradition in the post-exilic period. The steady shifting of beliefs from human terms to theological concepts greatly increased the dissonance resistance of the hopes though it also tended to lessen their cognitive force. A community settled in Jerusalem over which Yahweh was king could be interpreted as the fulfilment of all the prophetic expectations originally posited of the royal house. The achievement of such a resolution of dissonance caused by the dynasty's collapse was the work of the followers and interpreters of Isaiah's vision who, over the centuries, worked on his oracles and provided them with a hermeneutic for the future.

Second Isaiah and his circle

The destruction of Jerusalem in 587 must have deeply disappointed those who believed that the city was inviolable because it was Yahweh's residence. Disintegration of cult, community and city must have created serious dissonance for any Judaeans who expected Yahweh to intervene on their behalf to defend his people. As the long exile progressed the hope of restoration must have faded for many sincere Yahwists. Indeed those who had been deported to Babylon settled down to a normal way of life there and established the roots of what was to become one of the major areas of Jewish life for the next two millennia. Prophecy had been damaged by the collapse (cf. Lam. 2.14; Ps. 74.9) and had revealed very serious defects as a social movement in society. The majority of Judaeans had survived the catastrophe and had settled down to a meagre existence in and around Jerusalem. It was a time of consolidation and lack of vision. Traditions were collected and edited but mainly in order to show how inevitable the destruction had been (cf. Lamentations, the deuteronomic history etc.). For those who had believed that Yahweh would protect his own people it must have been a time of serious loss of faith after the holocaust.

Within fifty years of the fall of Jerusalem the Babylonian empire fell to the Persians under Cyrus. With the (imminent) fall of Babylon there emerged a prophet who proclaimed the change of political fortunes to be the long awaited salvation of Israel by Yahweh. The salvation oracles of this prophet are to be found in Isa. 40–55. The incorporation of these oracles into the traditions associated with

Isaiah shows that the tradents understood them to be the fulfilment of the expectations carefully nurtured by the interpretation of Isaiah already undertaken.

This anonymous prophet greeted the rise of Cyrus to power as the occasion of Yahweh's salvation of community and city. Thus the prophetic task was no longer one of denunciation and critique of society but a proclamation of comfort and forgiveness: 'Comfort, comfort my people, says your God. Speak tenderly to Jerusalem, and cry to her that her warfare (service $ṣᵉbā'āh$) is ended, that her iniquity is pardoned, that she has received from Yahweh's hand double for all her sins' (40.1, 2). The thrust of his message was that something *new* was about to happen (cf. 42.9; 43.18, 19; 48.6–8). The message itself was preached with great rhetorical flourishes and grandiose metaphors which depicted the immediate future in triumphalistic terms. The people would return to their own land, the city would be rebuilt, nature would be transformed and the nations would acknowledge Israel's leadership (49.7, 22, 23; 55.5). The legends of the old exodus would be surpassed in this new exodus from Babylon across the desert (now turned to springs). So in the late sixth century prophecy asserted that finally the day of salvation had arrived, the time of waiting was over and the nations would witness the triumph of the previously despised little nation of Israel.

Second Isaiah's preaching was by far the most sustained, confident assertion of the actuality of Israel's salvation and therefore it provides the best paradigm in prophecy for dissonance analysis. His oracles were an attempt to resolve the dissonance caused by the continued failure of the positive aspects of prophecy by identifying the release of the Babylonian captives with the expected salvation. Whether he envisaged such an actual return or only attempted to encourage the exiles to seize their opportunity by turning the events of their time into the great act of salvation cannot now be determined. Whatever his motives and thinking may have been he imbued the occasion with far greater significance than it actually turned out to have had. Few returned from captivity and the few that did found a territory still suffering the effects of the Babylonian invasion. Between the proclamation and the response fell the shadow but between the proclamation and the reality fell an even greater shadow. Such a gap between expectation and experience is the essence of dissonance and the preaching of Second Isaiah only created greater dissonance for those who took his vision seriously.

Nothing is known about the prophet so we do not know whether he worked in Babylon or Palestine, whether he was a peripatetic preacher or a cult prophet, or to whom he preached.[17] Viewing him as a cult prophet would account for the gap between proclamations of salvation (a motif strongly associated with the cult) and their realizations in reality because the world of the cult had its own values and to relate them to the real world would be category confusion. However the importance of Second Isaiah's oracles for this study is in terms of their relation to Isaiah's work as fulfilment of that vision and especially the dissonance aroused by them that had to be resolved by his followers. The proclamation of a salvation so vivid in its details and so absent in its realization constitutes the essence of dissonance arousal. If the prophet had followers then they will have had to provide explanatory schemes, at some stage after Second Isaiah's preaching, to account for the failure of the vision. So it is the work of his circle that concerns the analysis here.

Appended to the oracles of Second Isaiah is a collection of discrete oracles (56–66) which includes a number of dissonance reduction moves. Because his followers and those who preserved his oracles accepted the truth of their master's vision they therefore had to show how that expectation was true but had not yet materialized for reasons that would preserve the truth of the original vision from falsification. The reduced circumstances under which the Jerusalem community functioned forced the prophetic party to come to terms with this problem because there was no alternative social structure which would have provided them with support. Although the various oracles in 56–66 date from different periods and belong to various literary genres together they constitute a pattern of dissonance resolution which clearly indicates some of the problems caused by the failure of the predicted salvation.[18]

The predicted salvation was accepted as the basic commitment of the group so there was no attempt to deny that cognition. If there was nothing wrong with the predicted event then the fault must have been in the community and so the oracles argued. In Second Isaiah's preaching there had been no stress on the ethical requirements of the community because the exile was understood as having expiated the nation's sins (40.2)[19] Now his followers laid down demands that had to be met by the community, e.g. keeping the sabbath (56.2–7), or made accusations against the community for failing to keep the sabbath (58.13), for dietary offences (65.4; 66.17), for having false attitudes to fasting (58.1–5), for indulging in immorality and idolatry (57.3–10, 13; 65.1–7), and for general sinfulness (59.1–15). So the fault lay with the community! 'Look, Yahweh's hand is not shortened, that it cannot save, or his ear dull, that it cannot hear; but your iniquities have made a separation between you and your God, and your sins have hid his face from you so that he does not hear,' (59.1, 2). It is the old story of the human factor which had frustrated the deity yet again. Given this type of explanation it is difficult to conceive of a prediction that could not be preserved from dissonance. The future *we* have proclaimed has failed to appear because *you* are such miserable sinners! The ethical factor in prophecy rescued the expectation from failure by accounting for its absence.

A different form of explanation can be seen in the statement in 56.1 'Thus says Yahweh: "Keep justice, and do righteousness, *for soon my salvation will come (kî-qᵉrōbā yᵉšûʿātî lābōʾ)*, and my deliverance be revealed."' Apart from the note of ethical demand which is similar to the other accusations against the community, the distinctive explanatory device is that 'soon'. How striking a contrast this note of delay makes with the 'now' of Second Isaiah's insistent assertion of salvation. It has not yet happened but *soon* it will arrive. It looks like a classic dissonance reduction ploy. This note of soon (*qārōb*) will be found more frequently in prophecy as the community struggled with the problem of delayed realization (cf. 10.25). It is coming but it has not quite arrived yet so everybody behave properly until it does arrive. Perhaps this was the first confident explanation for the non-appearance of the expected salvation but as the years passed the explanations turned to accusing the community of being at fault. Concealed prescriptions were being introduced into the scenario to reduce the growing dissonance as hopes went unrealized.

A third form of explanation can be found in the oracles and it approximates to the conspiracy theory account of events. Others are to blame for the state of affairs, they have excluded the servants of Yahweh from the sanctuary, and in the coming action of Yahweh they will be destroyed (cf. 63.18, 19; 65.5, 13–16). The opponents (ṣārīm) referred to in 63.18 may have been other prophetic groups, or civil and cultic leaders whose policies for redeveloping Jerusalem did not include the followers of Second Isaiah.[20] That the tradents distinguished clearly between two sets of people, Yahweh's servants and the others, is obvious from 65.13–16; 66.5. Perhaps they were excluded from power and therefore could only denounce the opposition as certain targets of divine judgment whenever it appeared. The presence of an anti-cult bias in some of the oracles (cf. 57.1–13; 58.1–5; 65.1–7; 66.1–4, 17) suggests that some of the prophetic circle may have opposed the current cult leaders in Jerusalem and therefore would have received very little sympathy from the leaders of the community. Excluded from the sanctuary and lacking effective power in the community they saw their opponents' policies as one of the reasons for the delay of their expectations (and also one more very good reason for hoping they would be realized soon).

The element of direct divine action already noted in the additional oracles interpreting Isaiah can also be found in the oracles of 56–66. This appears in 63.1–6; 65.17–25; 66.12–16. No human effort was adequate to the task so the deity himself acted and brought about the victory. At least that was the hope of the interpreters of Second Isaiah, that the transcendental dimension would resolve the problem. The old dreams of a transformed nature would be realized when Yahweh created the *new* heavens and *new* earth (65.17, 25; cf. 11.6–9 which is abbreviated in 65.25). In this celebration of the divine initiative prophecy struggled to maintain the tension between human freedom and corruption and the divine act which transcends man's situation and his will. The failure of the prophetic vision for the future forced the reinterpretation of prophecy further down the line of stressing transcendental resolutions, already very apparent in the interpretation of Isaiah, that was to end in the apocalyptic vision.

In isolating these various responses of delay of expectation, the iniquities of the community as prevention of salvation and conspiracies by other groups as responses to dissonance in Isa. 56–66 I hope to have indicated some of the evidence for dissonance theory in the interpretation of prophecy. We do not know how effective such responses may have been but they probably convinced some of Second Isaiah's circle to their own satisfaction sufficiently for them to have preserved the oracles of the prophet along with their own interpretations. They were able to go on working because they had provided sufficient dissonance reduction by these explanatory schemes.

The one instance of a more realistic and reflective outlook in Second Isaiah is his extended metaphor of Israel as the servant suffering humiliation and injustice at the hands and on behalf of others (52.13–53.12). This view of the nation (assuming that that is the correct interpretation of a very complex, enigmatic poem) is in striking contrast to the more characteristic triumphalism of Israel's role in the world. Metaphors are extremely difficult to pin down for meaning so the vision of the servant humiliated by suffering injustice easily eludes any one definite interpretation. If the meaning of the poem can be taken to include the post-exilic experiences of the nascent community then it may represent a statement adjusting vision to reality. Instead of the glorious triumph fully expected by the prophet there is the darker side of reality incorporated into the vision of the community. Israel remains Yahweh's servant, not as the ascendant to the throne but as the bearer of judgment against iniquity. It is only a temporary condition but it does recognize the reality of events immediately following the Persian liberation. It would be foolish to imagine that treating the section as a prophetic response to the dissonance caused by the failure of the original expectation would solve the many problems associated with the interpretation of that highly influential but dense poem. However in drawing a darker picture of Israel's role in the world the prophet accommodated himself to the reality the community bitterly experienced. It was his hope that such a role would not be a permanent one – yet in that vision he produced his most seminal metaphors for the future life of the community.

Looking at the Isaiah traditions as a whole it is clear that the oracles of Isaiah of Jerusalem underwent a continual reinterpretative process over a long period. This activity centred on Jerusalem and the community living there. The core of the activity centred on the salvation of city and community and this entailed regular attempts to identify such events as indicating the realization of this salvation. Wherever possible interpretations were provided that facilitated such a reading of history or helped to explain why the expectations had not yet been realized. In struggling with these problems the tradents created a very rich hermeneutic that enabled the prophetic vision to survive long after its day and to influence subsequent events in the community's life in Jerusalem. The flexibility created by the interpretative processes gave prophecy a good defence against dissonance arousal and kept alive hope and vision for the community. Some of the ways these were achieved are best illustrated by the Isaiah traditions but other prophetic traditions also demonstrate the continual transformation of the vision.[21]

Text and Interpretation II

For the analysis of prophecy using dissonance theory to be most effective it must concentrate on areas of specified events capable of being disconfirmed. As the main traditions in the prophetic tradition are concerned with critiques of contemporary society and anticipations of the immediate future little scope is provided for response to dissonance arousal. However in the case of additional oracles or editorial material appearing in the traditions it is then possible to check for evidence of awareness of dissonance caused by the failure of expectations. Such awareness can only have been caused by specific events not having occurred or not having measured up to expectations to the extent that the parties concerned had to produce explanations for the apparent failure. Hence the analysis has to focus on the exilic and early post-exilic period because that was the time when expectations of the realization of future hopes were at their greatest. The responses of Second Isaiah's followers to the failure of his expectations have already been discussed so in the following texts further responses and reinterpretative devices will be considered as ways of reducing dissonance caused by expectation failure.

Haggai-Zechariah

A time of crisis and the responses it generates is the best time to observe how structures react, disintegrate and are reconstructed. The crisis brought on by the collapse of Jerusalem in 587 led to the eventual editing of prophetic traditions that had announced such a disaster (e.g. Jeremiah, Ezekiel), brought to an end the history of the kings of Israel and Judah (the deuteronomic history) and was lamented in a collection of poems about the fall of the city (Lamentations).[1] The possibility of restoration inaugurated by the new policies of Cyrus saw a resurgence of prophecy (Second Isaiah, Haggai, Zechariah). The restoration of the gods to their original places, the rebuilding of their sanctuaries and the return of deportees to their own countries were part of the reorganization of the empire undertaken by Cyrus.[2] Among the beneficiaries of this enlightened policy were the Judaeans who had been exiled by the Babylonians. Their return involved provision for the rebuilding of the destroyed temple of Yahweh in Jerusalem (cf. Ezra 1.2–4; 6.1–5). So the prophetic vision of a restored community living in a prosperous homeland was about to be realized: expectations were about to be confirmed.

Hopes may have been raised but they were not realized because, in spite of the resources at their disposal, there was no great movement back from Babylon to Jerusalem. This lack of response to prophetic proclamation is not difficult to account for: most of the deportees had grown up and lived all their life in Babylon. Few would have been still alive after fifty or sixty years since the fall of Jerusalem or the original deportation. During that long period they would have settled into patterns of organized community life (cf. Jeremiah's letter to the deportees of 597 in Jer. 29.1–9). The journey from Babylon to Jerusalem was a long hazardous one and the territory of Judah uninviting. These factors will not have deterred all the exiles for a few did return to an unwelcoming land. There they encountered a hostile community centred on the ruined city of Jerusalem and constituted a further drain on the limited resources available for sustaining the community. Apparently the foundations of the temple were laid but twenty years later the building had not been completed so the community must have been apathetic towards the project (cf. Ezra 5.11–16).[3]

This poor response to expectations was the context for the work of the prophets Haggai and Zechariah. Crises within the empire and the community produced the prophets whose work consisted mainly of encouraging the community to seize the opportunity of creating the new age. The accession of Darius resolved the succession crisis of the empire and the preaching of the prophets encouraged the continuation of the temple project. The link-up between the few returned exiles and the pro-temple Yahwists constituted one party in the community which may have had to face considerable opposition from groups opposed to temple politics on economic or religious grounds (cf. Isa. 66.1–4). There was certainly opposition and antagonism in the community and the prophets attempted to impose their scheme of restoration by regarding the temple project as a necessary stage in the realization of the expected salvation.

There are two central elements in the oracles of Haggai and Zechariah: a concern with the building of the temple and the support of Zerubbabel's claim to be the rightful occupant of the Davidic throne. Both may be seen as responses to the dissonance caused by the failure of the expected transformation of land and people in that they were attempts to create the conditions for the fulfilment of expectations. Their diagnosis of the prevailing conditions saw in the lack of temple and royal leadership the obstacles to the realization of the new age. Therefore the activity of Haggai in relation to the temple and both prophets' attitude to Zerubbabel provide focal points for the analysis of post-exilic prophecy in terms of dissonance theory.

The temple. The preaching of Haggai focused on the contrast between a community living in houses and a temple in ruins: 'is it a time for you yourselves to dwell in your panelled houses, while this house lies in ruins?' (1.4). In the community's estimation it was not the right time to rebuild the temple (1.2). The prophet then connected these attitudes with the poor social and economic circumstances of the community and linked them together in causal terms. The community was poor and shabby because the temple lay in ruins (1.5–11). The prophet interpreted the lack of well-being, the failure of the harvests, and the general poverty of spirit in the community as being due to neglect of Yahweh's house and its building programme. The prophetic argument, classically stated in Amos 4.6–11, that disaster was as much the activity of Yahweh as prosperity was used by Haggai to relate current poverty to the state of the temple. Ironically Amos's critique had been directed against a people all too willing to attend to the sanctuary and to offload gifts and sacrifices on to the deity, whereas Haggai's complaint was that they ignored the sanctuary yet expected to prosper. Haggai's stance was more than a criticism of the ruined condition of the temple, it was an indictment of the community's lack of a genuine religious concern for Yahweh's presence among the people.[4] A people limited to caring only for their own welfare displayed an incapacity for understanding the nature of true religion. So Haggai advised the people to gather the materials for the building project and then they would experience prosperity and expectations would materialize (1.8, 9; 2.18, 19).

The oracles of Haggai are an interesting example of a prophet trying to explain to his people why they should be suffering great deprivation in a time hailed by some prophets as one of abundant salvation (e.g. Second Isaiah). The flaw between expectation and reality was caused by the people's own fault. They had not built the temple! Thus what was absent in Second Isaiah's preaching, namely a precondition of Yahweh's great act of salvation, has been here made the cause of the delay of prosperity. The followers of Second Isaiah explained the delayed salvation as having been caused by the community's general sinfulness and cultic heterogeneity whereas Haggai accounted for the delay in terms of the unbuilt temple. Each explanation resolved the dissonance by creating conditions for the fulfilment of the expectation, conditions that had not yet been fulfilled and therefore there could be no confirmation of that expectation until they were fulfilled. Thus in the early post-exilic period of reconstruction the prophetic parties acknowledged the delay in the realization of the new age but accounted for the delay in terms of the community's lack of preparedness to be worthy of receiving such salvation. On these two counts, delay and failure to maintain standards (what may be called concealed demands or conditions for fulfilment), the preaching of the prophets must be seen as typical responses to the dissonance caused by the non-appearance of their expectations. Both responses belong to the explanatory scheme reduction of dissonance in that they rationalize the failure of prediction by positing prior conditions of fulfilment to account for the delay of fulfilment (the small print of prophecy not provided by the original proclamation).

The appeal to the human factor as an explanation for delay or non-realization of expectations provides a foolproof argument for protecting predictions. It glosses all predictions with a conditional clause so that even the most transcendental statement may be explained later in terms of human failure. The deuteronomistic doctrine of repentance (as stated in Jer. 18.7–10) also provided a similar control for predictions by stressing the importance of the human response. No expectation could be said to have failed, rather it was a case of the community having repented or having failed to repent. Of course it does not follow that the prophets necessarily saw their explanations as attempts to resolve dissonance so much as attempts to understand and explain the circumstances prevailing at the time of preaching. However the effect of such ploys is to provide a paradigm resolution of all failed predictions and to indicate some of the problems entailed by the tensions between human decision and divine decree in the prophetic traditions.

The construction of the temple was bound up with the coming event of salvation thus: 'Once again, in a little while (*'ōd 'aḥat m'ʿaṭ hî'*), I will shake the heavens and the earth and the sea and the dry land; and I will shake all nations, so that the treasures of all nations shall come in, and I will fill this house with splendour, says Yahweh of hosts.' (Hag. 2.6, 7).[5] The long expected event would shatter the nations and lead their wealth to Israel's temple; the phrase literally translated as 'yet one, that a little one' indicates the immediacy of this coming event. An immediacy which also gave the community time to make the right response because until the temple was rebuilt the wealth of nations could not flow into it. So the rebuilding of the temple had become a prerequisite for the expected event of salvation. Although the prophets and their interpreters never seemed to allow that the events they proclaimed might be delayed they often allowed that a little time was still left between expectation and event. The event was regularly pushed further into the future. Such a move had the effect of protecting the expectation from immediate failure and also provided an avoidance of dissonance explanation. It also afforded the community time to change and therefore again stressed the importance of human response for realizing prophetic expectations.

Zechariah was also aware of the delayed realization of the expected well-being of Jerusalem (1.12) and concurred in Haggai's assessment that the community's poverty was linked to the state of the temple (cf. 8.9–13). He also encouraged the rebuilding of the temple (1.16) and associated this project with Zerubbabel (4.6–10). Embedded in this support for the building programme was a claim to prophetic authenticity by Zechariah (4.9). Thus not only was the building of the temple the *sine qua non* for the new age but it was also necessary for Zechariah's credibility (6.15). For Haggai and Zechariah then the temple was the key to the transition from the old age to the new age. Its continued existence as a ruin meant that there would be no salvation for the community. It may be to read too much into their preaching to say that the temple was the guarantee of blessing but the prophetic rhetoric certainly gives that impression. They were staking their reputations on that project and until it was built they were able to account satisfactorily for the non-appearance of the new age. In this way they were able to reduce the initial dissonance caused by the failure of the expected salvation. Once the temple was built they may have had to face further dissonance which would have required different explanations but the temple project provided the community with a positive programme of activity that could be achieved and in that achievement lay the community's salvation (cf. Ezek. 40–48).[6]

Zerubbabel. The religious and political cohesion of the pre-exilic Judaean state had been maintained by the Davidic dynasty and the temple cult in Jerusalem. With the collapse of the city both dynasty and temple had ceased so that the surviving community had neither centre nor cohesiveness. So when the Persians permitted a return to Palestine with authority to reconstruct the sanctuary the Jerusalem community was given the opportunity to recreate a centre and restore its identity. Part of the old identity had been the monarchy so there were now attempts to restore the Davidic ruler. A rebuilt temple and city with a legitimate scion of the house of David would certainly have constituted the new age as anticipated by some prophetic traditions. They would have realized the hope to be found in various prophetic fragments about 'the booth of David that is fallen' (Amos. 9.11), 'a shoot from the stump of Jesse' (Isa. 11.1), 'a legitimate branch (*ṣemaḥ ṣaddîq*) for David' (Jer. 23.5), and 'my servant David shall be prince among them' (Ezek. 34.24). Haggai and Zechariah were supporters of such hopes for the future and a number of their oracles supported the governor of the community, Zerubbabel ben Shealtiel, in terms drawn from the traditional view of the Davidic king.

The hopes of the prophets centred on Zerubbabel can be seen

clearly in the following oracles: 'The word of Yahweh came a second time to Haggai on the twenty-fourth day of the month, "Speak to Zerubbabel, governor of Judah, saying, I am about to shake the heavens and the earth, and to overthrow the throne of kingdoms; I am about to destroy the strength of the kingdoms of the nations, and overthrow the chariots and their riders; and the horses and their riders shall go down, every one by the sword of his fellow. On that day, says Yahweh of hosts, I will take you, O Zerubbabel my servant, the son of Shealtiel, says Yahweh, and make you like a signet ring (*kaḥōtām*); for I have chosen you, says Yahweh of hosts."' (2.20–23). 'This is the word of Yahweh to Zerubbabel: Not by might, nor by power, but by my spirit, says Yahweh of hosts. What are you, O great mountain? Before Zerubbabel you shall become a plain; and he shall bring forward the top stone amid shouts of "Grace, grace to it!" Moreover the word of Yahweh came to me, saying, "The hands of Zerubbabel have laid the foundation of this house; his hands shall also complete it. Then you will know that Yahweh of hosts has sent me to you. For whoever has despised the day of small things shall rejoice, and shall see the plummet in the hand of Zerubbabel."' (Zech. 4.6–10). 'Thus says Yahweh of hosts, "Behold, the man whose name is the branch (*ṣemaḥ*): for he shall grow up in his place, and he shall build the temple of Yahweh. It is he who shall build the temple of Yahweh, and shall bear royal honour, and shall sit and rule upon his throne. And there shall be a priest by his throne, and peaceful understanding shall be between them both."' (Zech. 6.12, 13).

Haggai and Zechariah obviously believed in Zerubbabel's royal status, his role in completing the building of the temple and his designation as bearer of the prophetic title 'branch'. He was the one who would be the focus of the divine action when the kingdoms were overthrown and he would occupy the royal throne. The new age was about to dawn and Zerubbabel was the key figure in that new age. So the expectations of the prophets are clear in terms of what would have been required to confirm or falsify them: thus the Haggai-Zechariah oracles provide good material for dissonance theory analysis. What is less clear is whether there is evidence within the traditions to indicate how the prophets might have reacted to the failure of their hopes.

Zerubbabel had been appointed governor of the province of

Judah by the Persian authorities with the commission to see that the community's restoration was carried out in accordance with Persian policy. This was part of the Persian strategy of restoring order to the empire by reorganizing the provinces and having them overseen by officials seconded by the imperial court. Whether the attempt to make Zerubbabel king was strictly in keeping with that policy – a Judaean understanding of the significance of the Persian action – or a dangerous overstepping, even a misreading, of the situation is not now possible to determine. From a Persian viewpoint the mission of Zerubbabel was as a civil servant controlling an outlying province in the empire; from a Judaean stance it was the beginning of the fulfilment of the prophetic hopes long held about the Davidic dynasty. The two viewpoints were not necessarily incompatible in that Zerubbabel's credentials as a member of the Davidic house may have been known to the Persians and utilized as a means of commanding the territory's loyalty.

The prophetic party's support of Zerubbabel and their designation of him as the royal branch, with the allusions that carried reverberating through the community, is an interesting example of post-exilic prophecy's tendency to adjust or correct earlier prophecies. Haggai and Zechariah threw their support behind Zerubbabel's claim to the throne whereas the prophet Jeremiah had written off that particular family's future as occupants of the throne (Jer. 22.24–30). According to Jeremiah Jehoiachin's future was such that even if he had been a signet ring (*ḥōtām*) on Yahweh's right hand he would have been torn off and thrown away. The force of the statement 'write this man down as childless' was not that the man had no children (according to I Chron. 3.17, 18 he had seven sons), but that none of his children would actually sit on the throne of David. Assuming Haggai and Zechariah knew such was the opinion of Jeremiah they certainly did not share it. For them Zerubbabel, a descendant of Jehoiachin, was to be Yahweh's signet ring (a reversal of Jeremiah's judgment) and so would provide the line of Jehoiachin with a successor to the throne.[7] In the long run Jeremiah's foresight was much keener than that of Haggai and Zechariah but they presumably set out to reverse an older prophetic judgment. Few prophets seem to have contemplated the possibility that the Davidic dynasty would simply disappear during or after the exile and never be replaced. The convention of monarchical government was for them a near absolute (with the exception of Second Isaiah cf. 55.3–5) so that after the exile the earliest prophetic endeavours included the attempt to reinstitute the dynasty.

Despite the great hopes for Zerubbabel the movement to restore the throne did not succeed. After a certain point Zerubbabel disappeared from the picture and it is not known what happened to him. Various speculations have been put forward for the failure of the movement: the Persian authorities moved swiftly against him, had him recalled, executed or assassinated.[8] Perhaps he continued in office and was not associated with the prophetic outlook which may have had such little support that it constituted no danger at all to the Persian authorities. Perhaps Zerubbabel retired from office to farm some land outside Jerusalem. We do not know. The movement failed for reasons of state and community organization: it was not an auspicious time to restore the monarchy, there were too many factors and parties against such a move, and the prophets simply did not have the weight of support in Judaean society that we are sometimes tempted to posit for them. Whatever the causes of the failure of the prophetic vision fail it did and with that failure prophecy failed yet again.

I have devoted some space to the Zerubbabel case because it provides an example of a clearly confirmable instance of prophetic prediction. After a certain period of time the expectation was equally clearly disconfirmed. The pertinent question for the analysis is: can we find evidence of an awareness of such disconfirmation and is there any evidence of an attempt to explain the failure of the expectation? It is at this stage of the enquiry that the difficulties of applying dissonance theory to biblical traditions are most evident. The nature of the material is such that the expectations are well delineated in it but little or no attempt was made to indicate the outcome of such expectations. Without editors like the deuteronomistic historians who had a thesis to establish by their rewriting of history the prophetic traditions have not been constructed on a prediction – fulfilment basis. The fall of Jerusalem was sufficient to confirm the negative oracles of most of the prophets whereas the fewer positive oracles were left open-ended because there was nothing that could be pointed to in the same way.

Furthermore supposing the small prophetic group that supported Zerubbabel under the aegis of Haggai and Zechariah had eventually

become aware that their hopes were never going to be realized –
how would we know? They could have given up their support for
such a policy, retired into discreet silence from public activity, or
simply have changed their outlook and assisted with the cultic
reorganization of the community by building the temple. None of
these reactions would have been registered in the oracles. Their
credibility as prophets might have been damaged but Zechariah had
wisely confined the confirmation of his credibility to the building of
the temple (4.9; 6.15). The two-pronged nature of the proclamation, temple and ruler, allowed them to fall back on the temple
project as a means of saving face. Later oracles were added to their
work to develop and transform the expectation of the coming king
(Zech. 9–14; cf. 14.16, 17). The lack of information about the
public reception of prophetic proclamations in the prophetic traditions militates against our analysing effectively those traditions for
evidence of reactions to failure of expectations. However the additional material already noted as having been appended to Isaiah and
Zechariah constitutes some evidence of a continuing concern with
the interpretation of such hopes in the traditions.

In the light of such negative considerations finding evidence of
actual awareness of and response to dissonance is a very difficult
task. I have no doubt that the supporters of the prophetic expectations for Zerubbabel were disappointed and suffered dissonance
when their hopes were not realized but there appears to be only one
piece of evidence that might be construed as actual response to
failed expectations. Zech. 6.11, 14 refers to crowns for Joshua the
high priest: 'Take from them (certain exiles) silver and gold, and
make crowns (*ᵃᵉṭārōt*) and set upon the head of Joshua, the son of
Jehozadaq, the high priest; and say to him . . . and the crowns
(*ᵃᵉṭārōt*) shall be in the temple of Yahweh as a reminder to Heldai,
Tobijah, Jedaiah, and Josiah the son of Zephaniah.'[9] The section
omitted is verses 12, 13 which refer to Zerubbabel rather than the
high priest so that verse 11 could have originally had Zerubbabel as
the recipient of the crowns. The plural crowns may have been
intended for king and priest and the subsequent failure of Zerubbabel to become king necessitated the removal of his name at this
point.[10] With the changing fortunes of the community in the Persian
empire the original plan to place Zerubbabel on the throne came to
nothing so he was removed from the coronation reference and the

theocratic nature of the community was recognized with a reference to the coronation of Joshua the high priest. Such an explanation would suit admirably the claim of dissonance theory: the expectation having been disconfirmed the sources were edited to reflect that disappointment by changing the original cognition. As confirmation of that interpretation it may be noted that the text itself is far from clear and has not been well preserved at this point. However there are other explanations which might equally account for the reference to Joshua: the high priest could have been crowned before Zerubbabel arrived in anticipation of his arrival and as an earnest of peaceful co-operation between them (cf. verse 13). The crowns could have been symbols relating to the pair of them, though that would still entail Zerubbabel having been edited out of verse 11. The editing has been done badly nor has the book of Zechariah been consistently edited to remove the hopes associated with Zerubbabel. Yet the absence of Zerubbabel in a text dealing with coronation suggests that at some stage there was an attempt to read the text in the light of failed expectations and this constitutes response to dissonance.

The failure of the Zerubbabel expectation was in many ways typical of prophecy in ancient Israel, i.e. allied to a trenchant critique of the norms of society went a naïve belief in transcendental solutions based on conventional royal models. Perhaps such predictions were just regarded as the stock-in-trade of prophets designed to keep in with the royal authorities and therefore were not taken seriously outside the royal court. Yet such beliefs in the royal house persisted and can be found in the Isaiah, Jeremiah and Ezekiel traditions. These elements in the traditions point to the survival of hopes for the dynasty which long outlasted the dynasty and were to contribute significantly to the messianic ideology of Roman times. Other elements in the traditions stressed the kingship of Yahweh and either played down the Davidic material or transformed it completely into a distinctive view of the nation. This seems to have been the case with Second Isaiah's view of the dynasty, for he transferred the functions of David to the nation itself.[11] The substantial changes brought about by the Persian organization of the empire included the impossibility of Judah existing as an independent state with its own king. Second Isaiah had recognized the demise of the dynasty and therefore did not encourage the community to place any hopes in the revival of monarchy. Haggai and Zechariah took a different view of the situation and supported Zerubbabel as a candidate for the throne. It would be unfair to accuse them of being shortsighted in that they may have thought that circumstances would change so rapidly and fundamentally that it was quite likely that the monarchy could be sustained. They failed to appreciate the serious changes that had taken place but their oracles were preserved because once they had been an important element in the reconstruction of the community after the exile. The Zechariah tradition was supplemented by various oracles, some of which transformed the beliefs about the future of the house of David (cf. 9.9; 12.7–9, 10–14; 13.1) and others took the line that in the future Yahweh would be the king (cf. 14.9, 16, 17). Thus there are family resemblances between the reinterpreted Isaiah traditions and the reinterpreted Zechariah traditions.

Texts indicative of delay

In the analysis of prophecy as reinterpretation in response to dissonance it has been emphasized that one such response was to talk about the delay of the expectation (cf. Isa. 10.25; 56.1). However delay is probably not quite the term that the biblical writers would have used. Delay is a negative term and implies some sort of hold-up in the implementation of the programme. It is a programmatic word relating to schedules and time-tables, but prophecy did not work with such entities. The 'not yet' of prophecy took the view that the event or expectation was about to happen, soon it would happen, it was imminent. All these terms can be seen as positive versions of the more negative notion of delay. By interpreting various notes on imminence in the prophetic traditions as hints of deferment or delay it is possible to see in them responses to or awareness of dissonance caused by the non-appearance of expectation. The interpreters of the traditions were compelled to emphasize the nearness of the event in order to encourage the community to be faithful and to reaffirm their faith in the reliability of the expectation. Each text should be seen as an answer to the question foremost in the consciousness of the prophetic groups: 'when?' or 'how long?'. Thus prophecy in its struggle with the disintegration of the vision faced this type of question with the continued assurance that the answer was 'soon, very soon'.[12]

Isaiah 10.25. This text has already been noted (above ch. 4, pp. 147–8) but here it may be more fully considered in terms of its stress on the shortness of the present period of suffering and the imminence of the expected deliverance. The key phrase is 'for yet a very little while' (*kī-ʿōd mᵉʿaṭ mizʿār*) or 'for there is still a very brief period'. Similar phrases occur elsewhere in Isaiah, thus 'is there not yet a brief period?' (*hᵃlōʾ-ʿōd mᵉʿaṭ mizʿār* 29.17) and 'like a brief moment' (*kimʿaṭ-regaʿ* 26.20). In 29.17 the emphasis is on how soon it will be that the prosperity of the land will be restored, the blind will see and the deaf hear – the general transformation of land and community is imminent. In 26.20 the wrath of Yahweh is about to be directed against the nations and the people of Israel are called to hide themselves until it is past (*ʿad-yaʿᵃbār-zāʿam* 'until the wrath has passed' – an echo of the passover legend?). In 10.25 the short period refers to the time remaining for Israel's domination by the Assyrians. In this oracle there is an explicit reference to the exodus (verse 26) and the assurance that only a little time remains before the Assyrians themselves are destroyed suggests that there was such an expectation in the community, an expectation here being reaffirmed. The stress on the shortness of the period before deliverance is the biblical equivalent of admitting to there being a short delay before expectations would be realized. The regular experience of a devastated land and foreign domination must have disheartened many generations of Judaeans but still the interpreters of the prophetic traditions kept up the word of reassurance as their answer to questions raised by experience.

The placing of 10.24–27a in its present context is an example of the balancing of negative elements by positive ones: 10.20–23 indicated that 'a full destruction is decreed . . . a full and determined end in the midst of all the earth' and that in such a terrifyingly complete devastation only a few survivors of Israel would return to Yahweh. The focus of verses 24–27a is on the short time left for Israel's suffering and the oracle stresses the Assyrians as the object of Yahweh's wrath. This reassuring oracle was then placed before the depiction of the Assyrian invasion of Israelite territory (27b–32), perhaps as a word of comfort balancing the threat of that onslaught. Its note of 'not quite yet' was the community's last hope against the despair of dissonance caused by the failure of its expectations.

Habakkuk 2.2, 3. Habakkuk was a cult prophet during the time of Jeremiah who preached salvation and whose work is essentially liturgical. The prophet may have been trying to combat elements in his own time that were sceptical about the prophetic vision ever materializing. Against such a background the oracle should be read: 'And Yahweh answered me "Write the vision; make it plain upon tablets, so he may run who reads it. For still the vision awaits its time; it hastens to the end – it will not lie. If it seem slow, wait for it; it will surely come, it will not delay."' The key phrases are 'if it lingers, wait for it; it will certainly come, it will not delay' (*'im-yitmahmāh ḥakkē-lō kī-bō' yābō' lō' y*ᵉ*'aḥēr*).[13] What the prophet seems to be saying is: 'although it delays, wait for it; it will most certainly arrive, it will not be late'. In other words, 'in spite of appearances everything is on schedule'. The admission of delay (*mhh*) quickly followed by a denial of delay indicates the problem facing the prophet. By giving the vision a fixed time (*mō'ēd*) Habakkuk provided a schedule for it and could therefore dismiss the possibility of delay by reassuring the community of the certainty of its realization. Whatever the popular belief in a delayed deliverance the prophet was convinced that the vision would be fulfilled on time, in its own season. A communal context of pessimism and questioning is here contradicted by an assertion that any *seeming* delay must not be considered to be an *ultimate* delay.

The oracles of Habakkuk provide many interpretative problems so this analysis must inevitably be a tentative one. As a salvationist prophet operating from a cult base he foresaw the judgment of Yahweh in the encroaching Babylonians (1.6) but as the liturgy in chapter 3 reveals he believed that Yahweh would act to save his people. The vision assured the community that deliverance would eventually come, without delay and in its own time. In spite of the apparent delay of the expected deliverance the prophet could maintain his faith in Yahweh (cf. 3.17–19). Such faith in Yahweh's power to save the community was the central tenet of Israel's cult, hence the assertion 'the righteous shall be sustained by his faithfulness' (2.4). Whether such a group of cult prophets were able to maintain that invincible faith as the Babylonian army tore down the city walls and destroyed the temple we do not know. However the exhortation 'wait for it, it will not be late' could cover all exigencies and provided an attitude for living through the dark days that followed the destruction of Jerusalem. With such tolerance of bitter disappointment the prophetic group might just have been able to stave off the dissonance caused by the failure of the vision.

Joel 1.15; 2.1. Joel was another cult prophet whose work consisted of identifying the coming day of Yahweh as one of terrible destruction directed against the earth. The motif 'day of Yahweh' (*yōm yhwh*) was one regularly used by the prophets to indicate a future day of fearful judgment (cf. Amos 5.18; Isa. 2.12–21; 13.6–16; Ezek. 7.5–9; Zeph. 1.7, 14). Its origins are obscure but judging by Amos's transformation of it (5.18–20; 8.9, 10) it may have been viewed popularly as a great time when Yahweh would save his people and destroy their enemies.[14] In Joel, the cult prophet, both elements functioned: the terrible doom associated with the day by the prophets could be averted by repentance and cultic observations such as fasting and mourning (cf. 1.15–2.11; 2.12–17) and eventually it would be a time of salvation for the nation when foreign nations would be judged (3.1–21 (Heb. 4.1–21)).

However, the concern here is with the statements in 1.15; 2.1 about the arrival of the day of Yahweh: 'Alas for the day! For the day of Yahweh is near (*kî qārōb yōm yhwh*), and as destruction from Shaddai it comes (*yābō*'). Blow the trumpet in Zion; sound the alarm on my holy mountain! Let all the inhabitants of the land tremble, for the day of Yahweh has come (*kî-bā' yōm-yhwh*), it is near (*kî qārōb*).' The Hebrew is ambiguous when translated into English so that the phrase *kî qārōb* can mean 'it is near/it has come/it is coming/it is approaching'. The phrase *kî-bā*' can also have a variety of tenses 'it has come/comes/is coming'. The appended *kî qārōb* in 2.1 may be an (intentional) indicator that the phrase *kî-bā' yōm yhwh* should be understood as 'the day is coming – it approaches'. It looks suspiciously like a gloss as it overloads the line and it may have been a marginal note to indicate that the verse should be interpreted as referring to a future event rather than a past or present one.[15] The assertion that the day had actually arrived was considered by a later editor to be incorrect (in view of his belief that it would be a day of salvation for Israel) so he marked the margin to indicate that it was still in the future, therefore *kî-bā*' 'for it has come' should be understood in the sense of 'is coming', i.e. 'approaches' (*kî qārōb*; in 1.15 *qārōb* is balanced by *yābō*', i.e. 'approaches . . . will come'). It

would then constitute a response to the failure of the original vision
and act as a correction indicating an awareness of dissonance caused
by the failure of the prophet's identification of the item of salvation.

It has to be admitted that all the phrases used in Joel on this point
are inherently ambiguous – the day may have actually arrived or
only have been approaching. Such ambiguity was an essential part
of the prophetic mode of proclamation and ambiguity is a strong
dispeller of dissonance because it prevents statements being made
that can be clearly verified or falsified. The two levels of destruction
and salvation associated with the day of Yahweh could be used to
interpret current events in terms of one or the other. The various
invasions and catastrophes could be seen as the negative aspect of
the day, the positive element could be retained as a hope for the
future. The question whether these texts (Isaiah, Habakkuk, Joel)
indicate *awareness* among the prophets of the possibility of delay
and an attempt to reduce dissonance caused by such delay by
incorporating the delay into their schemes is very difficult to answer.
Delay implies schedules and programmes and it is unlikely that the
prophets had such a programmatic outlook on the future. Yet
consciousness of the continued lack of deliverance for the community must have disturbed the interpreters of the traditions and even
some of the cult prophets so it may not be unreasonable to interpret
these notes on delay as indications of an awareness that events were
not working out as expected. The incorporation of waiting into the
vision (especially in Habakkuk) would then provide evidence that
some dissonance was experienced and that steps had been taken to
explain it sufficiently to preserve the integrity of the vision.

Adaptive prediction

The generality of so many predictions and the ambiguity of others
meant that they could be used in a variety of different ways.
Prophecies of doom could always be reused because the context of
Israel's existence was one of constant political manoeuvres by various states to gain power over other states. In such a context invasion, siege and conquest were regular experiences of the small
nations as empires advanced and retreated throughout the Ancient
Near East. Therefore threats of woe and destruction could be
regularly reused to indicate yet another visitation of the wrath of

God. In this section two examples of the category of adaptive prediction will be considered as evidence for the open-endedness of prophecy and also certain aspects of the nature of prophecy.

Jeremiah. Some of Jeremiah's early oracles include predictions about an enemy from the north: 'Raise a standard toward Zion, flee for safety, stay not, for I bring evil from the north and great destruction,' (4.6). The importance of the enemy from the north motif for Jeremiah can be seen in the vision of the boiling pot included in the introductory material to Jeremiah (1.13–19). The significance of the boiling pot facing away from the north was 'out of the north evil shall break forth upon all the inhabitants of the land' (1.14; cf. 4.5–31). The cycle of poems in 2–4 most likely belongs to the earliest period of Jeremiah's preaching and the impending doom foreseen there may well have been the impetus that made him a prophet. Whatever the identity of the foe from the north may have been the possibility of a formidable enemy invading Palestine in the mid-620s evoked the response in Jeremiah that here was the judgment of Yahweh against a corrupt Jerusalem: 'your ways and your doings have brought this upon you. This is your doom, and it is bitter; it has reached your very heart' (4.18).[16] However no such invasion took place then and the land of Judah survived for another three decades before the first Babylonian incursion took place. The poems about the invader from the north were sufficiently indefinite to be then re-utilized for the later Babylonian threat. Perhaps when originally delivered Jeremiah had not had any particular foe in mind, simply a people coming from the north country (cf. 6.22–26), but much later when the Babylonians appeared he identified them as the long threatened enemy from the north. Some three decades of proclaiming such an advent might well have earned him the nickname 'terror on every side' (cf. 20.10).

This open-endedness of a prophet's proclamation gave it less cognitive force but more adaptability so that a motif such as 'the foe from the north' could have indicated a mythological enemy from the home of the gods, a localized military action north of Judah or the invasion by the Babylonians. It could be used time and again to interpret different events. With the exception of Egypt all Judah's enemies inevitably came from the north so it was capable of great adaptation. Thus the depiction of the activities of Antiochus IV in the book of Daniel is in terms of 'the king of the north' (cf. 11.6, 7, 11, 13, 15, 40). Even what could be considered successful predictions (from the viewpoint of the traditions), e.g. the seventy years of Jeremiah (25.11, 12; 29.10; cf. Zech.1.12; 7.5), were capable of being adapted for different purposes.[17] The Chronicler regarded the seventy weeks as having a sabbatical significance (II Chron.36.20, 21), whereas the author of Daniel adapted them as a time indicator for the period from the exile until the destruction of the oppressor of Jerusalem (9.24–27). Thus in some sense the occurrence of the Maccabaean struggle against Antiochus IV was seen as the fulfilment of prophecy. Such an adaptive approach to prediction greatly enlarged the scope of prophecy and made specific failures of predictions less important because they were capable of being reapplied to new situations and events.

Ezekiel. Ezekiel devoted a number of oracles to denouncing Tyre in very strong metaphors which depicted the city as being overwhelmed by the sea and the forces of death and the underworld (26–28). The gist of the small collection of oracles against Tyre is: 'I will bring you to a dreadful end, and you shall be no more; though you be sought for, you will never be found again, says Yahweh God' (26.21). The collection is dated around 586 and was partly motivated by the Tyrian reactions to the fall of Jerusalem. However the predicted devastation of Tyre did not happen in the manner or to the extent foreseen by Ezekiel. Tyre surrendered to the Babylonians and had to accept that empire's domination but the prophetic rhetoric was well wide of the mark.[18] One more example of unfulfilled prophecy? In this instance there is something more interesting than an unfulfilled prediction; there is a variation on the principle of adaptive prophecy.

The adaptation of the original oracles appears in the collection of prophecies against Egypt (29–32): 'In the twenty-seventh year, in the first month, on the first day of the month, the word of Yahweh came to me: "Son of man, Nebuchadrezzar king of Babylon made his army labour hard against Tyre; every head was made bald and every shoulder was rubbed bare; yet neither he nor his army got anything from Tyre to pay for the labour that he had performed against it. Therefore thus says the lord Yahweh: Behold, I will give the land of Egypt to Nebuchadrezzar king of Babylon; and he shall carry off its wealth and despoil it and plunder it;[19] and it shall be the wages for his army. I have given him the land of Egypt as his recompense (*šākār*) for which he laboured, because they worked for me, says the lord Yahweh"' (29.17–20). So the failure of the vision against Tyre was adapted along lines which showed how Egypt would be ransacked to pay the Babylonians for their unrewarded troubles against Tyre. Two points may be made about this oracle: (1) it provides clear evidence of *awareness* of a prediction lacking fulfilment; (2) it is also evidence of the phenomenon of prediction after the event (*vaticinium ex eventu*).[20] Awareness that a prediction had not been realized completely did not so much cause dissonance as permitted a switch of position on the subject. If the first expectation did not measure up fully to the prediction then a further oracle could be produced to incorporate the failure into it. The oracle against Egypt has taken account of the failure of the Tyrian destruction, i.e. the long campaign of Nebuchadrezzar against Tyre ended without that city being plundered or destroyed, and has assimilated the hindsight provided by such a partial failure of expectations.

The ability to adapt predictions in the light of reality shows that the prophets were not necessarily at the mercy of their visions, be they as general as Jeremiah's destruction from the north or as specific as Ezekiel's against Tyre. Explanations by means of adaptation could be found for the apparent failure of such predictions and these moves must have considerably reduced any dissonance arising out of non-fulfilment. Some theologians justify such moves by appealing to the transcendental aspects of prophecy, thus Eichrodt writes of this adaption by Ezekiel: 'The predictions of prophets . . . are always associated with that to which the prophets testify, a direct awareness of the whole control of providence, so they subordinate each single historical event to its context in the activity of God which makes the whole development of history serve his kingdom. Their limitation consists in the fact that they are trying to show the way along which God is leading, whereas that God is always transcendent and far above all human capabilities, and so his march through history cannot be imprisoned in human words. He carries his plans home and attains his objective with all the freedom of the Creator; so, while prediction can make statements clarifying the plan and assuring us of its existence, it can never determine the exact line it will take or calculate beforehand its individual stages. So prediction demands humble obedience to the mystery of the divine work of realization and, like the rest of what prophets preach, it confronts the hearer with the question of a faith which refuses to let itself be led astray by unexpected delays, changes of front, or reconstructions.'[21]

This is a good example of the transcendental dimension of prophecy securing it from failure. However, it would take this book off in a direction beyond my competence and detrimental to its length to become involved in the complicated theology behind Eichrodt's statement. I do not see how such a statement differs from an insistence that even if the core of the prophetic message had been wrong it would not damage the theology of prophecy. Eventually Eichrodt's position must lead to a legitimation of whatever turned out to be the case having been the will of Yahweh. If prophecy had been entirely wrong it would not be possible to make such a judgment using the transcendental explanation for being wrong could have been God's way of vindicating his word! Yahweh may have possessed the sovereign freedom to have fulfilled predictions in whatever way seemed good to him (whatever that may mean) but at what point along such a scale do we stop? Would the non-fulfilment of an oracle preserve God's freedom in a more distinctive way then anything approximating to a correspondence between word and event? I ask these questions not out of scepticism at such theology so much as out of wonderment that in preserving the freedom of God to be God some theologians have come perilously close to installing Humpty Dumpty ('a word means what I choose it to mean') as his prophet.

The delay of expectations and the manipulation of oracles adapted for different purposes may have contributed to the bad name prophecy had among the citizens of Jerusalem in the closing decades of the Judaean state. Jeremiah complained about popular scepticism towards his preaching – 'Look, they say to me, "Where is the word of Yahweh? Let it come"' (17.15). The oracle in Ezek. 12.21–25 contains the popular proverb 'The days grow long, and every vision comes to nought', i.e. the predictions were not being realized. The fact of delay was also admitted: 'I Yahweh will speak the word which I will speak, and it will be performed. It will no longer be delayed (*lō' timmāšēk 'ōd*), but in your days, O rebellious house, I will speak the word and perform it, says the lord Yahweh,' (12.25). The sense of deferment or postponement shows that there was awareness of the non-realization of the vision among the public (cf. 12.26–28), though the prophets struggled to avoid such conclusions. The adaptive principle also indicates that the prophetic movement was not entirely unconscious of difficulties involved in their visions in relation to their fulfilment and therefore it provides a useful analytical device for the tracing of dissonance response in the traditions.

Corrective prophecy

One aspect of the reinterpretation of prophecy carried out by the prophetic parties and their followers was the correction of earlier statements by further oracles. Whereas some of the hermeneutic moves were designed to amplify or extend the earlier oracles the correction of prophecy was intended to contradict the earlier expectation and to replace it with a more up-to-date insight. Sometimes the correction simply involved inverting the earlier statement so that the dialectic of judgment and salvation could be maintained. This technique of inversion has already been noted in Isa. 27.2–6 where Isaiah's song of the vineyard has been inverted to provide a word of salvation. Also in Isa. 32.1–4 the inversion of Isaiah's inaugural vision (6.9, 10) has been partially achieved. A similar type of inversion can be found in the book of Joel where the statement 'Proclaim this among the nations: Prepare war, stir up mighty men. Let all the men of war draw near, let them come up. Beat your ploughshares into swords, and your pruning hooks into spears' (3.9, 10 (Heb. 4.9, 10)) contains the inversion of the oracle in Isa. 2.4 and Micah 4.3.

The principle of corrective prophecy can only be drawn from the edited traditions or the later prophets because it arises out of the reflection of prophets on the earlier traditions. In the post-exilic period prophecy began to reflect upon itself and became aware of the tradition of prophecy (cf. Zech. 1.4–6; 7.7) as a tradition in itself so there was a conscious dialogue between earlier and later prophecy. The tendency to correct earlier prophecy has also been seen in the distinctive attitudes to Zerubbabel of Haggai and Zechariah as opposed to Jeremiah's dismissal of that royal line. So the oracles of Zechariah will be considered as evidence for this corrective principle.

In the vision of Zech. 11.7–14 there is an obscure piece of play with two rods (*maqlōt*) relating to shepherds and sheep.[22] The relevant statement for the principle of corrective prophecy occurs in verse 14: 'Then I broke my second rod Union (*haḥōblîm*), annulling the brotherhood between Judah and Israel.' Whatever the precise date of this oracle the background is most probably that of the conflict between the community reorganized around Jerusalem and neighbouring communities, especially the Samaritan community (cf. Neh. 5; 7). However an important element in the vision is its opposition to the earlier visions of Ezekiel about the reunification of the two nations, Israel and Judah, under the image of two sticks being joined together.[23] Ezekiel stressed the union of the nations under the leadership of a Davidic king in a peaceful land (cf. 37.15–28). The Zechariah vision reversed those predictions in an oracle which not only depicted the annulment of the union but also delineated the corruption of the community's leaders (verses 15–17). This worthless leader destroying the community should be seen as a polemic directed against Ezekiel's vision which saw the community led by David (34.23, 24), for Ezekiel's shepherd is in striking contrast to the worthless shepherd of Zech. 11.15–17. The covenant of peace presided over by king David (Ezek. 34.26–31; 37.24–28) becomes doom and desolation in Zechariah (11.17; 13.7, 8). The great changes in the community's circumstances in the fifth century had rendered the hopes of the exilic prophet void and the visionaries of the later period had to fight against false hopes engendered by such outmoded predictions. Thus their oracles were intended to be the corrective of visions created by earlier prophets.

The attack on the corruption of the community's leadership in Zech. 11.4–17 might to some extent reflect not only the contemporary prophetic dissatisfactions with their own society but also hint at the illusions shattered by the failure of the earlier Zerubbabel movement. This would indicate a further link between the oracles of Zech. 9–14 and the tradition of Zech. 1–8.[24] By the time the material in Zech. 14 had been produced hope for the emergence of a great Davidic figure who would heal the wounds of the community had been replaced with the hope that Yahweh himself would become king. 'Yahweh will become king over all the earth . . . then every one that survives of all the nations that have come against Jerusalem shall go up year after year to worship the king, Yahweh of hosts'

(14.9, 16). Such a replacement of the Davidic hope with the more generalized belief in the kingship of Yahweh and his special presence in Jerusalem became a corrective to earlier ideas. By changing its terms and correcting older ideas and hopes the later stages of prophecy kept abreast with the changing circumstances in the world about them, and also modified dissonance caused by the failure of expectations by switching its expectations to a more transcendental level of reference.

Prophecy should not be regarded as having been a static or monolithic phenomenon in ancient Israel. It was constantly changing, developing, reinterpreting and reacting to various changes in society. Many diverse patterns of thought and opinion were meshed together to construct the multiplex traditions of prophecy and these represented part of an ongoing hermeneutic process in the community centred on Jerusalem. Awareness of disappointments and dissonance arousing lack of confirmation kept the tradents busy interpreting the traditions so as to maintain the vision and discern the way of Yahweh in relation to the community's historical experiences. If it were possible to question the prophetic groups in the post-exilic period about the steady failure of many of the visions of the past and how they survived such disconfirmations we might receive an answer along the following lines (assuming the question would have been meaningful to them at all). 'Of course our predecessors were often wrong and we have had to correct their visions with other visions given in our time. Yet we still believe, as they did, that Yahweh of hosts rules and is shaping the powers that be according to his own ends; eventually he himself will come and everything will be subjected to him. It is our task in this period of waiting to maintain the vision but interpreted in keeping with the newer insights of our own time. We have but built on the earlier prophecies and would count ourselves part of that long tradition of men who mediated the word of Yahweh to the people of Yahweh.' If such speculation is not entirely wrong then we may be able to discern how the later correction of prophecy contributed to its reinterpretation along lines which helped to protect it from being subsumed by dissonance altogether. Such an evolution of prophecy gave it a flexible and open structure that made it far less vulnerable to dissonance because it had developed the capacity to absorb disconfirming information into its hermeneutic systems.

Realized expectations

It would be misleading to give the impression that prophecy was a complete failure and that the post-exilic community bemoaned prophecy as such. For the negative visions of many of the prophets were clearly confirmed when Samaria or Jerusalem fell – 'Yahweh has done what he purposed, has carried out his threat; as he ordained long ago, he has demolished without pity' (Lam. 2.17). However there were also beliefs that the positive vision, a people living at peace in its own homeland with temple and priesthood, had been achieved. Such beliefs took the kernel of the salvation oracles, land and community, and saw in the existence of the post-exilic community in Jerusalem the fulfilment of prophecy. So in circles that held such a belief about the community the possibility of dissonance did not arise because prophecy had been fully confirmed. Two examples of this interpretation of prophecy may be considered as one of the dominant ways of reading prophecy in the age of the second temple.

Ezra. The vision engendered by Second Isaiah was maintained by his followers and became the inspiration and aspiration of a few in the restoration programme of the new community in Jerusalem. If Ezra's return to Jerusalem from the court of Artaxerxes, nearly a century later, be seen as a cultic procession intended to be a second exodus then it may have been an attempt to fulfil Second Isaiah's prophecy (cf. Ezra 7.1–8.36).[25] Ezra left in the first month (8.31), of the seventh year (7.7) – a year of liberation? (the sabbath principle cf. I Macc. 6.49, 53) – he even refused a military escort (8.22), perhaps reflecting Second Isaiah's reassurance that the way through the desert would be free of obstacles (cf. Isa. 43.2, 16–21; 45.2; 48.20, 21). Ezra also refused to leave Babylon without a company of levites (8.15–20). When he arrived in Palestine he separated the people there from the heathen round about (9; 10). When the feast of tabernacles was celebrated in the seventh month that year it was celebrated in a fashion not seen since the Israelites had arrived in Palestine under the leadership of Joshua (Neh. 8.17). The impression conveyed by the accounts in the books of Ezra and Nehemiah supports the thesis that Ezra deliberately modelled his remove from Babylon along the lines of the first exodus and in response to Second

Isaiah's proclamation. Klaus Koch observes: 'All these details of the Ezra record are understandable only if the historical Ezra intended to fulfil the promises or, better, to be the instrument of fulfilment of the promises of the exilic prophets about a marvellous return of the exiles, which will be the foundation of a second Israel and the opening of a new *Heilsgeschichte.*'[26]

The preaching of Second Isaiah echoed through the next century and awoke in Ezra the vision of a new exodus which he instigated and also successfully achieved. The failure of prophecy in historical terms became an aspirational factor in the life of the community and was transformed into reality by Ezra. The reforms of Ezra and Nehemiah reorganized the community in Jerusalem and provided the roots of the movement that led on to Judaism and the survival of the community with a distinctive identity and history. The future seldom turns out as expected and so it was with Second Isaiah's vision. Couched in language at once too transcendental and traditional it functioned in the struggling community as a vision to be created by their own efforts. The scribe Ezra saw that vision and translated it into practical terms and so achieved, to a certain extent, the realization of the vision. Thus were the predictions of Second Isaiah fulfilled, though not in the transcendental way the prophet had envisaged. Ezra 'showed that the prophetic outlook into the future of Israel is not only pious theory, not only utopia in the sense of that which will never come to pass, but that it is also an instruction for practice, a power to change the conditions of contemporary society, even under the evil circumstances of an overwhelmingly strong foreign empire, if such a change is necessary'.[27]

The Chronicler. At some period in the fourth century the Chronicler produced his version of the history of Judah. A comparison of it with the deuteronomistic history shows that his concern was with the southern kingdom and especially with David and the levitical organization of the temple. His vision of David was so lavish and distorted that perhaps it was the case that he was a supporter of the surviving members of the royal house and hoped to revive, with his work, the aspirations of the house of David to take over power in the community.[28] The purpose of his presentation of the temple with the emphasis on the levitical organization of it may well have been to demonstrate that the theocracy, the original purpose of the exodus, had been realized in Israel, particularly in his own day.[29] If the purpose of the exodus had been to take the people from Egypt and settle them in Palestine worshipping Yahweh in the great temple virtually founded by the great king David, then the fact that the present community worshipped Yahweh in the rebuilt temple in Jerusalem indicated that the goal of the exodus had been achieved. So the Chronicler produced his version of the history of mankind up to the edict of Cyrus, but concentrated on David (I Chron. 12–29) to indicate that all expectations had been realized and that, apart from a possible hope that the royal family might once again rule, the present condition of the community was what it should be. Thus the Chronicler aligned himself with those who denied that Judah's expectations lay in the future and insisted that prophecy had been realized in the community centred on the temple. So again we cannot talk about the failure of prophecy but have to indicate a further source that was of the opinion that the future expectations had been realized and that the current cultic community (theocracy) was the embodiment of those expectations (though there might just have been the hope that the Davidic line had still a more dominant role to play in the community).

Summary

We have now considered a number of texts and their interpretation as well as a number of interpretative moves within the traditions which indicate ways in which dissonance was experienced, reduced or resolved, or did not arise in the first instance. The various techniques of resolution or avoidance were not all of a piece but came from different groups that worked on the traditions, maintaining where they could or reinterpreting where necessary. The meshing of all these approaches together made for a very complex network of prophetic traditions held in tension by sophisticated hermeneutic moves. Such a series of traditions does not permit a facile analysis for dissonance awareness or concomitant resolution. Demonstrating the failure of prophetic expectations depends upon a linguistic turn that insists upon a correspondence between word and event of a strict kind. Taken as creative impulses prophecy may be seen as having had a significant role to play in the formation and maintenance of the post-exilic community. Such a modification of its terms does not rule out an acknowledgment that some parties took the predictions more literally and maintained the hope that the visions would be realized at some stage in the future. Out of such groups came the apocalyptists with their expectations of destruction and messianic destiny. For many centuries such groups tended to represent minority interests and to be of peripheral influence in the community but they kept alive certain perceptions of prophecy that were to become seminal influences in later Judaism. In the growth of the traditions we should see many discrete and distinctive movements which built up and expanded earlier insights and maintained the transformational capacities of the prophetic vision alive in the community during the Persian, Greek and Roman periods. Once Torah and the histories had been written only prophecy provided the possibility of further interpretative transformations of material of a creative nature which could afford a commentary on current events in the light of certain theological values. Those traditions which designated the community as the sphere of realized expectations were also very influential in the development of various Jewish communities, e.g. Qumran and certain of the early Christian communities.[30] So in the dialectical struggle produced by expectation and dissonance among the prophetic groups the prophetic traditions became the repository of their insights, corrections, reinterpretations, adaptations and the whole range of hermeneutic activities that were necessary to ward off the triumph of dissonance over hope.

➳ **6** ➳

The Limits of Prophecy

In this chapter on the interpretation of prophecy certain limiting factors will be considered as they bear on the understanding of the nature of prophecy. These limiting factors indicate further complications for the analysis of the prophetic traditions using dissonance theory and contribute to building up a picture of the complexities of prophecy as a hermeneutic phenomenon in Israelite society. The more complex a structure is the less it yields to a simple interpretative approach and this is nowhere more evident than in the interpretation of biblical prophecy from the standpoint of cognitive dissonance theory. However it is necessary to discuss these factors because they involve important features of the traditions, without which it is not possible to give a comprehensive account of the relevant aspects of prophecy for this analysis.

Prophetic conflict

Recent studies of prophecy have been much concerned with the issues involved in conflict between the prophets and with criteria for determining 'false consciousness' among prophets.[1] The problem of truth and falsehood among the prophets became an important issue in the period before the collapse of Jerusalem. Conflict between prophets had been a part of Israelite society for centuries (e.g. Elijah on mount Carmel) but it became a matter of some concern towards the end of the existence of Judah as a state. The conflict was intensified by the fact that there were so many prophets prophesying different things in Jerusalem at the time that confusion and hostility were inevitable. Quarrels and controversies between the prophets were symptomatic of the disintegration of Judaean society and did little to persuade the community to heed what prophecy had to say. Prophecy had always been dependent upon people listening to and accepting its proclamation so the state of conflict militated against such acceptance during a critical period of Judaean history.[2] It was therefore a serious problem for the theologians who regarded certain prophets highly and attempts were made to regulate prophecy by way of criteria of authenticity. These attempts and the data provided by the Jeremiah and Ezekiel traditions constitute the scenario for prophetic conflict.

Deuteronomy. The central problem was one of distinguishing the authentic prophet from the one with a false vision. The legislators saw the problem and in Deuteronomy provided two simple criteria for regulating the behaviour of the prophets. The first regulative principle concerned the prophet who attempted to lead the community away from Yahweh by preaching in the name of another god; such a prophet was *ipso facto* false and should be executed as a rebel against Yahweh (13.1–5). This ruling dispensed with all prophets of other cultures but hardly touched the problem of the Yahwistic prophets who all prophesied in the name of Yahweh, only the content of their oracles differed significantly.

The second regulative principle dealt with the issue of determining which prophet spoke the word of Yahweh: 'And if you say in your heart, "How may we know the word which Yahweh has not spoken?" – when a prophet speaks in the name of Yahweh, if the word does not come to pass or come true, that is a word which Yahweh has not spoken; the prophet has spoken it presumptuously, you need not be afraid of him' (18.21, 22). There we have it – a straightforward falsification principle allowing the community to distinguish between the prophet with the word of Yahweh and the prophet lacking that word. So the two criteria for identifying the authentic prophet were: he must speak in Yahweh's name and the word so spoken must come to pass. The two were cumulative in that if he spoke in some other god's name and the word came to pass it did not count (cf. 13.1, 2), whereas if he spoke in Yahweh's name but the word did not come to pass he had acted presumptuously. Both kinds of prophetic action were punishable by death (13.5; 18.20).

Reflection on the criteriology of Deuteronomy will quickly reveal serious defects in it. In the first place it was too oversimplified an approach to the complex matter of prophecy. No doubt it accurately reflected the deuteronomistic outlook because their historians produced a very lengthy account of the monarchies using such principles of prophecy as part of the construction of that history. In the second place it put a good deal of emphasis on hindsight in that only by waiting until the prophetic word had come to pass would the community have been able to ascertain the prophet's authenticity. Such a hindsight assessment factor ignored or outlawed long term predictions (cf. Ezek. 12.27), yet other deuteronomists were prepared to include in their history long term predictions (cf. I Sam. 2.31–36; I Kings 13.2; II Kings 13.15–19) and their edition of Jeremiah contained a seventy year prediction (Jer. 25.11, 12; 29.10)! Furthermore it operated with a simplistic model of prophecy as a predicting of events that could be checked off a list as they occurred. However prophecy as it appears in the prophetic traditions was essentially a preaching for a decision type of activity. To have asked for a suspension of judgment until the catastrophe had happened would have vitiated the whole prophetic endeavour. So would a 'wait and see' reaction to their preaching have outraged prophets such as Amos, Isaiah or Jeremiah. Thus the criteria of Deuteronomy were both theoretical and unrealistic and probably far removed from the reality of the working prophets. This inadequate and unrealistic criteriology was probably due to a combination of the writers' lack of experience of prophecy in action, lack of serious reflection on the subject, part of their ideological approach to the subject and the great difficulty of clearly establishing adequate criteria for determining prophetic authenticity.

The demand for short term predictions which could be assessed for truth within the memory of the audience must have been highly idealized in view of the more complex features of the prophetic traditions. It also would have falsified many of the prophets whose traditions contain fulfilled and unfulfilled expectations. Any criterion that would falsify so much was not a helpful one. If the problem could have been resolved as simply as Deuteronomy thought we would not have had such lengthy reinterpretative editings of the prophetic traditions. Nor did it take into account the fact that a genuine prophet might on occasion be false and a so-called in-

authentic prophet might speak the truth (cf. I Kings 13). The distinguishing features between prophets who declared 'Yahweh will
save his people' and prophets who proclaimed 'Yahweh will destroy
his people' were complex matters of judgment that few communities can have had the time or the ability to work out.

The interpretation of predictive prophecy is not simply a matter
of asking 'what actually happened?' (*wie es eigentlich gewesen*) in
relation to what the prophets said – they were not weather forecasters charting the immediate future but men attempting to shape
the destiny of the community. They were not only concerned with
the likelihood of certain events but with *why* they were happening
and the ways in which the community should respond to such
possibilities. The criteria of Deuteronomy provided for a
falsification paradigm of prophecy whereas prophecy was a much
more complex affair altogether. Part of their proclamation was that
certain events would happen *because* of conditions in the community; they were not providing information about the future so much
as a critique of the community's current activities. What they were
doing is analogous to predictions of the kind that assert 'the village
of *x* will be destroyed because its people are bad neighbours, do not
pay their taxes and are unkind to immigrants'. How could that sort
of prediction be verified? The village might be destroyed but for
other reasons (e.g. new motorway plans). Would such destruction
count as the fulfilment of the prediction? Such predictions are
neither verifiable or falsifiable because of the explanatory factor
incorporated into the prediction. A modern example which approximates quite well to the biblical form of prophecy, and which illustrates the logical fallacy involved, would be the following reading of
modern history.

The European Jews were destroyed by the Nazis because of
their corrupt way of life and their departure from the law of God.
Furthermore God used the Nazis to punish the Jews and also was
punishing the European nations for permitting communism to exist
in Russia. There can be no denying that the Jews and Europe
suffered terribly during the second European war but this explanation for such suffering is not verified by the fact of a destructive war.
Few biblical scholars would tolerate such an equation between
event and explanation yet many might be tempted to do so in terms
of biblical prophecy and accept the fall of Samaria and Jerusalem as

confirmation of the prophetic diagnostic predictions. Why is this so often the case? Is it because people can readily believe that the ancient Israelites were particularly immoral and therefore deserved to be destroyed by the Assyrians and Babylonians? Whereas they cannot believe that the European Jews were particularly wicked (certainly no worse than non-European Jews or Gentiles) nor that such a grossly wicked machine as the Nazi regime should be regarded as a suitable executive for the divine will. Yet were Assyria and Babylon so much more virtuous than Israel or Judah that they could be freely used to punish the smaller nations? Such ways of discussing the matter belong more to biblical ideology than modern thought but they do illustrate some of the problems inherent in the interpretation of the prophetic traditions. Prophecy was not simply about predicting events in the future but entailed a religious ideology about the nature of society. Behind the deuteronomistic handling of prophecy was an acceptance of such an ideology and an attempt to legitimate it by depicting Israelite history as the unfolding of the prophetic word. A shared ideology made the deuteronomists support (from hindsight?) the prophets, hence the edition of Jeremiah presented him as a peripatetic preacher of the covenant (cf. Jer. 11.1–11).

Given elements of a shared ideology that included the equation between event and explanation of the prophetic critique it is hardly surprising that Deuteronomy produced an inadequate criteriology for establishing prophetic authenticity. Their criteria justified the prophets who had preached in Yahweh's name and whose negative oracles had been confirmed as Yahweh's word by the destruction of Israel and Judah. The inadequacy of such criteria was probably due to their being concerned to provide such justification but not to give a comprehensive account of prophecy. It was clear to them that the prophets who had preached of war and destruction (cf. Jer. 28.8) were authentic prophets and by their criteria all the others were necessarily false. Deuteronomy legislated in the service of a particular view of prophecy and in order to justify those prophets as legitimate. Beyond that it was not interested in providing a sophisticated discussion of prophetic complexities.

Jeremiah. The book of Jeremiah contains a substantial amount of material on the subject of prophetic conflict. The main oracles of

Jeremiah directed against the community contained various criticisms of the prophets (cf. 2.8, 26, 30; 4.9; 5.13, 31; 6.13, 14; 8.10) but the gravamen of his charges against them was gathered together into one place (23.9–40). For a prophet such as Jeremiah, who spent so much of his time announcing that the community was doomed because of its immorality and idolatry, the existence of other prophets preaching the salvation of the community must have posed serious problems. Not only problems of explanation and assessment of his own rightness but problems of communicating his views to the community. If different prophets announced contradictory viewpoints in public what notice will the community have taken of them? The citizens of Jerusalem did not have the hindsight of the later historians so they could not employ the criterion of Deut. 18.22, but the sight of so many prophets squabbling in public (cf. Jer. 28) must have given rise to a certain amount of scepticism about prophecy. Allied to the difficulties of determining the authenticity of a prophet such scepticism must have contributed to the hostile reception some of the prophets received from the community.

The charges made by Jeremiah against the other prophets in 23.9–32 provide further criteria for distinguishing between prophets. The first charge was one of immorality, particularly sexual immorality (23.9–15). The charges of immorality and idolatry were very general ones and have been made by prophets against communities for centuries. Part of the argument included the point that such immorality encouraged others in doing evil (verse 14) and again we find the prophetic charge that Jerusalem was like Sodom and Gomorrah (14 cf. Isa. 1.10). We do not know to what extent these were real or formal criticisms for Jeremiah had a tendency to make blanket charges against every member of the community (cf. 5.1–5; 6.13; 9.4–6 (Heb. 9.3–5)). However no doubt there was some truth in the accusations but the force of the charge depends very much on the connections made between what people say and what they do.

The second charge was that of raising false hopes in the people because their visions were purely self-induced rather than divinely inspired (23.16, 17). Again the charge included the element of encouraging evildoers by such visions of hope: 'They say continually to those who despise the word of Yahweh, "It shall be well with

you (*šālōm yihyeh lākem*)".' Presumably Jeremiah's grounds for
such charges must have been his conviction that he was right and
that therefore anybody who prophesied peace in this time to this
people had to be wrong.

The third charge developed this point, but also introduced the
notion of Yahweh's council (23.18, 22). In contrast to the well-
being (*šālōm*) preached by the other prophets Jeremiah was aware
that the storm of Yahweh (*sa ʿªrat yhwh*) had gone forth against the
wicked. Furthermore, although the prophets had spoken they had
not been sent by Yahweh. Proof of this for Jeremiah was their
failure to turn the people from their evil ways. Had these prophets
had access to Yahweh's council they would have known about
Yahweh's storm and would have tried to turn the community from
its wicked ways.

The fourth charge (23.23–32) included accusations of lying,
deceit and stealing each other's oracles. For Jeremiah the distinction between genuine and false prophecy was similar to the difference between wheat and straw (23.28). Further elements in the
charge were criticisms of the techniques of the prophets: they used
dreams and borrowed (stole) each other's oracles as well as using
the correct formula for their oracles. 'I am against the prophets, says
(*nᵉʾum*) Yahweh, who use their tongues and say, "Says Yahweh"
(*wayyin ʾªmō nᵉʾum*)' (23.31).

The various charges provide a criteriology of genuine prophecy
from Jeremiah's viewpoint. Prophets who were immoral or idolatrous, encouraged evildoers, led people astray, preached *šālōm*
instead of destruction, used dreams and borrowed oracles from
each other were all false. Their force as arguments depends, to a
great extent, on the assumption that Jeremiah was a true prophet
and that his descriptions of the other prophets were accurate in so
far as it was possible to make such judgments. However there are a
number of problems involved in the criteria presented by
Jer. 23.9–32 which need to be examined in order to demonstrate
further the difficulties of determining authenticity in prophets.

The general charges of immorality and idolatry may have been
the standard form of abuse directed at opponents which was characteristic of all the prophets. The vilification of one's opponents
became a normative feature of biblical polemic (cf. the New Testament attitudes to the Pharisees). If it be misleading to use the

synoptic gospels as a basis for describing the Pharisees then it is also fallacious to use the prophetic traditions as evidence for the beliefs and practices of the other prophets. Such polemics included a good deal of prejudice and abusive rhetoric that exaggerated the differences between the prophets. That the other prophets were preaching lies and deceit would only have been true if they were *deliberately* lying and deceiving the people. Yet they may have been preaching what they honestly believed to have been the truth as they saw it and as they imagined Yahweh had inspired them. Jeremiah's obsession with falsehood in the community and his critique of the structures as all false included the other prophets as false also.[3] Their visions may have been false but not necessarily intentionally false. Jeremiah's argument that had the prophets stood in Yahweh's council they would have turned the people from evil (23.22) has a curious lack of cogency about it. Jeremiah had singularly failed to turn the people from evil yet presumably was an authentic prophet with access to the divine council. Taking the force of verse 18 as 'Who is it that has stood in Yahweh's council?', then the answer to the question would be 'the prophet who knows that Yahweh's immediate activity is one of sending storms not peace'.[4] As a corollary of that knowledge the prophet would turn the community from evil (v. 22). However, even Jeremiah, who presumably had that knowledge, failed to turn the people from evil (cf. the editors' assessment of his first twenty-three years of preaching 25.3–7) so by his own criterion of standing in the council even he was unsuccessful.[5] Perhaps the force of 23.22 should be reduced to the more modest proposal that access to the council made a prophet *try* to turn people from evil-doing by *preaching against evil*. It is a reduction of Jeremiah's rhetoric to a more rational level but necessary in order to balance Jeremiah's tendency to exaggerate.

The attack on the formal techniques of the other prophets, e.g. their use of dreams (23.25–28) and other prophets' oracles (23.30), also raises interesting problems about prophetic conflict. The biblical traditions indicate that dreams were a legitimate medium of revelation in ancient Israel (cf. the stories of Joseph and Daniel; Gen. 28.12–17; I Kings 3.5–15; Joel 2.28 (Heb. 3.1)). Even the deuteronomists recognized that Yahweh might use dreamers of dreams (13.1, 3), though perhaps they had in mind that such uses were strictly for negative purposes (cf. Jer. 29.8, 9). Can it be that

Jeremiah either did not dream very much or had no inspirational dreams? He used the word whereas his opponents used the word and dreams so he dismissed their dreams as an illegitimate source of inspiration. He then attacked their words as having been stolen from each other. He admitted that what they had was Yahweh's word ('*my* word' 23.30) but dismissed their possession of the divine word on the grounds that they had not acquired it properly. Having conceded that they had Yahweh's word he had to rationalize his opposition to them by accusing them of theft. This curious charge could be made against many of the prophets represented in the biblical traditions because so much of the material there consists of reworked oracles and elements common to different prophets. Thus Isa. 2.2–4 and Micah 4.1–3 are essentially the same oracle, Amos 1.2, Jer. 25.30 and Joel. 3.16 (Heb. 4.16) all use the same element, and shared elements can be found between Isa. 10.27b–32 and Micah 1.10–15, Isa. 5.8–10 and Micah 2.1–3, Jer. 49.7–22 and Obad. 1–9. Many more shared elements among the prophets could be instanced but these examples suffice to make the point. Furthermore the influence of earlier prophets on Jeremiah should be contrasted with this attack on the other prophets so as to indicate the pejorative nature of his description of their activity as stealing. The polemic against the prophets had here a certain hysterical note of desperation induced by the frustration experienced by Jeremiah as he tried to make a coherent and cogent case against the prophets. The unsatisfactory nature of his criteria against them was part of the difficulty of producing a criteriology for distinguishing one prophet from another as the authentic spokesman of Yahweh.

The charge of immorality made against the prophets by Jeremiah (23.11–15; 29.21–23) has been extended to the canonical prophets by Crenshaw.[6] He sees Hosea's marriage to Gomer, the cult prostitute, as immoral; also Isaiah's sexual relations with the prophetess (Isa. 8.1–3), and his wandering about half-naked (Isa. 20.2). Jeremiah was guilty of telling a lie to protect King Zedekiah (Jer. 38.24–27), Micaiah deceived King Ahab (I Kings 22.16), Elisha intrigued with Hazael and used deception against Ben-hadad (II Kings 8.7–15), and his cursing the children resulted in the death of forty-two of them (II Kings 2.23, 24). The activities of Elijah and Elisha caused various bloodbaths in Israel (I Kings 18.40; II Kings 1.9–12; 9; 10) and some of these massacres were remembered later as a cause for divine judgment (cf. Hos. 1.4). In defence of the prophets it should be said that many of these actions are immoral by our ethical standards but not by Israelite ethics, e.g. Isaiah's intercourse with another prophet did not constitute an unethical action (assuming she was not married) but it would offend certain modern bourgeois notions about sexual morality. However the examples cited do sufficiently muddy the waters to the extent that they raise questions about the behaviour of the canonical prophets and therefore indicate that, as a criterion of genuine prophecy, Jeremiah's charge of immorality against the prophets was inadequate. Further difficulties are involved in the argument that morality so validates a message that immorality would invalidate it. This is the old problem of 'would a good man make a better pair of shoes than a good cobbler?'. To pursue this line of reasoning would take the argument beyond the needs of this section but the complicated arguments involved in determining the relation between morality of speaker and speaker's utterance (in terms of its truth value) indicate that the matter is a good deal more complex than Jeremiah's easy equation of life style and falsity of message.

The one charge that probably best reflects the difference between the two sets of prophets was the one that the prophets did not speak out against evil (23.17, 22). Assuming this to have been true about the prophets (for a similar criticism that is unsatisfactory see I Sam. 2.22–25; 3.13) then it may have reflected the prevailing political commitment of the majority of the prophets who did not speak out against the evil of their time. They may have been party to a conspiracy of silence against corruption in society and politics. However this principle must not be used as a blanket condemnation of prophets for the same charge could be made against Second Isaiah whose oracles proclaimed salvation and liberation rather than criticism of the community. In a time of oppression by the powerful in the community it was the prophet's duty to preach against it, but when the community was oppressed by foreign powers it may have been his task to proclaim liberation. Yet these were not two separate stages of historical existence for the Jerusalem community; often foreign domination externally was matched by internal oppression of the weak (they are analogous). So the duty of a prophet in relation to what was happening in the community was a complex task of discerning the true nature of reality and preaching accordingly. That different prophets made distinct, and often incompatible, judgments on that issue was the very basis for prophetic conflict. Conflict was inevitable as may be seen in the encounter between Jeremiah and Hananiah.

The editors of the book of Jeremiah collected together further elements in the conflict between Jeremiah and the other prophets as part of their presentation of the authentic prophet in contrast to the inauthentic ones (27–29). After the deportation of 597 the predictions of the prophets who had maintained salvation rather than destruction as the future activity of Yahweh were falsified. Their reaction to this setback (assuming Hananiah had been one of that party) provides a good example of dissonance reduction by changing original cognition: now it was announced that the exile would be very brief ('within two years' 28.3). First they had announced 'no deportation', then when deportation took place they announced 'a very brief period of deportation'. This ability to vary the message with changing circumstances gave prophecy great strength against dissonance arousal, but it may not have increased its credibility with the community.

Hananiah announced that within a couple of years the deportees would return along with the exiled king and the temple vessels (28.2–4). Theologically speaking Hananiah might have been right, hence Jeremiah's cautious reception of the oracle and the time taken to think about it before making a reply.[7] Initially Jeremiah did not react in his usual belligerent fashion but listened to what was said and gave it some thought. Now if Jeremiah had to respond so carefully to the announcement and only received guidance later on (28.12), how much more difficult must it have been for the ordinary citizen to have determined the truth of what prophets had to say. Eventually Jeremiah accused Hananiah of deceiving the people with a lie (28.15) but initially Hananiah had given him cause to think before acting and to make sure of his ground before replying.

The deuteronomistic account of Jeremiah's initial response to Hananiah's prediction provided a paradigm of verification of such predictive statements: 'The prophets who preceded you and me from ancient times prophesied *war, famine, and pestilence against* many countries and great kingdoms. As for the prophet who prophesies peace, when the word of that prophet comes to pass, then it will be known that Yahweh has truly sent the prophet' (28.8,

9). An impractical solution but in keeping with the principle stated in Deut. 18.21, 22. The editing of Jeremiah has produced the curious feature that Hananiah's prediction for two years ahead is followed by a section that includes Jeremiah's prediction for seventy years ahead! Hananiah's prediction could at least have been verified within the experience of the community whereas Jeremiah's could not, but the editors worked from hindsight and the principle that Jeremiah was a genuine prophet. The tradition that the prophets had preached 'war, famine, and pestilence' also was in keeping with the presentation of prophecy in the deuteronomic history.

Hananiah's viewpoint might have reflected the salvation outlook typical of a cult prophet and the clash between the two prophets might have been between two different perceptions of Yahweh's activity in history in relation to the current situation.[8] Hananiah drew from Israelite theology the notion of the saviour Yahweh who would save his people, especially after having just punished them. Jeremiah, on the other hand, did not regard the recent deportation as the full extent of the destruction so maintained that further disasters were to come (the editors had the benefit of hindsight in the preparation of the account). In the temple sermon (7.1–15) the paradigm of divine action had been made the destruction of Shiloh whereas for salvation oracles the criterion was confirmation by actual occurrence. In theological terms there was little to distinguish between Jeremiah and Hananiah for using the traditions of Yahwism either might have been right about the future. Hindsight shows that Hananiah was wrong because his hope was premature but who could have decided that point when he made his prediction? Determining the nature of the prevailing circumstances was so difficult that very few prophets got it right and even fewer for the right reasons. Buber makes the point on this issue of salvation or judgment oracles: 'It is not whether salvation or disaster is prophesied, but whether the prophecy, whatever it is, agrees with the divine demand meant by a certain historical situation, that is important. In days of false security a shaking and stirring word of disaster is befitting, the outstretched finger pointing to the historically approaching catastrophe, the hand beating upon hardened hearts; whereas in times of great adversity, out of which liberation is liable now or again to occur, in times of regret and repentance, a strengthening and unifying word of salvation is appropriate.

Jeremiah opposes the dogmatics of a guardian deity, Deutero-Isaiah the dogmatics of a punishing deity; both of them venerate the living God Who is exalted above all dogmatic wont, and His historically expressed will, which they interpret.'[9] It does not, however, contribute to a criteriology of determining in a given situation which prophet has correctly understood what was happening and been able to convey that discernment to the community in an effective way.

Polarization between elements of destruction and salvation within Yahwism would appear to have taken place among the prophets of Jeremiah's time so that they fragmented into camps opposed to one another. Such hostility between the prophets cannot have improved the community's attitude towards them. Jeremiah's criteria for maintaining that the other prophets were inauthentic lacked a cutting edge that would have made such a distinction clear to the community. Ultimately a prophet depended upon his own sense of calling and rightness to convince himself, if not others, of his genuineness.[10] If the community rejected that conviction then a prophet would have had great difficulty in getting his message across to them. The certitude with which Jeremiah berated his prophetic opponents as false and deceitful contrasts with the doubt and uncertainty that his confessions show he suffered from (cf. 15.18; 20.7-9). A prophet who inwardly admitted that the deity had deceived him and then publicly accused the other prophets of being deceitful had problems which may have been compensated for by the public denunciations. The polemical oracles did not claim that the other prophets had been deceived by Yahweh but an oracle in a different collection makes that point: 'Ah, lord Yahweh, surely thou hast *utterly deceived* this people and Jerusalem, saying, "It shall be well with you" (*šālōm yihyeh lākem*); whereas the sword has reached their very life' (4.10). This was obviously a reference to the prophets who preached *šālōm* (cf. 6.14; 8.11) but as an explanation it was not incorporated into his attack on the prophets. The point will be considered later as a further limiting factor for the interpretation of prophecy.

Ezekiel. If Jeremiah only hinted at the possibility of divine deception as an explanation of what happened to the community Ezekiel developed the motif further. The problem of false consciousness in prophecy was one that concerned Ezekiel as well as Jeremiah and a number of oracles were devoted to it (13; 14.1–11). The spirit of his arguments was very similar to Jeremiah's in that he accused the prophets of deception and using lying visions. They used the correct terminology ('they say, "says Yahweh"' *hā'ōmrim n^eum-yhwh* 13.6, 7) but Yahweh had not sent them. Ezekiel's attack on the prophets was more graphic in its use of metaphors than Jeremiah's, e.g. he described the prophets as 'foxes in ruins' (13.4). The prophets had misled the people and whitewashed the situation (13.10–12), the prophetesses were involved in magical practices (13.17–19) and the result of such false prophecy was the disheartening of the righteous in the land (13.22). The material in 14.1–11 concerns rather different issues dealt with by Ezekiel in relation to idolaters. Where an idolater had inquired of a prophet for a word from Yahweh and the prophet, being deceived, had spoken a word then that prophet had been deceived by Yahweh (14.9) and would be destroyed. The notion of a divine deception in a context of idolatry agrees with Deut. 13.3 where the false prophet or dreamer was seen as a test from Yahweh.

The elements involved in prophetic conflict provide a number of insights for the study of prophecy in terms of dissonance theory. Once again the complexities of biblical prophecy are underlined and the difficulty of reading dissonance response off the surface of the traditions demonstrated. The principle of hindsight as the method for verifying a prophet accounts, to a certain extent, for the particular prophetic traditions preserved in that those prophets who had predicted catastrophe were reckoned to have been genuine because of the exile. Where hindsight operates dissonance can be strictly controlled. The confirmation of the doom oracle prophets helped to carry the salvation oracles of the cult prophets who were among the preservers of the traditions. Doom (confirmed) and hope (expected) held together the dialectic in terms of past and future. Thus prophecy was considered to have verified itself in the past and yet to have been open towards the future. Hindsight and expectation governed the subsequent interpretation of prophecy along lines rarely vulnerable to dissonance arousal, yet of direct relevance to the community in so far as it was prepared to pay any attention to prophecy.

The analysis of the criteria for distinguishing the authentic prophet from the rest has shown that they were too ambiguous to be helpful and that 'one must admit that there is no such thing as an external test by which to tell true prophecy from false, such as all reasonable persons may safely apply'.[11] This being the case it is small wonder that the community gave little heed to the prophets except to register the complaint about their falseness (cf. Lam. 2.14). Any social phenomenon as ambiguous and opaque as prophecy, as torn by conflict, polemic and abuse, must have been a defective vehicle for mediating effectively the divine will in ancient Israel. After the exile the power blocks in the new community were the priesthood and the wise men whose epistemologies were based on much less subjective factors than that of prophecy. At some stage in that reconstruction of the community the prophet came to be regarded as a disreputable figure as may be seen in the attacks on them in Jer. 23.33–40; Zech. 13.2–6 and the satire on the prophet in the book of Jonah.[12] Community rejection of the prophets will have pushed experience of dissonance at the failure of their visions to the periphery of society, though it will have been accentuated to a certain degree by such unreliability.

The decline of prophecy brought on by many reasons, not least the inability of the prophets to convince the community that they were reliable, contributed to substantial changes in the movement that were to redirect its course in the direction of apocalyptic.[13] These changes helped to transform prophecy so that it survived and maintained both visions and traditions in the subsequent centuries, but never again as the producer of individuals who challenged community and cult. Two further limiting factors to be considered here arise out of the late developments in prophecy, the problem of divine deception which was used to explain the exilic destruction and the movement towards apocalyptic which preserved the prophetic expectation open to the future.

Divine deception and the demonic

Deuteronomy, Jeremiah, Ezekiel and the deuteronomists all recognized that Yahweh could and did deceive communities and individuals. The widespread agreement on this motif in the traditions indicates that it came to be taken very seriously as a part explanation for the exile. Without a complex account of causality, a sophisticated psychology of human perception and behaviour or a general theory of political economy the biblical writers were forced to use a primitive transcendentalism to explain problems of prophetic conflict and the destruction of the community.[14] The Hebrew doctrine of causality attributed to Yahweh the one effective will in creation so that he was behind everything that happened or was done. He it was who killed and made alive (cf. I Sam. 2.6), created wellbeing (*šālōm*) and catastrophe (*rā'* Isa. 45.7; cf. Amos 3.6), and caused manslaughter (cf. Ex. 21.13). If Israel regularly experienced evil destruction and lived on the edge of disintegration then Yahweh was the source of such terrors. There were, of course, also tendencies to refer to secondary causes such as men's rebelliousness and crimes as the cause of disasters but such references appear in the traditions alongside the standard account of causality. The two may be seen in the reactions of Jeremiah and Ezekiel to the same phenomenon, the passing of the children through the fires of Moloch. Jeremiah (or the deuteronomists) saw such practices as the contradiction of what Yahweh wanted, in spite of a popular belief that he had commanded them (Jer. 7.31). On the other hand Ezekiel viewed such practices as commandments of Yahweh, evil indeed but designed as a primitive form of aversion therapy to shock the people (20.25, 26).

The notion of the deity deceiving people through the medium of prophecy is given classical form in the account of Micaiah ben Imlah's prophetic conflict with the royal court prophets: 'Therefore hear the word of Yahweh: I saw Yahweh sitting on his throne, and all the host of heaven standing beside him on his right hand and on his left; and Yahweh said, "Who will entice (*y'patte*) Ahab, that he may go up and fall at Ramoth-gilead?" . . . Then a spirit came forward and stood before Yahweh, saying, "I will entice him." And Yahweh said to him, "By what means?" And he said, "I will go forth, and will be a lying spirit (*rūaḥ šeqer*) in the mouth of all his prophets." And he said, "You are to entice him, and you will succeed; go forth and do so." Now therefore behold, Yahweh has put a lying spirit in the mouth of all these your prophets; Yahweh has spoken evil concerning you' (I Kings 22.19–23). A similar principle is embodied in the claims of Jeremiah and Ezekiel that Yahweh had deceived community and prophet (Jer. 4.10; 15.18; 20.7; Ezek. 14.9). Now if Yahweh used the false prophets or the idolaters to deceive community and individuals, or if he tested the community by false dreamers or prophets (Deut. 13.3), in what sense were Jeremiah and Ezekiel right to claim that Yahweh had not sent the prophets who proclaimed such false visions (Jer. 23.21; Ezek. 13.6)? For the two claims are incompatible in that prophets cannot have been sent by Yahweh with a deceitful message and at the same time have produced messages out of their own minds. The inclusion of the two motifs in the traditions illustrates the difficulties the prophets had accounting for the disaster of the exile and the behaviour of various prophets.

The main thrust of the relevant prophetic traditions made the disaster of the exile the result of the community's corruption and its failure to turn. Such corruption did not require assistance from prophets sent by Yahweh to deceive the community so why is the motif so prominent in the traditions? Perhaps there was an attempt to answer a question raised by some in the community: 'how could a people have been so blind to all the warnings they received from the prophets if it had not been Yahweh's will all the time to destroy it?' Isaiah had come to a similar conclusion when he reviewed his failure to turn the people from evil (Isa. 6.9, 10). However the motif of Yahweh deceiving the people through lying prophets is to be understood its place in the traditions has to be recognized and integrated into any account of prophecy. Such an integration does not make prophecy any more amenable to dissonance theory analysis but emphasizes just how complex it had become by the time of the fall of Jerusalem. It provided one more account of why the disaster had befallen the community and was the Israelite equivalent to other cultures' polytheistic notions of gods that deceived so as to destroy the community against the wishes of other gods, e.g. Homer's account of the Trojan war.[15]

Throughout the biblical narratives there are incidents of an irrational nature recounted about the deity's fierce desire to kill. Thus Yahweh tempted Abraham to murder Isaac (Gen. 22), the demonic attack on Jacob at the brook Jabbok was identified with the deity (Gen. 32.24–30), Yahweh attempted to kill Moses on the road to Egypt (Ex. 4.24–26), he hardened the mind of the Pharaoh in order to increase the destructive slaughter of the Egyptians (Ex. 5–12), he destroyed Saul's mind (I Sam. 16.14; 19.9, 10), tempted David to number the people in order to destroy thousands of them (II

Sam. 24), and permitted the terrible torturing of the mind and body of Job (Job. 1, 2). All these examples present the deity as a force for evil and destruction in the community, a negation of life and health; in short, a demonic power. Whatever we may call it – the dark side of God, the negative mysteriousness at the centre of all life, time and chance, or death and necessity – its place in the biblical traditions is eloquent testimony to a dimension of reality that Israel could only describe as terrifying because it was so irrational and random. On the occasions when Israel experienced these demonic attacks good and bad were seized and the innocent slaughtered. The only way to survive these attacks was to incorporate them into the community's theological holdings, hence the demonic was identified with Yahweh.[16] To a certain extent the biblical writers were trying to be realistic and true to their experience of the world: all life is constantly threatened by the irrational, the accidental, the unforeseen and such forces attack at random and are in no way restricted along ethical lines. A small nation like Israel lived at the mercy of the larger nations and was regularly invaded by imperial forces, hence the realism of the accounts of the demonic in the traditions. Israel's monist outlook forced it to attribute such destructive forces in the world to Yahweh. It lacked a sophisticated demonology which could take the responsibility for the negative aspects of life so it had to attribute death and evil to Yahweh. The advantages of monist systems include coherence of accounts of the world and economy of hypotheses, but their disadvantages can be seen in relation to the reality of evil and the facility with which dualist systems can cope with evil. Living among cultures with complex systems of demons, ghosts and spirits the Israelites could only subsume such forces under modified systems of expiatory blood rites regulated by the cult of Yahweh.[17]

Yet we must keep the demonic in the biblical traditions within proper proportions for the dominant motifs were about the providence of Yahweh rather than his destructive aspect. The appeal to the demonic was only made on occasions of deep crisis and horror, e.g. the exile. The collapse of the life and history of the people was explained as prophetic deception caused by the deity – an aspect of the hidden god enigma (cf. Isa. 8.17; 45.15; 54.7, 8). This explanation for the exile was only one of many given by different traditions. Other attempts to explain the exile included the view that it was caused by the corruption and injustice prevalent in society (the prophets), the long history of idolatry and cultic heterodoxy practised by the kings and the community (the deuteronomic history), and also provided the land with the opportunity to keep sabbath (II Chron. 36.21). It is difficult to determine to what extent the prophets were blamed for the exile, either as preachers of it or deceivers of the community, but their stock in the community steadily declined after the exile. Proclaiming the judgment of Yahweh as an imminent event was characteristic of prophecy but the horrors of siege, famine, rape and torture (cf. Lam. 5.1–17) were too brutal to be tolerated other than in the abstract. The prophets were identified with their message and therefore must have been the object of resentment after the success of some of their preaching. The possibility that some of the prophets had misled the people by false visions (Lam. 2.14) and that others had prevented the community from turning (cf. Isa. 6.9, 10) cannot have improved the standing of the prophets in the period of reconstruction. Yet such strange explanations had to be employed to deal with the phenomenon of a shattered community.

The aspect of divine deception provides a further difficulty for producing a rational account of prophecy because it stresses the transcendental dimension that could be used to explain the curious behaviour of prophets and the resultant catastrophes for society. One of the more obscure prophetic legends in the first book of Kings illustrates some of the problems involved here. The legend tells how a Judaean man of God prophesied against the altar at Bethel, was involved in a *contretemps* with King Jeroboam and refused to receive hospitality because he was under Yahweh's command not to do so (I Kings 13.1–10). On his return journey home the man of God was met by an old prophet from Bethel who persuaded him to return to Bethel because a subsequent revelation had been received to that effect (a lie); at the meal in Bethel the old prophet received a further divine message denouncing the man of God for disobeying the original command and warning him of his imminent death, which occurred when he met a lion on the way home (verses 11–25).[18] The unfortunate prophet was lied to and believed that lie to have been the word of Yahweh. In that he was wrong he paid the penalty for his error but there was no way that he could have determined the truth of the old prophet's claim to have received the word of Yahweh from an angel (13.18). The editor was aware of what was happening (cf. 'but he lied to him' in verse 18) but the prophet did not have that kind of hindsight. That the message had changed could not have been grounds for knowing it to have been false because part of the groundrules was that Yahweh was free to change his mind. The irony of the story was that the genuine prophet was killed whereas the false (lying) prophet was capable of declaring the word of Yahweh. That vulnerability to personal disaster brought on by human or divine deception was a constant possibility for prophets. The story illustrates, as Barth notes 'the abyss on whose edge, as is clear from this passage, every man of God and every genuine prophet walks'.[19] It is important as a further limiting factor in the interpretation of prophecy because, among other things, 'this passage deals the death knell to every attempt to specify absolute criteria by which to differentiate the true from the false prophet, for the ultimate criterion to which contemporary scholarship appeals (the charismatic intuition of a true prophet) fails in this instance'.[20]

The fact that Yahweh was believed to operate occasionally by lies and deceit to the detriment of individuals and communities constitutes the demonic in relation to prophecy. As such the motif of divine deception belongs to the transcendental dimension of prophetic explanation which makes dissonance theory analysis so difficult. It renders explanations less precise because it poses an alternative explanation and stresses the ambiguous nature of prophecy and its lack of self-validating criteria. The failure of expectations could then be explained as intentional due to the deity deceiving the community. Such an explanation would not differ from a similar one which saw in the demonic a response to dissonance caused by failure of expectation but it cannot be clearly shown which is the correct approach to the issue. In this way divine deception as the demonic form of prophecy must be treated as a limiting factor in the analysis of the prophetic traditions for evidence of dissonance response.

Many problems may be associated with the divine deception motif but the one that had most consequence for the prophets was the problem it caused for any community that tried to take prophecy seriously. The appearance of a prophet preaching a specific message could have been taken as a genuine message from Yahweh or a message designed to deceive. How could the community determine which it was? If the community accepted the prophet's message and it turned out to have been false then it had been deceived into destruction. If it exercised caution and did not accept the message and it turned out to be genuine then the community was destroyed because it failed to heed a prophet sent by Yahweh. Such a double bind must have contributed considerably to the decline of prophecy as a significant force in the community. If very few people in the community paid much attention to prophecy it was because of this acute problem posed by the many prophets active in Judah during the period leading up to the exile. Where prophecy was followed it was believed to have been responsible for deceiving the people (cf. Jer. 4.10; Lam. 2.14). From the fact of the exile the (prophetically influenced) historians deduced the necessity and inevitability of it. Those prophets who had warned the community were not obeyed (cf. Jer. 7.25, 26; 25.3–7), those who were listened to by the people misled them (cf. Ezek. 13.1–16). Given the prophetic tendency to use divine causality as a principle of action in the world such a state of affairs must have been divinely intended or induced. Either way prophetic activity was vindicated as the outworking of the divine will. Under such circumstances dissonance could have been controlled quite well by complex theological motifs which explained, to the satisfaction of certain parties, that what had been intended had happened and the purpose of Yahweh had been achieved (cf. Lam. 2.17). Thus the limiting factor of divine deception could be extended to show that there never was, nor could have been, a problem of dissonance. However it is doubtful that such a coherent account was ever produced by the prophets or their editors and tradents, but the elements for such an account are there in the traditions.

The rise of apocalyptic

The catastrophe of the exile did much to discredit prophecy as a movement central to the development of Israelite society. Furthermore the failure of expectations of salvation and the poor response to Second Isaiah's visions created further problems for prophecy. The sweeping changes in political structures introduced by the Persian empire helped to diminish the role of the prophet in

Judaean society. All these changes brought about substantial changes in prophecy and slowly transformed it in the direction of apocalyptic. The relation of apocalyptic thought to prophecy is important for my thesis on the grounds that the transformation of prophecy into apocalyptic was assisted by the efforts of post-exilic prophecy to respond to the collapse of its hopes by means of reinterpretative changes in direction. The impetus to change came from their response to dissonance caused by the failure of the vision and combined with changed circumstances to maintain the prophetic traditions and to develop in certain directions. The internecine struggles and quarrels that typified the post-exilic reconstruction period saw the emergence of a group whose transformation of prophecy rescued its positive vision from complete failure. The whole period of the second temple was dominated by the twin motifs of community and conflict so this transformation was only a minor part of what was happening, but it was important for the survival of the prophetic vision. Dissonance response should not be seen as the creator of apocalyptic but as an element that gave rise to the reinterpretation of prophecy and therefore as an important contributory factor to the creation of apocalyptic. *With its roots in prophecy apocalyptic became the resolution of the dissonance caused by the lack of fulfilment of prophecy in the early post-exilic period*: such is the thesis of this section.

The account of the rise of apocalyptic followed here is that given by Paul Hanson.[21] His account of the matter makes eschatology the bridge between prophecy and apocalyptic. He defines prophetic eschatology as: 'a religious perspective which focuses on the prophetic announcement to the nation of the divine plans for Israel and the world which the prophet has witnessed unfolding in the divine council and which he translates into the terms of plain history, real politics, and human instrumentality; that is, the prophet interprets for the king and the people how the plans of the divine council will be effected within the context of their nation's history and the history of the world.' Apocalyptic eschatology is defined as: 'a religious perspective which focuses on the disclosure (usually esoteric in nature) to the elect of the cosmic vision of Yahweh's sovereignty – especially as it relates to his acting to deliver his faithful – which disclosure the visionaries have largely ceased to translate into the terms of plain history, real politics, and human instrumentality due to a pessimistic view of reality growing out of the bleak post-exilic conditions within which those associated with the visionaries found themselves. Those conditions seemed unsuitable to them as a context for the envisioned restoration of Yahweh's people.'[22]

The shift in prophecy which made it become apocalyptic in outlook was caused by the failure of the earlier expectations and the breakdown in confidence brought on by the prevailing conditions in post-exilic Palestine. The prophetic crisis of confidence occurred during a period when various groups were competing for power during the reconstruction of temple and city. According to Hanson the key to the matter is the collection of Second Isaiah's oracles (40–55). A comparison of these oracles with the earlier prophetic traditions reveals the increased use of mythological material in the later strand. Thus post-exilic prophecy was beginning to move away from the vision of a historically determined future towards a more mythologically constructed scheme of the future in which the warrior God fought for his people against their enemies and the forces of chaos. The followers of Second Isaiah continued this mythologization of the proclamation (cf. Isa. 63.1–6). They wished to participate in the coming salvation of the community but found themselves excluded from the sanctuary because they did not belong to the more powerful group whose ideology had been constructed round the priestly vision of a renewed temple (cf. Ezek. 40–48). Excluded from power they denounced those in power and the fierce opposition already seen in their oracles was directed against the group controlling the rebuilt temple. No longer were these prophets concerned to translate their vision into historical reality nor did they see their expectations as applying to the whole Judaean community. As the struggle got harder for them their mythology began to dominate their outlook and out of that ideological struggle apocalyptic was born.

To make this case Hanson uses a set of sociological analyses derived from the work of Max Weber, Karl Mannheim and Ernst Troeltsch.[23] Weber saw the prophet as a breaker with established order and the priests and nobility as preservers of the *status quo*. So for Hanson the visionary group functioned over against the ruling classes and challenged the structures of their power base. From Mannheim Hanson has taken the distinction between 'ideological' and 'utopian' mentalities: the proponents of ideology support absolute structures and their ideas system is designed to maintain power; the utopian outlook takes the opposite view and challenges the structures on behalf of the oppressed. Hanson also uses Troeltsch's distinction between 'church' and 'sect' as the two types of religious organization: the church as an institution is overwhelmingly conservative, dominating the masses and preserving the existing social order in working relationship with the powers that be. It is characterized by a hierarchy and tolerates all social and political orders as qualifying for membership. The sect, on the other hand, is fiercely intolerant of laxity and draws its members from lower class elements and maintains a rigorous opposition to the world in the name of salvation for its few members. Compromise is not permitted with the orders of society and the sect tends to regard the church as a corrupt, immoral institution. Thus Hanson treats the visionaries as challengers of the newly established order in post-exilic Jerusalem, as utopian opponents of the ruling class ideology, and as a sect opposed to the corruption of the community and its leaders. Their opponents were the prophets, priests and followers of Ezekiel who believed that in rebuilding the temple they were creating the new age. These he identifies as the Zadokites who maintained power in the new sanctuary and who 'stood in unbroken continuity with the ruling classes of the temple prior to the exile'.[24] This hierocratic party compromised itself with the ruling Persian powers so as to preserve itself as the ruling party in Jerusalem. Defeated in the struggle for power and recognition the visionary group abandoned its vision of the older prophetic hope and began to develop a more mythologically constructed view. Thus prophecy moved from treating of the mundane world to the transcendental and in doing so became the first stage of apocalyptic.

The fact that Haggai and Zechariah provided prophetic legitimation for the temple reconstruction shows that not all the post-exilic prophets were visionaries of the utopian type. The temple was the great factor of continuity (cf. Ezra's concern to establish the law of Moses and Zechariah's awareness of the *former* prophets) so its reconstruction became the first priority for the community. The project was a very practical one that everybody could contribute to so the reconstruction programme was a practical means of implementing the vision. The emergence of a particular priestly power such as the Aaronites eventually gave the community the shape and direction it needed.[25] The failure of the followers of Second Isaiah to achieve any position of influence in the community meant the frustration of their vision so they sought in other ways to reshape their vision to take into account the new reality and to oppose it by denunciation and threats. Hanson claims that the main objections of the visionaries to the ideology of the realists were: (1) their regard for the pagan emperor; (2) their exclusivization of the temple; (3) their lack of an eschatology.[26] Typical of the spirit of compromise with the powers that be is the statement 'they finished their building by the command of the God of Israel *and by the decree of Cyrus and Darius and Artaxerxes king of Persia*' (Ezra 6.14).

Hanson suggests that the development in this period should be seen as taking the following course: Second Isaiah may be described as proto-apocalyptic; Isa. 24–27; Zech. 9, 10 as early apocalyptic; Zech. 12 as middle apocalyptic; and Zech. 14 as full blown apocalyptic. In terms of dating that would yield the second half of the sixth century for proto-apocalyptic, early apocalyptic somewhere between end of sixth century and early fifth century, the first half of the fifth century for middle apocalyptic, and full blown apocalyptic between 475–425.[27] Hanson's datings radically differ from those offered by the manuals of critical orthodoxy. The roots of apocalyptic are now seen to be firmly in Israelite prophecy rather than in Zoroastrianism or Hellenistic thought and the so-called dualism of apocalyptic can be traced to the opposition between the two groups struggling for power in the early period of the second temple.[28] The first steps towards apocalyptic were taken by the followers of Second Isaiah as they contrasted the expectations aroused by his oracles with the reality of their deprived status in the community. Unable to bridge the gap between such expectations and reality they retreated further into a mythic interpretation of the divine action in the future. This myth of the divine warrior fighting on behalf of his beleagured followers rescued the vision at the expense of the more universalistic elements incorporated into it. Instead of salvation for the whole Israelite community there was now a polarization of the community into the servants of Yahweh and the usurpers of power in the sanctuary (cf. Isa. 63.18; 65.13–16; 66.5, 6). Divine intervention in human affairs became the great apocalyptic myth.[29]

The general thesis of Hanson is that Israelite apocalyptic was not foreign but, to use his own allegorical analogy, was born of Jewish parents on Jewish soil, the parents being prophecy (mother) and father unknown (possibly royal).[30] It was essentially a transformation (metamorphosis) of prophecy brought about by the failure of the earlier prophetic vision to be realized and the resolution of that failure by retreat into mythology. Its origins are to be traced to the struggle for power in the period of the temple reconstruction. Hanson's main analysis is a vigorous exposition of the texts of Isa. 56–66 and Zech. 9–14 using, what he calls, the contextual-typological method.[31] Prophecy survived the collapse of its world by an accelerated use of myth and a polarization of entities into antithetical forms, e.g. continuity: change, realized eschatology: futuristic eschatology, hierocratic: prophetic. Lacking power the visionaries cursed their opponents and looked forward to a cataclysmic transformation in the near future. After the missions of Ezra and Nehemiah apocalyptic eschatology stopped developing and the opposing factions in the community appear to have become more tolerant of each other (see the Chronicler's work).[32] The next upsurge of apocalyptic fervour was not until the next critical period of the community's history, the Maccabaean struggle against Hellenistic domination.

This introduction to Hanson's work has been necessarily long because his book was not published in Britain and therefore is not as accessible as it ought to be. His analysis has many good features, not least his use of sociological categories against which to read the prophecies. This gives his account of the origins of apocalyptic a depth and a dimension often lacking in older accounts. His demonstration of the growth of apocalyptic out of prophecy is a persuasive account of the matter and agrees with views put forward by earlier scholars.[33] The lengthy treatment of specific sets of texts gives his work a solid content, even though some of his specific interpretations are open to dispute. Many of the texts dealt with are extremely difficult and obscure sections of the prophetic traditions and therefore his engaging with them is to be commended. I find his general thesis and the texts utilized in the exposition of it convincing and, in view of other treatments of these texts and alternative accounts of the origins of apocalyptic, the best account of the matter to date.

There are, however, substantial criticisms that can be made of his work. I find his use of polarities obsessive and oversimplified.[34] The polarity he draws between myth and history cannot, I feel, be sustained (the opposite of myth is nature not history).[35] Definitions at this point might have been welcome. His thesis that the pre-exilic prophets did not use myth seems to me to be wrong in that the notion of Yahweh as the king enthroned in Zion's temple was as mythic in Isaiah as anything in Second Isaiah and his followers. All the prophets appear to have believed in a divine intervention in history or, at least, control of the forces of history. 'The Hebrew prophets in the periods of successive disaster found what might almost be called new patterns in history; but the word pattern itself is too hard to be applied to anything so elastic as history, and I see no harm and possibly some good if we call these things rather myths, using the word myth not to represent something untrue or something which did not happen, but to typify an essential process in history.'[36] To what extent the prophets were political realists is also a disputable point. If there had been a realism in politics in that period it lay with the wise men with whom Isaiah appears to have had many quarrels (cf. Isa. 5.19–24; 29.14–16; 30.1–5).

Part of one's critical response to Hanson depends upon one's attitude to the Albright-Cross school of biblical scholarship which dominates so much non-Jewish American biblical scholarship. The influence of the Albright-Cross school is very apparent (and acknowledged) in Hanson's prosodic analyses of texts and its linear development models for pottery and poetry have influenced his linear typology of apocalyptic genres. Where the defects of his presentation become important is at the centre of his thesis where he polarizes the post-exilic community into two groups, ideological and utopian. Although his sociological analysis is an advance on other treatments of the material it does involve him in the defects of his sources. The separation of utopian and ideological does not necessarily mean that the utopian lacked an ideology – there are a number of senses in which social scientists use ideology, of which one is certainly Hanson's sense of a system of ideas aimed at maintaining the power structures.[37] Utopians also have an ideology, a system of ideas, though not one devoted to maintaining the power structures of the community. The church: sect analogy only works for the post-exilic period if there had been a monolithic structure in existence comparable to a church. Such may have developed over the centuries but hardly as early as Hanson's dates for apocalyptic (550–425). The struggle was probably much more complex and ideological than Hanson allows and the eventual emergence of a power group that still required the Persian authorities for its legitimation was a long, slow process. Whether the party that eventually came to power had an eschatology or not depends upon the status granted to realized eschatology – is it an eschatology or not? We have already seen the active elements of prophetic influence in Ezra's mission and the possibility of a futuristic element in the Chronicler's work. Again it is a problem of the avoidance of an oversimplification of terms, material and analysis in relation to a shadowy area of history about which we know so very little.

These criticisms of Hanson should not be taken as a rebuttal of his thesis but should be seen as an attempt to clarify some elements of it. His identification of the group producing the apocalyptic visions as an oppressed disenfranchised section of the community makes good sense of the period, as well as of the climate and content of the oracles. It also makes good sense of the subsequent periods of apocalyptic activity – the Maccabaean period, the early Christian era typified by the Roman assaults on Jerusalem, the disintegration of the medieval world, the time of Luther and Müntzer, the puritan revolution in England, and in the twentieth century (1914–18, 1933–45 and the 1960s). It is the oppressed and disenfranchised who engage in such activities and who are sustained by the apocalyptic vision with its insistence on the transformation and transvaluation of everything: the making of a new world after the destruction of the corrupt old world. This vision of the creation of a new heavens and a new earth (Isa. 65.17) was to become very important in the development of apocalyptic thought and to give rise to various movements that have shaped the history of the past two millennia. A consideration of the biblical traditions and the movements to which they gave rise would show that thoughts and expectations about the future (eschatology) could be active or passive. Hanson's distinction between lack of eschatology (ideology) and eschatology (utopian) may have to be restructured to take into account such a distinction between active and passive hopes for the future. Prophecy gave rise to both types of hope and apocalyptic movements tended to contain a variety of responses to the vision of the future. Such responses included waiting for the destruction of the kingdoms by transcendental forces (e.g. Daniel) and working towards a vision of the future by transforming the present structures through human activity (e.g. Ezra and all those political movements of the Roman period that attempted to throw off the yoke of foreign domination).[38]

The significance of the rise of apocalyptic for this study is that it provides further evidence for the view that dissonance in prophecy was met by substantial responses of reinterpretation. By reinterpreting the concern of prophecy and realigning its solutions to the problems posed by the existence of the post-exilic community apocalyptic showed a way out of the disconfirmations of expectation. Apocalyptic provided a context for further transcendental resolutions of the problems but also made possible a series of practical responses whereby groups attempted to transform society in accordance with the expectations. The transformation of prophecy into apocalyptic (a long, slow process) helped to reduce the dissonance caused by the failure of the vision after the exile by a series of changes in cognitions and expectations. These changes accommodated the various social, political and ideological shifts of the post-exilic period and allowed prophetic groups to maintain their visions in spite of serious drawbacks and changed circumstances.

The three limiting factors of prophetic conflict, the demonic motif and the rise of apocalyptic indicate some of the interpretative problems involved in dealing with prophecy, especially in relation to dissonance theory analysis. They each provide ways of evading dissonance by explanatory schemes which can conceal the failure of prophecy. The difficulty of determining the authentic prophet, the possibility of prophecy deceiving and the subsequent need for prophecy to change in the direction of apocalyptic severely limited prophecy as a reliable element in society. Yet the capacity of prophecy to survive through change reveals its inner toughness and its ability to cope with substantial dissonance. One answer to the question 'how did prophecy survive the failure of Second Isaiah's vision of the immediate future?' was formulated by those prophets who developed in the direction of apocalyptic thought. There were other answers but all involved changes of cognition and readjustment to new circumstances. The future of prophecy was determined by these changes and its role in the post-exilic period was fairly

minor. Yet the visions were maintained, interpreted and transformed so it is necessary to recognize that prophecy survived (in a
much altered state) in spite of what should have been a spirit
annihilating experience of dissonance.

The survival of the prophetic vision in much reduced circumstances and under great difficulties was facilitated by its turning into
apocalyptic. Apocalyptic may be considered the triumph of the
imagination over reality. A triumph brought about by the felt need
to overcome the restrictions of grim reality on the realizations of the
vision. This could only be achieved by faith and imagination and the
visionaries had such in great supply. It is as Joshua Bloch says: 'The
apocalyptic writings are a strange and magnificent literature. They
serve as a testament to once widely prevalent ideas about God and
man, the universe and the various forces operating in it; they also
testify to the *sovereignty of imagination* and to the recognition of a
like prevalent claim that this sovereign faculty is helpless unless it
works with and through the substance of reality. What gives
apocalyptic literature its particular quality is that in it imagination is
exercised upon material so exotic that it seems to partake of fantasy
and legend. In existence now longer than two millennia and available in many languages, its scope is enormous and takes the reader
to the remote outposts of the divine empire and transports him to
the farthest reaches of the spirit.'[39] The earlier prophets had produced imaginative visions of what the future could be like and their
post-exilic followers continued that imaginative process in ways that
gradually transformed prophecy into apocalyptic. Combined with
this capacity for creative fantasy must have been a fair degree of
negative capability in order for them to have lived with the dissonance created by the failure of their hopes. Together these virtues of
the human spirit kept the vision alive and transformed it into the
apocalyptic matrix that was to become so seminally important in the
Roman era.

Conclusions

The examination of the prophetic traditions for evidence of response to dissonance yields both positive and negative results. The negative results stem to a great extent from the nature of the traditions preserved and the unlikelihood of prophetic disintegration brought about by disconfirmation of expectations being recorded. Because the future outlook of prophecy was, by definition, open-ended the traditions only record the expectations and the subsequent responses of the prophetic community in the future are not known to us. Whatever the motivations behind the preservation of the prophetic traditions may have been it is clear that the destruction of Jerusalem and the experience of the exile greatly facilitated the maintenance of those traditions which contained criticisms of the community and warnings of impending destruction. The fact that prophets of doom and prophets of salvation, as well as prophets who combined both outlooks, were so active in Judah meant that whatever the outcome of history might have been some of the prophets will have been confirmed by subsequent events. The continued survival of the Jerusalem community throughout the exile and after also allowed the more positive aspects of prophecy to be retained as possibilities for the future. Thus the broad sweep of prophecy could, in an uncritical way, be viewed as a successful delineation of history (cf. the presentation of prophecy in the deuteronomistic history) and as holding out hope for the future (hence the preservation of the individual traditions). In such general terms any analysis of the traditions for dissonance response will meet with failure.

The positive results of the analysis emerge in the examination of details, in the treatment of the text as text rather than as the bearer of vague generalities. Dissonance can be tested for where predictions of a specific nature exist and where it is possible to show that as such they lacked specific fulfilment. Yet again the dissonance experienced by the failure of such expectations need not be recorded in the tradition so textual evidence for dissonance experience and response may be entirely lacking. In order then to show that dissonance has been experienced it is necessary to work inferentially. The work of inferring from the text is assisted by the structures of dissonance response constructed by the theory of cognitive dissonance. This approach is assisted by the fact that the prophetic traditions underwent various interpretative developments over a long period of time and some of the factors in this growth were related to problems of non-fulfilment of earlier expectations. Some of the hopes in the traditions were maintained centuries after their original construction and in spite of such a long period of disconfirmation so we must conclude that either explanations that satisfactorily resolved the dissonance were provided or such groups did not regard continuing non-confirmation as a significant defect in the original expectation.

The main thrust of my argument for the existence of response to dissonance in the prophetic traditions is the amount of *re*interpreted material in those traditions. The accumulated growth of the prophetic traditions incorporated numerous responses to problems of failure and seriously modified motifs that had become obsolete. Changes in social and political circumstances destroyed the realization of the hope for a Davidic king but interpretative elements within prophecy transformed the hope into one of the city as the throne for the *divine* king (e.g. Jer. 3.17; cf. Isa. 28.5; 33.17, 21; Ezek. 48.35). Such reinterpretative shifts protected prophecy from ultimate failure by rescuing motifs and incorporating them into broader theological streams associated with community and city. Where there is such a capacity for reinterpretation from the narrow to the larger range of motifs then there is great scope for protecting expectations along lines amenable to piety. The transference of terms from the concrete to the abstract or metaphoric (e.g. from king David to king Yahweh) may have tended to empty them of content but did make them more impervious to disconfirmation. Furthermore it also opened up the way for identifying possible fulfilment of expectations along modified lines. This type of interpretation has been noted in relation to Ezra's organization of the community and the Chronicler's view of the temple served by levites as the goal of Israelite history. A community faithfully serving Yahweh in his temple could well have been understood as the fulfilment of the prophetic expectations for the future. In such ways dissonance could have been modified or even avoided by those determined to see in their own time the realization of prophecy.

A special case of reinterpreted prophecy along such lines can be seen in the treatment of prophecy in the New Testament where the early Christian communities regarded the life and teaching of Jesus as the fulfilment of biblical prophecy and also viewed themselves as participants in the eschaton. This interpretation of prophecy obviously did not believe that prophecy had failed and certainly glossed over the passage of centuries as irrelevant. However it was only an *interpretation* of prophecy, an accommodation of prophecy to reality. It could only be sustained by the transformation of the terms of prophecy into modified or metaphoric levels of interpretation. There was no public fulfilment of prophecy (i.e. clear, unequivocal and demonstrable to the public at large): no David occupied the throne, there was no transformation of nature or the nations, the enemies of Israel had not been destroyed, universal peace and prosperity had not set in nor was the temple the focus for international worship. Yet in so far as there existed a small community that believed prophecy had been fulfilled there dissonance had been overcome. It is a classical example of fulfilment by reinterpretation of all the basic premises and by redefinition of all the ground rules. It avoids dissonance by emptying the original terms of their content and provides a linguistic account of fulfilment by matching the original set of expectations to an entirely different set of explanations. It provides the *unexpected* as the fulfilment of the expected and so constitutes a radical discontinuity as the means of maintaining continuity. Yet it also displays all the inherent weaknesses of dissonance resolution by reinterpretations of original expectations for meaning is manipulated by such conventionalist stratagems.[1] Where meaning becomes indeterminate the spectre of Humpty Dumpty stalks all interpretation. Furthermore such a transformation may in turn require for itself subsequent manipulations of language and expectation in order to be sustained, e.g. the dissonance aroused by the failure of the parousia entailed a series of dissonance reducing explanations and reinterpretations among the early Christian communities.[2]

A further level of dissonance reduction or resolution may be found in the prophetic traditions that emphasize the need for the exercise of faith as the proper response to the prophetic vision (Isa. 7.9; cf. Hab. 2.1–4). This element is not articulated in the traditions but has the capacity for providing a very effective way around dissonance arousing events or experiences. In contrast to the overwhelming devastations threatening the community the Isaiah traditions offer the possibility of a safe foundation in relation to which 'he who believes will not be in haste' (Isa. 28.16; cf. 30.15). The precise meaning of the statement is far from clear but the motif of faith as a way of responding to the prophetic proclamation is there.[3] Now faith is a very slippery concept indeed and will provide endless ways around problems, resolve dilemmas and sustain conviction against overwhelming dissonance. In the centuries during which the prophetic traditions were created and maintained only faith can have kept the prophetic vision of a transformed future alive. In Qumran, among apocalyptic groups and Christian communities only faith in their own distinctive outlooks can have reinforced the determination to maintain the vision in spite of the increasing delay in its realization. Within a religious or political context faith is a way of avoiding dissonance by refusing to treat with reality and compromising expectations. This is particularly so in religious matters when so often faith in God and fidelity to the vision are inextricably bound up together.

What makes faith such an effective avoidance of dissonance is its irrefutability. It cannot be gainsaid, rebutted, shown to be wrong or effectively argued with, though it can, of course, be given up or lost. To the person with faith nothing counts against a position nor could anything count against it. The faith that can move mountains cannot be refuted because the faith that fails to move the mountains is either insufficient or unreal. This kind of faith is always of the type 'if you have *sufficient* faith you can move mountains' so that any failure to achieve such transportation is not a refutation of the principle. Of course few individuals or communities could sustain such an abstract principle for very long and usually the principle is modified to cover only metaphorical issues but the refutation-free principle is there for defence against sceptics. Where faith can be tested modifications have to be introduced or the group will suffer serious dissonance on occasions. A good example of the principle of faith modified by experience so as to prevent disruption of the

community through dissonant experiences may be seen in the
development of that curious religious sect that takes the apocryphal
ending of Mark's gospel literally to the point of having incorporated
the handling of snakes into their cult rituals. Among the snake
handling fundamentalists of the southern areas of the United States
the occasional believer is bitten to death by a poisonous snake or
dies from drinking poison. Such occurrences are not seen as refutations of Mark 16.18 or as a failure of the victims to exercise
sufficient faith but have been incorporated into the sect's hermeneutic as being due to the completion of the individual's work for
God on earth and so are God's way of calling his servant home![4]
Faith and theology can meet any exigency likely to produce dissonance so the existence of the motif of faith in the prophetic traditions should be seen as having provided a potential way of handling
subsequent dissonance (though that may not have been its original
intention). In answer to the question 'how could the prophetic
vision of a transformed future be sustained in view of its continued
failure to be realized?' those who maintained the vision could
respond in terms of 'faith in Yahweh's promises to his people' or by
means of much reinterpreted expositions of the vision.

Reinterpretation and faith provided expectations with adequate
protection against dissonance for those who took the prophetic
traditions seriously. Furthermore the many variables and unknowns
(if not unknowables) involved in the interpretation of the traditions
(especially as outlined above in chapters 1 and 6) render all specific
interpretations open to question, so that it is far from clear what
would have constituted the fulfilment of particular expectations. On
the basis of a correspondence between language and event many of
the expectations (e.g. David on the throne, great prosperity,
unification of the tribes, defeat of enemies) were not realized but
using reinterpretative moves (often in response to dissonance
caused by such failures of expectations) it may have been possible to
explain their nonfulfilment or to have demonstrated fulfilment to a
group's own satisfaction. The prophets were not philosophers providing rational schemes but utopians when it came to positive
visions of the future.[5] Their visions were kept alive by various
groups and became the basis for expectations of a literal fulfilment
among some and a wide range of modified expectations and
identifications of fulfilment of such expectations among others.

Prophecy's capacity to yield so much variety of interpretation from so many specific statements was one of its strengths in the period of the second temple.

The analysis of the traditions for evidence of dissonance and how it may have been dealt with has always to bear in mind that prophecy was only one temporary element in the life of ancient Israel and that in the community of the second temple it was not a dominant force at all. Even in its own time it had been fragmented by diverse claims of authenticity by different groups of prophets and many Israelites must have regarded most, if not all, prophets as false deceivers of the community.[6] The subsequent interpretation of prophecy may have been an important activity for some in the community but the shaping force of the community's life was Torah. This provided an alternative theological stream to that of prophecy, though it also afforded an anchorage from which the maintenance and transmission of the prophetic traditions as development and supplementation of Torah may have been sustained.[7] The continued interpretation of prophecy met the needs of the prophetic group (and possibly the larger community) and struggled with the problems caused by dissonance. The hermeneutic life of the second temple community was a very rich, complex one and it is the argument of this book that among the various tensions in the community that gave impetus to the hermeneutic process was the experience of dissonance. Such dissonance must have been increased often by alternative interpretations in the community which identified the contemporary structures with the fulfilment of prophecy – for the actual or asserted fulfilment of prophecy is as much a cause of dissonance in many cases as the failure of prophecy is in others. Yet in spite of the failure of the prophetic vision and its ensuing dissonance the interpretation of the traditions was maintained until in the Roman era that hermeneutic process triggered a number of significant responses which transformed prophecy.

Abbreviations

AB	Analecta Biblica
ALUOS	*Annual of the Leeds University Oriental Society*
ANET	J. B. Pritchard (ed.), *Ancient Near Eastern Texts relating to the Old Testament*, Princeton 1969³
ANVAO	Avhandlinger utgitt av Det Norske Videnskaps-Akademi i Oslo
ASTI	*Annual of the Swedish Theological Institute*
ATANT	Abhandlungen zur Theologie des Alten und Neuen Testaments
BFCT	Beiträge zur Förderung christlicher Theologie
BHS	Biblia Hebraica Stuttgartensia
BKAT	Biblischer Kommentar. Altes Testament
BJRL	*Bulletin of the John Rylands Library*
BWANT	Beiträge zur Wissenschaft vom Alten und Neuen Testament
BZAW	Beihefte zur Zeitschrift für die alttestamentliche Wissenschaft
CBCNEB	Cambridge Bible Commentary on the New English Bible
CBQ	*Catholic Biblical Quarterly*
EJ	*Encyclopedia Judaica*
ExpT	*Expository Times*
FRLANT	Forschungen zur Religion und Literatur des Alten und Neuen Testaments
HSMS	Harvard Semitic Monograph Series
IEJ	*Israel Exploration Journal*
IESS	*International Encyclopedia of the Social Sciences*
JASP	*Journal of Abnormal and Social Psychology*
JBL	*Journal of Biblical Literature*
JCS	*Journal of Cuneiform Studies*
JJS	*Journal of Jewish Studies*
JNES	*Journal of Near Eastern Studies*
JQRMS	Jewish Quarterly Review Monograph Series
JR	*Journal of Religion*
JSS	*Journal of Semitic Studies*
JTS	*Journal of Theological Studies*
NS	New Series
OBO	Orbis Biblicus et Orientalis
OTL	Old Testament Library

OTS	*Oudtestamentische Studien*
PB	*Psychological Bulletin*
PR	*Psychological Reports*
RB	*Revue Biblique*
RSV	Revised Standard Version
SBLDS	Society of Biblical Literature Dissertation Series
SBLMS	Society of Biblical Literature Monograph Series
SBT	Studies in Biblical Theology
SGVSGTR	Sammlung gemeinverstandlicher Vorträge und Schriften aus dem Gebiet der Theologie und Religionsgeschichte
SJLA	Studies in Judaism in Late Antiquity
SNT	Supplements to *Novum Testament*
SSN	*Studia Semitica Neerlandica*
SSS	*Social Studies of Science*
ST	*Studia Theologica*
STL	*Studia Theologica Lundensia*
SVT	*Supplements to Vetus Testamentum*
TGUOS	*Transactions of the Glasgow University Oriental Society*
VT	*Vetus Testamentum*
WMANT	Wissenschaftliche Monographien zum Alten und Neuen Testament
ZAW	*Zeitschrift für die alttestamentliche Wissenschaft*

Notes

Introduction

1. Quoted in D. Torr, (ed.), *Karl Marx and Friedrich Engels: Correspondence 1846–1895. A Selection with Commentary and Notes*, London 1936, p. 225. In a letter to Dr Kugelmann (K. Marx, *Letters to Dr. Kugelmann*, London 1934, p. 25) written on 28 December 1862 Marx included the observation 'We are obviously approaching a revolution.'

2. The literature on this aspect of Marxian thought is beginning to develop, e.g. see R. G. Wesson, *Why Marxism? The Continuing Success of a Failed Theory*, London 1976.

3. Thus part III is now devoted to the exegesis of texts and the original section on the theory and methodology of hermeneutic has been omitted. It has, however, been rewritten as an independent paper 'What is hermeneutic?' (to be published in *Studia Theologica*). The best introduction to the modern philosophical treatment of hermeneutic is R. E. Palmer, *Hermeneutics. Interpretation Theory in Schleiermacher, Dilthey, Heidegger, and Gadamer*, Evanston 1969.

4. It would be impossible to catalogue all the failed predictions of mankind but for a fascinating collection of misjudgments and predictive errors typical of a certain type of human activity see N. Slonimsky, *Lexicon of Musical Invective*, Seattle and London 1965.[2]

Part I: The Prophetic Traditions

1. Interpreting the Prophetic Traditions

1. 'The whole must be understood in terms of its individual parts, individual parts in terms of the whole' and 'the whole of a work must be understood from its individual words and their combination but full understanding of an individual part presupposes understanding of the whole', W. Dilthey, 'Die Entstehung der Hermeneutik', *Gesammelte Schriften*, 5, Göttingen, 1964, pp. 317–37; quotations from pages 334, 330. The essay was written in 1900 and an English translation can be found in H. P. Rickman (ed.), *W. Dilthey: Selected Writings*, Cambridge 1976, pp. 247–63; quotations from pages 262, 259.

2. See especially J. Lindblom, *Prophecy in Ancient Israel*, Oxford 1962; also Y. Kaufmann, *The Religion of Israel*, New York 1972, part 3,

pp. 343–451; G. von Rad, *Old Testament Theology*, 2, Edinburgh and London 1965, parts 1 and 2, pp. 1–315. O. Eissfeldt, *The Old Testament: An Introduction*, Oxford 1965, B II, pp. 301–443; G. Fohrer, *History of Israelite Religion*, London 1973, part 2, ch. 3, pp. 223–91; part 3, pp. 316–29; *Introduction to the Old Testament*, London 1970, part 4, pp. 342–479; O. Kaiser, *Introduction to the Old Testament*, Minnesota 1975, part D, pp. 207–317. Details of specific prophetic books can be found in the various series of commentaries, e.g. Old Testament Library, SCM Press: London, Hermeneia, Fortress Press: Philadelphia, also Das Alte Testament Deutsch, Vandenhoeck & Ruprecht: Göttingen, Biblischer Kommentar Altes Testament, Neukirchener Verlag: Neukirchen-Vluyn.

3. On divination see Lindblom, op. cit., pp. 83–95; A. Guillaume, *Prophecy and Divination among the Hebrews and other Semites*, London 1938. For comparative prophecy see F. Ellermeier, *Prophetie in Mari und Israel* Theologische und Orientalistische Arbeiten I: Herzberg 1968; M. Weinfeld, 'Ancient Near Eastern Patterns in Prophetic Literature', *VT*, 27 (1977), pp. 178–95.

4. Cf. M. Smith, *Palestinian Parties and Politics That Shaped the Old Testament*, New York and London 1971, pp. 137–41, 260. He dates the core of the covenant code (Ex. 21–23) about 720. For the relation between prophecy and the law see R. V. Bergren, *The Prophets and the Law*, Monographs of the Hebrew Union College IV: Cincinnati 1974.

5. Cf. R. de Vaux, *Ancient Israel: Its Life and Institutions*, London 1965², pp. 312–517; G. Fohrer, *Theologische Grundstrukturen des Alten Testaments*, Berlin 1972, pp. 62–7; W. Zimmerli, *Grundriss der alttestamentlichen Theologie*, Theologische Wissenschaft 3: Stuttgart 1972.

6. Cf. B. Levine, *In the Presence of the Lord*, Studies in Judaism in Late Antiquity 5: Leiden 1974; J. Milgrom, *Studies in Levitical Terminology*, I, Berkeley 1970; *Cult and Conscience. The ASHAM and the Priestly Doctrine of Repentance*, Studies in Judaism in Late Antiquity 18: Leiden 1976; J. Neusner, *The Idea of Purity in Ancient Judaism*, Studies in Judaism in Late Antiquity 1: Leiden 1973; and most recently M. Haran, *Temples and Temple-Service in Ancient Israel*, Oxford 1978. M. Douglas, *Purity and Danger. An Analysis of Concepts of Pollution and Taboo*, London 1966 has been very influential in this development.

7. See A. R. Johnson, *The Cultic Prophet in Ancient Israel*, Cardiff 1962²; A. Haldar, *Associations of Cult Prophets among the Ancient Semites*, Uppsala 1945; Kaiser, *Introduction*, pp. 212–4.

8. Cf. Kaiser, ibid., p. 214 note 12; Fohrer, *Introduction*, pp. 429, 440, 459; and the commentaries on Habakkuk, Haggai, Joel, Nahum, Obadiah, Zechariah, Zephaniah.

9. One dominant analytical approach current in biblical studies is that of form criticism; see C. Westermann, *Basic Forms of Prophetic Speech*, London 1967; W. E. March, 'Prophecy', in J. H. Hayes (ed.), *Old Testament Form Criticism*, San Antonio 1974, pp. 141–77; also K. Koch, *The Growth of the Biblical Tradition: The Form-Critical Method*, London 1969;

R. Knierim, 'Old Testament Form Criticism Reconsidered', *Interpretation*, 27 (1973), pp. 435–68.

10. See A. W. Gouldner, *The Coming Crisis of Western Sociology*, London 1971, pp. 29–45. It matters little whether we call these assumptions domain or epistémé or ideology or worldview or paradigm the point being made remains the same.

11. Ibid., p. 33.

12. Cf. M. Smith, 'The Common Theology of the Ancient Near East', *JBL*, 71 (1952), pp. 135–47.

13. For the Moabite Stone see W. Beyerlin (ed.), *Near Eastern Religious Texts Relating to the Old Testament*, London 1978, pp. 237–40; J. C. L. Gibson, *Textbook of Syrian Semitic Inscriptions*, I, Oxford 1971, pp. 71–83. Gibson observes (p. 71) that the inscription 'reads almost like a chapter from the Bible'. For the Esarhaddon treaties see Beyerlin, op. cit., pp. 129–31; and the discussion in M. Weinfeld, *Deuteronomy and the Deuteronomic School*, Oxford 1972, especially pp. 59–157. An important study of the whole subject is B. Albrektson, *History and the Gods. An Essay on the Idea of Historical Events as Divine Manifestations in the Ancient Near East and in Israel*, Coniectanea Biblica: Old Testament Series 1: Lund 1967.

14. Lindblom, *Prophecy in Ancient Israel*, p. 104.

15. The conflict between prophet and wise man is well brought out in W. McKane, *Prophets and Wise Men*, SBT 44: London 1965.

16. Most books assume or state such a view; see J. Bright, *Covenant and Promise. The Future in the Preaching of the Pre-exilic Prophets*, London 1977; R. E. Clements, *Prophecy and Covenant*, SBT 43: London 1965; W. Eichrodt, *Theology of the Old Testament*, 1, OTL: London 1961; D. J. McCarthy, *Treaty and Covenant. A Study in Form in the Ancient Oriental Documents and in the Old Testament*, AB 21: Rome 1963; *Old Testament Covenant. A Survey of Current Opinions*, Growing Points in Theology: Oxford 1973. Clements has modified his view of the matter in his recent *Prophecy and Tradition*, Growing Points in Theology: Oxford 1975, pp. 22, 23.

17. See L. Perlitt, *Bundestheologie im Alten Testament*, WMANT 36: Neukirchen-Vluyn 1969; cf. E. Kutsch, *Verheissung und Gesetz. Untersuchungen zum sogenannten 'Bund' im Alten Testament*, BZAW 131: Berlin 1973. For his judicious remarks on both viewpoints see J. Barr, 'Some Semantic Notes on the Covenant', in H. Donner, R. Hanhart and R. Smend (eds), *Beiträge zur Alttestamentlichen Theologie*, Festschrift for W. Zimmerli: Göttingen 1977, pp. 23–38.

18. Cf. Fohrer, *History of Israelite Religion*, pp. 80–2.

19. Cf. Weinfeld, *Deuteronomy and the Deuteronomic School*, p. 81 n. 6.

20. This fact is recognized even by McCarthy, *Old Testament Covenant*, p. 46.

21. This is particularly so in his commentary on Romans (K. Barth, *The Epistle to the Romans*, London 1933[6]); on his theology as dialectical see T. F. Torrance, *Karl Barth. An Introduction to his Early Theology*

1910–1931, London 1962, pp. 48–95. On the other hand, Paul Tillich denies that Barth's theology was dialectical and regards it as paradoxical (like prophetic religion), *Perspectives on Nineteenth- and Twentieth-Century Protestant Theology*, London 1967, p. 242.

22. See Fohrer, *Introduction*, pp. 370–1; Kaiser, *Introduction*, pp. 208–9. Kaiser notes 'it is methodologically justified to work with the postulate that it is not the inauthenticity but the authenticity of the sayings ascribed to the prophets that needs to be proved' (pp. 208f.).

23. This third possibility is particularly relevant to the book of Jeremiah, see Kaiser, ibid., p. 248; M. Kessler, 'Jeremiah Chapters 26–45 Reconsidered', *JNES*, 27 (1968), pp. 81–8; E. W. Nicholson, *Preaching to the Exiles. A Study of the Prose Tradition in the Book of Jeremiah*, Oxford 1970.

24. Cf. von Rad, *Old Testament Theology*, 2, p. 171.

25. The oracle against Judah (2.2–4) is generally regarded as secondary, see J. L. Mays, *Amos*, OTL: London 1969, pp. 40–2; H. W. Wolff, *Joel and Amos*, Hermeneia: Philadelphia 1977, pp. 163–4. Whether 1.2 is to be attributed to Amos or to the editors is a disputed matter.

26. Cf. J. L. Mays, *Hosea*, OTL: London 1969, pp. 47, 87, 152; H. W. Wolff, *Hosea*, Hermeneia: Philadelphia 1974, pp. 48, 116–7, 194–5.

27. For the ambiguous nature of Isaiah's attitude to salvation see T. C. Vriezen, 'Essentials of the Theology of Isaiah', in B. W. Anderson and W. Harrelson (eds), *Israel's Prophetic Heritage*, Essays for J. Muilenburg: London 1962, pp. 128–46.

28. Buber, *The Prophetic Faith*, New York 1960, pp. 103–4.

29. On this see W. L. Holladay, *The Root ŠÛBH in the Old Testament with particular reference to its usages in covenantal contexts*, Leiden 1958, pp. 120–6.

30. Cf. 14.1–8 (Heb. 14.2–9); for the genuineness of the call to repentance here being attributable to Hosea see Mays, *Hosea*, pp. 184–90; Wolff, *Hosea*, pp. 233–4.

31. This problematic text will be considered later; that Isaiah's preaching was dominated by the thought of repentance is the argument of H. W. Hoffmann, *Die Intention der Verkündigung Jesajas*, BZAW 136: Berlin 1974.

32. Cf. R. E. Clements, 'The purpose of the book of Jonah', *SVT*, 28 (1975), pp. 16–28.

33. See J. Milgrom, 'The Priestly Doctrine of Repentance', *RB*, 82 (1975), pp. 186–205; *Cult and Conscience*; T. M. Raitt, 'The Prophetic Summons to Repentance', *ZAW*, 83 (1971), pp. 30–49; H. W. Wolff, 'Das Thema "Umkehr" in der alttestamentlichen Prophetie', *Gesammelte Studien zum Alten Testament*, (München 1964), pp. 130–50. For the later rabbinic view of repentance see J. J. Petuchowski, 'The Concept of "Teshuvah" in the Bible and the Talmud', *Judaism*, 17 (1968), pp. 175–85.

34. There is a large literature on the subject of the remnant which can be found gathered together and discussed in G. F. Hasel, *The Remnant. The*

History and Theology of the Remnant Idea from Genesis to Isaiah, Andrews University Monographs V: Berrien Springs 1972. For the negative view of remnant in the eighth century prophets see Fohrer, *History*, p. 271.

35. 'The "remnant of Joseph" is the Israel of the Day of Yahweh. This "remnant of Joseph" will consist of those who have returned to Yahweh by having sought good.' Hasel, *The Remnant*, p. 205.

36. For the theory of two Assyrian invasions see J. Bright, *A History of Israel*, London 1960, pp. 282–7; London 1972², pp. 296–308. Cf. B. Oded in J. H. Hayes and J. M. Miller (eds), *Israelite and Judaean History*, OTL: London 1977, pp. 446–51. The ambiguities and complexities of the issue are ably discussed in B. S. Childs, *Isaiah and the Assyrian Crisis*, SBT 2:3: London 1967.

37. This ploy is used by Hasel, *The Remnant*, pp. 204ff. who claims that Amos was the first to use the remnant motif in an eschatological sense.

38. Cf. Fohrer, *History*, pp. 252–3; *Introduction*, pp. 370–1; Kaiser, *Introduction*, pp. 222–3; *Isaiah 1–12*, OTL: London 1972, pp. 24–5, 53–4, 147; H. Wildberger, *Jesaja* BKAT X/1: Neukirchen-Vluyn 1972, pp. 153–4, 413–4, 442–6.

39. The usual fundamentalistic criticisms tend to be charges of rationalism or subjectivity, cf. R. K. Harrison, *Introduction to the Old Testament*, London 1970, p. 752; J. B. Payne, *Encyclopedia of Biblical Prophecy. The Complete Guide to Scriptural Predictions and Their Fulfilment*, London 1973, p. 11.

40. See Augustine, *Confessions*, Book 11 in A. C. Outler (ed.), *Augustine: Confessions and Enchiridion*, Library of Christian Classics VII: London 1955, pp. 244–69.

41. See B. de Jouvenal, *The Art of Conjecture*, London 1967; cf. D. Bell, 'Twelve Modes of Prediction – A Preliminary Sorting of Approaches in the Social Sciences', *Daedalus*, 93 (1964), pp. 845–80.

42. Trollope, *Phineas Finn*, I, The Oxford Trollope: Oxford 1949, ch. 25, pp. 226f. This is a well known and often stated principle; thus 'Prophecy is many times the principal cause of the events foretold' (Hobbes); 'Even so do predictions often cause that to happen which has been foretold, as it is supposed that the opinions the Mahometons hold on fate makes them resolute' (Leibniz); 'I have a great mind to make a prophecy and they say prophecies work out their own fulfilment' (Keats).

43. The example is de Jouvenal's, *The Art of Conjecture*, pp. 51–2. He makes the important point 'A principle of uncertainty characterizes the particular events which most directly interest us, inasmuch as any knowledge we acquire of them can incite us to an action which will contradict this knowledge.'

44. Chesterton, *The Napoleon of Notting Hill*, London 1914, p. 13. The first chapter (pp. 13–20) is devoted to 'Introductory Remarks on the Art of Prophecy'.

45. The phrase is Karl Popper's see *Conjectures and Refutations. The Growth of Scientific Knowledge*, London and Henley 1972⁴, pp. 123, 38 note 3.

46. Cf. A. K. Grayson and W. G. Lambert, 'Akkadian Prophecies', *JCS*, 18 (1964), pp. 7–30; W. W. Hallo, 'Akkadian Apocalypses', *IEJ*, 16 (1966), pp. 231–42; R. D. Biggs, 'More Babylonian "Prophecies"', *Iraq*, 29 (1967), pp. 117–32. For biblical *vaticinia ex eventu* see I Kings 13.2; Isa. 7.8b; Ezek. 26; 29.17–20; also the predictive material in the Pentateuch (Gen. 9.25–27; 15.13–16; 49.1–27; Num. 24.14–24). Cf. E. Osswald, 'Zur Problem der *vaticinia ex eventu*', *ZAW*, 75 (1963), pp. 27–44 (limited to a discussion of late Jewish apocalyptic works).

47. Cf. 'Even God's anticipation would have reference to action as choice among probabilities. He would not see what "is to happen", but the range of possible things among which what happens will be a selection. And he will see that a higher percentage of some kinds of things will happen than others, that is, he will see in terms of probabilities. This seems to be the only view of God's knowledge that does not make human freedom impossible, or that does not destroy the religious idea of God as perfect in goodness and wisdom.' C. Hartshorne, 'Three Ideas of God', *Reality As Social Process. Studies in Metaphysics and Religion*, New York 1971, pp. 161–2. In rescuing God process theology necessarily must jettison many biblical metaphors; the traditional alternative is to saddle the deity with the mistaken predictions of men.

48. Cf. Ludwig Wittgenstein's dicta 'We *cannot* infer the events of the future from those of the present. Belief in the causal nexus is *superstition*.' *Tractatus Logico-Philosophicus*, London 1966, §5.1361. The main arguments of the books of Job and Ecclesiastes would appear to have a different account of divine causality from that of the prophets.

49. Cf. Fohrer, 'Die Struktur der alttestamentlichen Eschatologie', *Studien zur alttestamentlichen Prophetie (1949–1965)*, BZAW 99: Berlin 1967, pp. 32–58; S. Mowinckel, *He That Cometh*, Oxford 1959, pp. 125–54; J. P. M van der Ploeg, 'Eschatology in the Old Testament', *OTS*, 17 (1972), pp. 89–99.

50. Cf. Bright, *Covenant and Promise*, pp. 15–24; Lindblom, *Prophecy in Ancient Israel*, pp. 360–75; H. D. Preuss, *Jahweglaube und Zukunftserwartung*, BWANT 87: Stuttgart 1968, pp. 205–14; von Rad, *Theology*, 2, pp. 99–125; T. C. Vriezen, 'Prophecy and Eschatology', *SVT*, 1 (1953), pp. 199–229.

51. Bright, *Covenant and Promise*, p. 111; cf., pp. 18, 19.

52. On this see K. H. Bernhardt, *Das Problem der altorientalischen Königs-ideologie im Alten Testament*, *SVT*, 8: Leiden 1961; J. H. Eaton, *Kingship and the Psalms*, SBT 2:32: London 1976; I. Engnell, *Studies in Divine Kingship in the Ancient Near East*, Oxford 1967²; A. R. Johnson, *Sacral Kingship in Ancient Israel*, Cardiff 1967²; S. Mowinckel, *The Psalms in Israel's Worship*, Oxford 1962, I, pp. 42–80.

53. Cf. von Rad, *Old Testament Theology*, 2, pp. 147–75; E. Rohland, *Die Bedeutung der Erwählungs-traditionen Israels für die Eschatologie der alttestamentlichen Propheten*, (Dissertation: Heidelberg 1956), pp. 112ff.

54. Cf. 'For the "eschatological" hope – in Israel, the "historical people par excellence" (Tillich), but not in Israel alone – is first always historical

hope; *it becomes eschatologized only through growing historical disillusionment.*' M. Buber, *Kingship of God*, London 1967³, p. 14 (my italics).

55. Cf. the way local holy men developed reputations for being wonder workers in the fifth and sixth centuries of the Christian era; see the lucid account in P. Brown, 'The Rise and Function of the Holy Man in Late Antiquity', *Journal of Roman Studies*, 61 (1971), pp. 80–101. Lack of primary data prevents a similar account being provided for the early Israelite prophets.

56. Cf. B. S. Childs, *Exodus. A Commentary*, OTL: London 1974, pp. 55–60.

57. See the commentaries at this point (e.g. Mays, *Amos*, pp. 137–9; Wolff, *Joel and Amos*, pp. 311–14) and the discussions by P. R. Ackroyd, 'A Judgment Narrative between Kings and Chronicles? An Approach to Amos 7:9–17', in G. W. Coats and B. O. Long (eds), *Canon and Authority. Essays in Old Testament Religion and Theology*, Philadelphia 1977, pp. 71–87; and G. M. Tucker, 'Prophetic Authenticity: A Form Critical Study of Amos 7:10–17', *Interpretation*, 27 (1973), pp. 423–34.

58. I would call this the 'Horatio principle' after the advice given by the dying Hamlet to his companion Horatio in order to prevent him killing himself:

> 'Horatio I am dead:
> Thou livest; *report me and my cause aright*
> To the unsatisfied . . . . . .
> . . . .
> If thou didst ever hold me in thy heart,
> Absent thee from felicity awhile,
> And in this harsh world draw thy breath in pain
> *To tell my story.*' (*Hamlet*, Act 5, Scene 2, lines 330–39).

59. See 'Masorah', *EJ*, 16, pp. 1401–82; also L. J. Yagod, 'Tradition', *EJ*, 15, pp. 1308–11; Z. Ben-Hayyim, *'mswrh wmswrt'*, *Leshonenu*, 21 (1957), pp. 283–92. Ben-Hayyim argues that *msr* in both places (Num. 31.5; Ezek. 20.37) means 'count'.

60. The Greek versions use different words to render the Hebrew but the LXX *en arithmō* 'in number' may point to the original Hebrew (*b*ᵉ*mispār* 'by number'); cf. W. Zimmerli, *Ezechiel*, BKAT XIII: Neukirchen-Vluyn 1962, p. 437.

61. So Smith, *Palestinian Parties*, p. 227 note 284. Recent biblical studies have begun to stress the importance of tradition: thus von Rad's *Theology*, is subtitled 'The Theology of Israel's Historical Traditions' (vol. 1) and 'The Theology of Israel's Prophetic Traditions' (vol. 2). See also W. Brueggemann and H. W. Wolff, *The Vitality of Old Testament Traditions*, Atlanta 1975; D. A. Knight, *Rediscovering the Traditions of Israel*, SBLDS 9: Missoula 1975; D. A. Knight (ed.), *Tradition and Theology in the Old Testament*, London 1977; for the discussion on *masorah* see M. Fishbane, 'Torah and Tradition', in *Tradition and Theology*, pp. 275–300.

62. Popper, 'Towards a Rational Theory of Tradition', *Conjectures and Refutations*, p. 134.

63. Cf. F. R. Leavis, *The Great Tradition: George Eliot, Henry James, Joseph Conrad*, London 1948; T. J. Reed, *Thomas Mann. The Uses of Tradition*, Oxford 1974; H.-G. Gadamer, 'The rehabilitation of authority and tradition', *Truth and Method*, London 1975, pp. 245–53; W. Heisenberg, 'Tradition in Science', in O. Gingerich (ed.), *The Nature of Scientific Discovery*, Smithsonian international symposia series 5: Washington 1975, pp. 219–36 (cf., pp. 556–73).

64. Gadamer, *Truth and Method*, p. 250. Cf. his statement 'Tradition is always porous, for what is handed on (*tradiert*) in it.' in 'Martin Heidegger and Marburg Theology', *Philosophical Hermeneutics*, Berkeley 1976, p. 211. On the other hand, T. J. Reed, *Thomas Mann*, p. 5 observes 'Mann's personal dialogue with tradition produced answers radically different from the ones which determined the fate of his country, even though it was the common tradition from which he began. Indeed, nothing more clearly illustrates *the neutrality of tradition*, its passive availability for present use and misuse than this divergence. *Tradition offers possibilities, for good and ill; the individual selects and uses.*' (my italics)

65. Marx, *The Eighteenth Brumaire of Louis Bonaparte*, (1852). Translation in R. C. Tucker (ed.), *The Marx–Engels Reader*, New York 1972, p. 437 (my italics). As an example of the crippling effect of conjuring up the past in the service of the present revolution Marx cites, among others, Luther donning the mask of the apostle Paul.

66. On the absence of the exodus traditions as a central motif of Isaiah's oracles see von Rad, *Old Testament Theology*, 2, pp. 156–75; Rohland, *Die Bedeutung der Erwählungs-traditionen Israels*, pp. 112ff.

67. Cf. 'The verb *bāḥar* (subject God – object people) is an original deuteronomistic coinage.' G. von Rad, *Das Gottesvolk im Deuteronomium*, BWANT 3rd series, book 11 (47): Stuttgart 1929, p. 28.

68. Transformational elements are one of the major features of eighth-century prophecy; cf. Amos 3.2; 4.6–12; 8.3, 10; 9.7; Isa. 1.21–26; 2.12–21; 3.18–24. I am at present preparing a paper entitled 'Transformational elements in eighth century prophecy' which is to be the first stage of a more substantial work with the provisional title *Tradition and Transformation*.

69. Cf. 'One thing is certain: this was not the cult practiced in the temple, or the prevalent cult of the people of Jerusalem . . . What Ezekiel sees are really shadows out of the past.' *The Religion of Israel*, Kaufmann, p. 430; see Smith, 'The Veracity of Ezekiel, the Sins of Manasseh, and Jeremiah 44:18', *ZAW*, 87 (1975), pp. 11–16.

70. For this approach see Smith, *Palestinian Parties*, pp. 15–56.

71. Cf. J. B. Segal, 'Popular Religion in Ancient Israel', *JJS*, 27 (1976), pp. 1–22; Kaufmann, op. cit., pp. 291–340.

72. I am assuming here that there was such a phenomenon as a Mosaic radicalization of religion and that its core was a view of deity inimical to other religious concepts; cf. my article 'The Aniconic God and the Cult of

Images', *ST*, 31 (1977), especially pp.60–64. For the emergence of a rational thrust to Israelite religion see M. Weber, *Ancient Judaism*, New York 1967, passim.

73. For the first see Clements, *Prophecy and Tradition*; for the second S. Mowinckel, *Prophecy and Tradition. The Prophetic Books in the Light of the Study of the Growth and History of the Tradition*, ANVAO II.3: Oslo 1946.

74. The authenticity of some of these references is disputed by some commentators, cf. Kaiser, *Isaiah 13–39*, OTL: London 1974, pp.293–4; Kaiser (*Introduction*, p.299) regards Isa.30.8 as an 'indisputably pre-exilic passage' but in the commentary appears to prefer to take the section as a piece of exilic theology.

75. Cf. R. C. Culley (ed.), *Oral Tradition and Old Testament Studies*, Semeia 5: Missoula 1976; Mowinckel, *Prophecy and Tradition*, pp.15–19, 26–33, 60–6; E. Nielsen, *Oral Tradition. A Modern Problem in Old Testament Introduction*, SBT 11: London 1954; also Kaiser, *Introduction*, pp.297–302.

76. Cf. A. H. J. Gunneweg, *Mündliche und schriftliche Tradition der vorexilischen Prophetenbücher als Problem der neueren Prophetenforschung*, FRLANT 73: Göttingen 1959, pp.77–118.

77. For the complex editorial features of the temple sermon see H. G. Reventlow, 'Gattung und Überlieferung in der "Tempelrede Jeremias", Jer.7 und 26', *ZAW*, 81 (1969), pp.315–52; cf. Kaiser, *Introduction*, pp.301–2.

78. Cf. D. Jones, 'The Traditio of the Oracles of Isaiah of Jerusalem', *ZAW*, 67 (1955), pp. 226–46; R. P. Carroll, 'Inner Tradition Shifts in Meaning in Isaiah 1–11', *ExpT*, 89 (1978), pp.301–4.

79. See the remarks on this point in J. Barr, *Old and New in Interpretation*, London 1966, pp.118–26.

80. Cf. J. L. Crenshaw, *Prophetic Conflict. Its Effect Upon Israelite Religion* BZAW, 124: Berlin 1971, pp.183–9. Cf. 'The Jews survived as a people because they cultivated wisdom rather than prophecy', L. S. Feuer, *Ideology and the Ideologists*, Explorations in interpretative sociology: Oxford 1975, p.201. In spite of antique sources Feuer's analysis of the prophets as ideologists (pp.197–202) has some percipient insights into an aspect of prophecy which is all too infrequently examined by biblical scholars.

81. On the relation between magic and religion see especially W. J. Goode, 'A Sociological Theory of Religious Action', *Religion Among the Primitives*, New York 1951, ch.3, pp.38–55; R. Towler, *Homo religiosus: sociological problems in the study of religion*, Sociology and Social Welfare series 10: London 1974, ch.3, pp.40–61; cf. J. Skorupski, *Symbol and Theory. A philosophical study of theories of religion in social anthropology*, Cambridge 1976, ch.9, pp.125–59. See also M. Douglas, *Purity and Danger*, pp.73–89.

82. For the role of magic in the Israelite cult see Levine, *In the Presence of the Lord. A Study of Cult and Some Cultic Terms in Ancient Israel*,

pp. 56–91. Much of Levine's analysis is an argument against Kaufmann's view (*Religion of Israel*, pp. 301–4) that the Israelite cult had no magical elements, apart from vestigial ones, in it.

83. Cf. Wittgenstein's assertion 'Philosophy is a battle against the bewitchment of our intelligence by means of language.' *Philosophical Investigations*, Oxford 1972, I. p. 109. On the roots of language see O. Barfield, *Poetic Diction*, London 1952²; *Saving the Appearances. A Study in Idolatry*, New York 1965.

84. Von Rad, *Theology*, 2, p. 86; see the whole chapter 'The Prophets' Conception of the Word of God', ibid., pp. 80–98. For the relevant literature on this concept and a critical examination which rejects the notion see A. C. Thiselton, 'The Supposed Power of Words in the Biblical Writings', *JTS* NS, 25 (1974), pp. 283–99. Thiselton argues in favour of a performative account of language rather than the theory that words were endowed with power in themselves.

85. Thiselton (ibid.) does not deal with the problem of unfulfilled prediction in relation to statements understood as the word of God.

86. Cf. L. S. Hay, 'What Really Happened at the Sea of Reeds?', *JBL*, 83 (1964), pp. 397–403; see also Childs, *Exodus*, pp. 218–29.

87. Cf. Mays, *Micah*, OTL: London 1976, pp. 152–69.

88. Cf. C. Westermann, *Isaiah 40–66*, OTL: London 1969, p. 8; Carroll, 'Second Isaiah and the Failure of Prophecy', *ST*, 32 (1978), pp. 119–31.

89. Cf. Kaiser's (*Isaiah 13–39*, p. 227) observation: 'A reading of 27.7–9 leaves an expression of obscurity and jerkiness. One can read these verses again and again without knowing exactly to whom they are referring and how they fit into their context.'

90. *Pensées* III Section X.687, L. Brunschvigg (ed.), *Oeuvres de Blaise Pascal*, XIV: Paris 1904, p. 125.

91. For examples of the extremer forms of interpretation of the prophetic oracles see Payne, *Encyclopedia of Biblical Prophecy*, passim. In this area where Humpty Dumpty ('When I use a word it means just what I choose it to mean – neither more nor less') is king a criteriology of valid interpretation is very important; on this see E. D. Hirsch, *Validity in Interpretation*, New Haven and London 1967.

92. J. L. Austin, *How To Do Things With Words*, Oxford 1976², pp. 99–100. On Austin's account of performative language see W. P. Alston, *Philosophy of Language*, (Foundations of Philosophy series: Englewood Cliffs 1964), pp. 32–49; also K. Graham, *J. L. Austin. A Critique of Ordinary Language Philosophy*, Sussex 1977, pp. 53–112.

93. Austin, op. cit., pp. 101–32, especially p. 107.

94. Ibid., pp. 151–64.

95. Ibid., p. 14; for a discussion of such infelicities see pp. 14–45, 136–61. On the more difficult question whether performatives can have a truth value see J. Houston, 'Truth Valuation of Explicit Performatives', *Philosophical Quarterly*, 20 (1970), pp. 139–49.

96. See von Rad, *Old Testament Theology*, 1, Edinburgh and London 1962, pp. 246–50, 260–2; also his 'Faith Reckoned As Righteousness', *The*

Problem of the Hexateuch and Other Essays, Edinburgh and London 1966, pp. 125–30.

97. So P. D. Hanson, 'Jewish Apocalyptic against its Near Eastern Environment', *RB*, 78 (1971), pp. 44–6. He writes of the prophets 'they were the ones responsible for historicizing Israel's religion, for translating cosmic vision into history, for causing myth to retreat before a more "secularized", "humanistic" view of religion.' (p. 46).

98. Wittgenstein, *Philosophical Investigations*, I.445. §§. 437–95 are relevant for the discussion about expectations; on prophecy he observes (§. 461) 'We are – as it were – surprised, not at anyone's knowing the future, but at his being able to prophesy at all (right or wrong). As if the mere prophecy, no matter whether true or false, foreshadowed the future; whereas it knows nothing of the future and cannot know less than nothing.' For commentary on the sections see G. Hallett, *A Companion to Wittgenstein's 'Philosophical Investigations'*, Ithaca and London 1977, pp. 480–1.

99. Only I Kings 14.11 adds the formulaic 'for Yahweh has spoken it'; see P. R. Ackroyd, 'The Vitality of the Word of God in the Old Testament', *ASTI*, 1 (1962), pp. 7–23.

100. R. G. Collingwood, *An Autobiography*, Oxford 1939, p. 31; see especially pp. 29–43; *An Essay on Metaphysics*, Oxford 1940, pp. 23–33.

101. See Collingwood, *The Idea of History*, Oxford 1973, pp. 269–74, 278–82. Cf. Barth's (*Romans*, p. 254) insistence on the need for questioning but in terms of justification and on the boundary between religion and divinity.

102. Gadamer, *Truth and Method*, pp. 333–41.

103. Ibid., p. 333. The phrase 'human sciences' is a translation of the German *Geisteswissenschaften*, (as opposed to the 'natural sciences' *Naturwissenschaften*).

104. Gadamer, 'Semantics and Hermeneutics', *Philosophical Hermeneutics*, pp. 88–9.

105. *Truth and Method*, p. 338.

106. Cf. J. J. M. Roberts, 'Of signs, prophets, and time limits: A note on Psalm 74:9', *CBQ*, 39 (1977), pp. 474–81. Cf. Amos 8.11, 12.

107. Most of Nietzsche's writings contain sections on Socrates but see especially *The Birth of Tragedy and The Genealogy of Morals*, New York 1956; authorities disagree about how Nietzsche viewed Socrates, e.g. W. Kaufmann, *Nietzsche. Philosopher, Psychologist, Antichrist*, New York 1968[3]; T. B. Strong, *Friedrich Nietzsche and the Politics of Transfiguration*, Berkeley 1975. Cf. W. J. Dannhauser, *Nietzsche's View of Socrates*, Ithaca and London 1974.

108. On this Barthian approach to religion see F. Ferré, *Language, Logic and God*, London and Glasgow 1970, pp. 117–37.

109. Collingwood, *The Idea of History*, pp. 269–70.

Part II: Dissonance Theory and the Traditions

2. The Theory of Cognitive Dissonance

1. Leon Festinger, *A Theory of Cognitive Dissonance*, Evanston 1957. The ubiquity of Festinger's influence is comparable to that of Thomas Kuhn's *The Structure of Scientific Revolutions*, International Encyclopedia of Unified Science II/2: Chicago 1970[2]. For a combination of the two theoretical approaches see E. L. McDonagh, 'Attitude Changes and Paradigm Shifts: Social Psychological Foundations of the Kuhnian Thesis', *SSS*, 6 (1976), pp.51–76.

2. Any competent introduction to social psychology will provide an account of the theory; see also the relevant articles in *JASP*, 52–60 (1955–60) and the bibliography by S. T. Margulis and E. Songer, *PR*, 24 (1969), pp.923–35. The following books I have found invaluable R. P. Abelson and others (eds), *Theories of Cognitive Consistency: A Sourcebook*, Chicago 1968; E. Aronson, *The Social Animal*, San Francisco 1976[2], pp.85–139; J. W. Brehm and A. R. Cohen, *Explorations in Cognitive Dissonance*, New York 1962; R. Brown, *Social Psychology*, New York 1965, pp. 584–609; A. R. Cohen, *Attitude Change and Social Influence*, New York 1964; M. Deutsch and R. M. Krauss, *Theories in Social Psychology*, New York 1965, pp.62–76; L. Festinger and others, *Conflict, Decision and Dissonance*, London 1964; S. Feldman (ed.), *Cognitive Consistency: Motivational Antecedents and Behavioral Consequents*, New York 1966; also the articles B. J. Calder and M. Ross, 'Attitudes: Theories and Issues', in J. W. Thibaut, J. T. Spence and R. C. Carson (eds), *Contemporary Topics in Social Psychology*, Morristown N.J. 1976, pp.3–35; R. B. Zajonc, 'Cognitive Theories in Social Psychology', in G. Lindzey and E. Aronson (eds), *The Handbook of Social Psychology*, Massachusetts 1968[2], 1, pp.320–411.

3. Zajonc, 'Cognitive Theories', in *Handbook*, p.359.

4. Brown, *Social Psychology*, p.584.

5. Festinger, *A Theory of Cognitive Dissonance*, p.11.

6. So M. L. J. Abercrombie, 'Small Groups', in B. M. Foss (ed.), *New Horizons in Psychology*, London 1966, p.386.

7. Festinger, *Theory*, p.13.   9. Ibid., p.28.

8. Ibid., p.18.   10. Ibid., p.31.

11. Ibid., p.83; also pp.260–6 for recapitulation of his theory; cf. Zajonc, 'Cognitive Theories', *Handbook*, pp.360–1.

12. Abelson, In *Theories of Cognitive Consistency*, p.6.

13. Matt.6.13. Cf. Paul Ricoeur's response to this prayer (*The Symbolism of Evil*. Boston 1969, pp. 325–6): '. . . the question remains: Is not God wicked? Is it not that possibility that the believer evokes when he prays: "Lead us not into temptation"? Does not his request signify: "Do not come to meet me with the face of the tragic God"? There is a theology of temptation which is very close to the tragic theology of blinding . . .' On the demonic aspect of the world see below ch.6, pp.198–204.

14. L. Festinger, H. W. Riecken and S. Schachter, *When Prophecy Fails* Minneapolis 1956, p. 28.

15. *Theory*, p. 202.

16. Job. 32.1. Cf. the similar 'wise in their own eyes' (Isa. 5.21; Prov. 3.7).

17. Cf. Festinger, *Theory*, pp. 134–7.

18. *When Prophecy Fails. A Social and Psychological Study of a Modern Group that Predicted the Destruction of the World.* For a fictional treatment of the matter see Alison Lurie's novel *Imaginary Friends*, London 1967.

19. *When Prophecy Fails*, pp. 139–73.

20. Ibid., p. 169.

21. 'Reactions to Disconfirmation', ibid., pp. 193–215.

22. Ibid., pp. 197–201.   24. Ibid., pp. 212–14.

23. Ibid., p. 208.   25. Ibid., pp. 3–32, 216–29.

26. See G. Scholem, *Sabbatai Sevi. The Mystical Messiah 1626–1676*, The Littman Library of Jewish Civilization: London 1973; also his 'Shabbatai Zevi', *EJ*, 14, pp. 1219–54; 'Redemption Through Sin', *The Messianic Idea in Judaism*, London 1971, pp. 78–141; M. Buber, *Mamre: Essays in Religion*, London 1946, pp. 99–121; W. D. Davies, 'From Schweitzer to Scholem: Reflections on Sabbatai Svi', *JBL*, 95 (1976), pp. 529–58. For Festinger's brief account see *When Prophecy Fails*, pp. 8–12.

27. *When Prophecy Fails*, p. 12. Festinger (ibid., p. 233) suggests that a more effective group might have turned disconfirmation into the beginning, rather than the end, of a larger movement. Perhaps the prime example of such a positive use of disconfirmation is the early Christian movement.

28. Scholem, *The Messianic Idea in Judaism*, p. 88 (my italics).

29. *When Prophecy Fails*, p. 4. A shortened version of the conditions appears on p. 216.

30. On the difficult question of the significance for early Christianity of the delayed parousia (*Parusieverzögerung*) see M. Werner, *The Formation of Christian Dogma*, London 1957; A. Strobel, *Untersuchungen zum eschatologischen Verzögerungsproblem*, SNT 2: Leiden 1961. For a critical assessment of these views see D. Aune, 'The Significance of the Delay of the Parousia for Early Christianity', in G. F. Hawthorne (ed.), *Current Issues in Biblical and Patristic Interpretation*, Grand Rapids 1975, pp. 87–109. Recently there has been a movement towards analysing the New Testament traditions using cognitive dissonance theory, see J. G. Gager, *Kingdom and Community. The Social World of Early Christianity*, Prentice-Hall Studies in Religion Series: Englewood Cliffs 1975, especially pp. 37–49; cf. H. Jackson, 'The Resurrection Belief of the Earliest Church: A Response to the Failure of Prophecy?', *JR*, 55 (1975), pp. 414–25; U. Wernik, 'Frustrated beliefs and early Christianity', *Numen*, 22 (1975), pp. 96–130.

31. K. E. Weick, 'When Prophecy Pales: The Fate of Dissonance Theory', *PR*, 16 (1965), p. 1272.

32. Zajonc, *Handbook*, p. 390.

33. Deutsch and Krauss, *Theories in Social Psychology*, p.76.

34. Cf. the principle 'man cannot live by consonance alone', Aronson, *The Social Animal*, p.138; and in *Theories of Cognitive Consistency*, p.26.

35. In a letter to George and Tom Keats dated 21,27(?) December 1817; see H. E. Rollins (ed.), *The Letters of John Keats 1814–1821*, Cambridge 1958, 1, No. 45, p.193.

36. Halmos, *The Personal and the Political. Social Work and Political Action*, London 1978, p.154. Throughout the book Halmos argues for a 'cult of uncertainty'.

37. Brown, *Social Psychology*, p.595. For his critical assessment of the theory see pp.601–4.

38. Ibid., p.602.

39. Festinger, *Theory*, pp.84–122. See also L. Festinger and J. M. Carlsmith, 'Cognitive consequences of forced compliance', *JASP*, 58 (1959), pp.203–10; C. A. Insko, *Theories of Attitude Change*, The Century Psychology Series: Englewood Cliffs 1967, pp.223–70. For a different approach see J. M. Nuttin, *The Illusion of Attitude Change. Towards a response contagion theory of persuasion*, European Monographs in Social Psychology: London 1974.

40. The most critical review of dissonance theory is N. P. Chapanis and A. Chapanis, 'Cognitive Dissonance: Five Years Later', *PB*, 61 (1964), pp.1–22.

41. Cf. Chapanis and Chapanis, ibid., p.21. Aronson (*Theories of Cognitive Consistency*, p.27) responds to their verdict of 'not proven' with the remark 'Happily, after ten years, it is still not proven; all the theory ever does is generate research!' One is reminded of J. N. Findlay's (*Proc. Aristotelian Soc.* supplement 35 (1961), p.242) observation on Wittgenstein's philosophy: 'Moreover, each of Wittgenstein's frequent rhetorical questions is such that, if answered in the sense *not* intended by the question, it will lead to an illuminating result; they are practically all arrows which, if read in the reverse direction, point unerringly to some truth. A philosophy of meaning so valuably wrong does not differ profoundly from one that is systematically right.'

42. So Aronson, op. cit., p.13.

43. J. A. Hardyck and M. Braden, 'Prophecy Fails Again: A report of a failure to replicate', *JASP*, 65 (1962), pp.136–41.

44. Brehm and Cohen, *Explorations in Cognitive Dissonance*, especially pp.7–11.

45. Daryl Bem, 'Self-Perception: An Alternative Interpretation of Cognitive Dissonance Phenomena', *PR*, 74 (1967), pp.183–200; see discussion in Calder and Ross, 'Attitudes: Theories and Issues', pp.25–30. They (30) regard the evidence as supporting dissonance theory rather than self-perception theory.

46. So Brehm and Cohen, op. cit., p.314.

3. Dissonance Theory and the Prophetic Traditions

1. I have already published a number of articles on the subject see

'Prophecy, Dissonance and Jeremiah XXVI', *TGUOS*, 25 (1976), pp. 12–23; 'Ancient Israelite Prophecy and Dissonance Theory', *Numen*, 24 (1977), pp. 135–51; 'Prophecy and dissonance: a theoretical approach to the prophetic tradition', *ZAW* (forthcoming).

2. Ramsey, *Religious Language. An Empirical Placing of Theological Phrases*, London 1967, p. 116; for his discussion of prophecy see pp. 112–22.

3. Ibid., p. 119.

4. E.g. D. Z. Phillips, *Religion without Explanation*, Oxford 1976. For the logical oddity of religious language see Ramsey, op. cit., ch. 3, pp. 90–150.

5. Georg Lukacs, 'What is Orthodox Marxism?' in *History and Class Consciousness. Studies in Marxist Dialectics*, London 1971, p. 1.

6. On this point cf. C. D. Darlington, *The Evolution of Man and Society*, London 1969), pp. 173–92.

7. Cf. C. R. North, *The Second Isaiah. Introduction, Translation and Commentary to Chapters XL–LV*, Oxford 1964, pp. 106–13; U. E. Simon, *A Theology of Salvation. A Commentary on Isaiah 40–55*, London 1953, pp. 84–90; J. D. Smart, *History and Theology in Second Isaiah. A Commentary on Isaiah 35, 40–66*, London 1967, pp. 85–7, 180–6.

8. On the phrases 'covenant of people' (*b'rît 'ām*) and 'light of nations' (*'ōr gōyîm*) in 42.6 see H. M. Orlinsky in *Studies on the Second Part of the Book of Isaiah*, *SVT* 14: Leiden 1967, pp. 97–117; cf. R. N. Whybray, *Isaiah 40–66*, New Century Bible: London 1975, pp. 74–5, 155–6.

9. Cf. 'The Deuteronomic term "torah" means the whole of the bestowals of Jahweh's saving will – in German the word can be rendered by the equally neutral term *Willensoffenbarung* (revelation of the will).' von Rad, *Theology*, 1, p. 222.

10. See on *haftora* L. I. Rabinowitz, 'Haftarah', *EJ*, 16, pp. 1342–5.

11. Barr, *Old and New in Interpretation*, p. 108.

12. On this see especially G. Steiner, *After Babel. Aspects of Language and Translation*, Oxford 1975; also E. A. Nida and C. R. Taber, *The Theory and Practice of Translation*, Helps for Translators 8: Leiden 1969.

13. For text and translation see J. F. Stenning (ed.), *The Targum of Isaiah*, Oxford 1949, pp. 62–5.

14. So Zajonc, *Handbook*, p. 391. For issues involved in biblical hermeneutic see A. H. J. Gunneweg, *Understanding the Old Testament*, OTL: London 1978; for more general aspects of hermeneutic see my (*ST* forthcoming) paper 'What is hermeneutic?'.

Part III: Hermeneutic of the Traditions

4. Text and Interpretation I

1. On this see Eissfeldt, *Introduction*, pp. 306–29; Fohrer, *Introduction*, pp. 365–72; Fohrer, 'The Origin, Composition and Tradition of Isaiah i–xxxix', *ALUOS*, 3 (1961–2), pp. 3–38; R. Lack, *La Symbolique du Livre*

d'Isaie. Essai sur l'image littéraire comme élément de structuration, AB, 59: Rome 1973, pp. 28–76; also J. H. Eaton, 'The Origin of the Book of Isaiah', *VI*, 9 (1959), pp. 138–57; R. B. Y. Scott, 'The Literary Structure of Isaiah's Oracles', in H. H. Rowley (ed.), *Studies in Old Testament Prophecy presented to Th. H. Robinson*, Edinburgh 1950, pp. 175–86. See also Ackroyd, 'Isaiah I–XII – presentation of a prophet', *SVT* 29 (1978), pp. 16–48.

2. Kaiser, *Introduction*, p. 224. His commentary (*Isaiah 1–12*) does not follow this line.

3. Jacob Milgrom, 'Did Isaiah Prophesy during the Reign of Uzziah?', *VI*, 14 (1964), pp. 165–82.

4. Kaiser, *Introduction*, p. 223; cf. his *Isaiah 13–39*, pp. 234–6.

5. Cf. F. Hesse, *Das Verstockungsproblem im Alten Testament. Eine frömmigkeitsgeschichtliche Untersuchung*, BZAW 74: Berlin 1955, pp. 83–91.

6. On this see especially Hoffmann, *Die Intention der Verkündigung Jesajas*.

7. Cf. B. Lindars, *New Testament Apologetic. The Doctrinal Significance of the Old Testament Quotations*, London 1961, pp. 159–67.

8. This depends upon how it is translated and related to the previous phrase; cf. Hasel, *The Remnant*, pp. 236–50; Wildberger, *Jesaja*, I, p. 234; also J. Sawyer, 'The Qumran Reading of Isaiah 6: 13', *ASTI*, 3 (1964), pp. 111–13.

9. See W. McKane, 'The Interpretation of Isaiah VII 14–25', *VT*, 17 (1967), pp. 208–19.

10. Cf. G. B. Gray, *A Critical and Exegetical Commentary on the Book of Isaiah*, Edinburgh 1912, I, p. 155.

11. Cf. von Rad, *Theology*, 2, p. 171.

12. See the form critical approach of B. S. Childs, *Isaiah and the Assyrian Crisis*.

13. Ibid., p. 120. Cf. Bright, *History*[2], pp. 296–308.

14. On this motif see J. H. Hayes, 'The Tradition of Zion's Inviolability', *JBL*, 82 (1963), pp. 419–26.

15. Cf. Kaiser, *Isaiah 13–39*, pp. 223–6. There is a vast amount of prophetic reinterpretation in the so-called Isaiah apocalypse but 27.2–6 will serve here as an example; on Isa. 24–27 see O. Plöger, *Theocracy and Eschatology*, Oxford 1968, pp. 53–78.

16. On the strange story of Eliakim (Isa. 22.20–25) see Kaiser, *Isaiah 13–39*, pp. 155–9; also E. Jenni, *Die politischen Voraussagen der Propheten*, ATANT, 29: Zürich 1956, pp. 42–8. For further elements of royal language applied to the deity see Isa. 28.5, 6.

17. On this cf. Eissfeldt, *Introduction*, pp. 339–40; Westermann, *Isaiah 40–66*, pp. 6–8.

18. Contrasting styles of form critical analysis of Second Isaiah and the oracles in 56–66 can be seen in Westermann, *Isaiah 40–66* and P. D. Hanson, *The Dawn of Apocalyptic*, Philadelphia 1975.

19. Westermann (op. cit., pp. 142, 288) regards 44.22; 55.7, where a call to turn (*šūb*) is proclaimed, as glosses.

20. Cf. Hanson, op. cit., p. 92. Westermann (op. cit., p. 394) understands *ṣārîm* as 'foreign armies'. The interpretation of Isa. 56–66 given in §3 is much indebted to Hanson's account of the matter (op. cit., pp. 32–208).

21. For the network of reinterpretative strands in Isaiah see further Jones, 'The Traditio of the Oracles of Isaiah of Jerusalem', *ZAW*, 67 (1955), pp. 226–46; and more briefly Carroll, 'Inner Tradition Shifts in Meaning in Isaiah 1–11', *ExpT*, 89 (1978), pp. 301–4.

5. Text and Interpretation II

1. On the history see F. M. Cross, *Canaanite Myth and Hebrew Epic. Essays in the History of the Religion of Israel*, Cambridge Massachusetts 1973, pp. 274–89; on Lamentations as response to the exile see B. Albrektson, *Studies in the Text and Theology of the Book of Lamentations*, *ST*, 21: Lund 1963, pp. 214–39. For a comprehensive treatment of the exilic period see P. R. Ackroyd, *Exile and Restoration. A Study of Hebrew Thought of the Sixth Century BC*, OTL: London 1968.

2. Cf. *ANET*[3], p. 316.

3. On the historical problems involved in reconstructing the period see Ackroyd, *Exile and Restoration*, pp. 138–52; G. Widengren in *Israelite and Judaean History*, pp. 515–23.

4. On this see Ackroyd, op. cit., pp. 155–62, 248; W. A. M. Beuken, *Haggai-Sacharja 1–8. Studien zur Überlieferungsgeschichte der Frühnachexilischen Prophetie*, *SSN*, 10: Assen 1967, pp. 27–49.

5. The LXX has *eti hapax* (= *'ōd 'aḥat*) but no equivalent for *m**'aṭ hî'*. Cf. BHS; also Ackroyd, op. cit., p. 153 note 3.

6. Cf. J. D. Levenson, *Theology of the Program of Restoration of Ezekiel 40–48* HSMS, 10: Missoula 1976.

7. Most sources make Zerubbabel the son of Shealtiel (cf. Hag. 1.1, 12, 14; 2.2; Ezra 3.2, 8; 5.2) but I Chron. 3.19 gives his father as Pedaiah the brother of Shealtiel; for one explanation see J. M. Myers, *I Chronicles*, Anchor Bible 12: New York 1965, p. 21.

8. Cf. Ackroyd, *Exile and Restoration*, pp. 147, 164–5; Widengren, *Israelite and Judaean History*, pp. 521–2.

9. For the difficulties in the text see BHS and RSV footnotes g, h, i, j. In spite of the plural form *'**ṭārōt* only one crown may be indicated cf. Job 31.36.

10. Cf. Ackroyd, op. cit., pp. 196–200; M. Noth, *The History of Israel*, London 1960[2], p. 312 note 2; Smith, *Palestinian Parties*, pp. 109, 246. This is only one possible interpretation of a difficult text; its badly preserved state may be evidence of interpretative development cf. R. A. Mason, *The Books of Haggai, Zechariah and Malachi*, CBCNEB: London 1977, pp. 62–3.

11. Isa. 55.1–5. Cf. O. Eissfeldt, 'The Promises of Grace to David in Isaiah 55.1–5', in *Israel's Prophetic Heritage*, pp. 196–207.

12. For the discussion that follows see also my paper 'Eschatological delay in the prophetic tradition?', *ZAW*, (forthcoming).

13. For *mhh* 'delay' cf. Gen. 19.16; Ex. 12.39; Judg. 3.26; 19.8; II Sam. 15.28. The word *hitmahm*ʿ*hū* (Isa. 29.9) is difficult, though it should be noted that the context appears to be about men's failure to relate to the prophetic vision, see Kaiser, *Isaiah 13–39*, pp. 269–72.

14. On this important but obscure motif see L. Cerny, *The Day of Yahweh and Some Relevant Problems*, (Práce z vědeckých ústavú 53: Prague 1948); G. W. Ahlström, *Joel and the Temple Cult of Jerusalem*, *SVT*, 21: Leiden 1971, pp. 62–97; von Rad, *Theology*, 2, pp. 119–25.

15. Cf. Wolff, *Joel and Amos*, pp. 34–5, 43–4. For the association of *bā'* and *qārōb* cf. *bā 'hā'ēt qārōb hayyōm* 'the time has come, the day is near' (Ezek. 7.7).

16. For the identity of the foe see J. Skinner, *Prophecy and Religion. Studies in the Life of Jeremiah*, Cambridge 1922, pp. 35–52; J. Bright, *Jeremiah*, (Anchor Bible 21: New York 1965), pp. lxxx–iv; cf. B. S. Childs, 'The Enemy from the North and the Chaos Tradition', *JBL*, 78 (1959), pp. 187–98.

17. On the wide range of possible meanings for the seventy years see Weinfeld, *Deuteronomy and the Deuteronomic School*, pp. 143–6; also Ackroyd, *Exile and Restoration*, pp. 240–3.

18. Cf. Zimmerli, *Ezechiel*, pp. 600–702, 716–23; W. Eichrodt, *Ezekiel. A Commentary* OTL: London 1970, pp. 365–412.

19. The phrase 'and he shall carry off its wealth' (*w*ʿ*nāśā' h*ʿ*mōnāh* verse 19) is omitted by the original Greek text (cf. BHS; Zimmerli, *Ezechiel*, p. 716) and would appear to be redundant in view of the following statement 'and he will certainly despoil it and surely plunder it'.

20. On this point see especially Jenni, *Die politischen Voraussagen der Propheten*, pp. 92–6.

21. *Ezekiel*, pp. 410–11. His principle is 'the sovereign freedom of God to fulfil a prediction of a prophet in whatever way seems good to him' (p. 410). For a similar stress on the freedom of God (outside the ranks of orthodox Barthians) see J. A. Sanders, 'Hermeneutics in True and False Prophecy', *Canon and Authority*, pp. 38–40.

22. On the interpretation of this passage see Hanson, *The Dawn of Apocalyptic*, pp. 337–54; B. Otzen, *Studien über Deuterosacharja*, Acta theologica Danica 6: Copenhagen 1964, pp. 252–60; M. Saebo, *Sacharja 9–14. Untersuchungen von Text und Form*, WMANT, 34: Neukirchen-Vluyn 1969, pp. 234–52.

23. It should be noted that the term used in Ezek. 37.15–28 is *'ēṣ* rather than *maqqēl* (*maqqēl* occurs in Ezek. 39.9).

24. Cf. Mason, *The Books of Haggai, Zechariah and Malachi*, pp. 78–82; idem, 'The Relation of Zech. 9–14 to Proto-Zechariah', *ZAW*, 88 (1976), pp. 227–39.

25. Cf. K. Koch, 'Ezra and the Origins of Judaism', *JSS*, 19 (1974), pp. 173–97.

26. Ibid., p. 188.

27. Koch, ibid., p. 189.

28. Cf. Fohrer, *Introduction*, p. 248; von Rad, *Theology*, 1, p. 352;

H. G. M. Williamson, *Israel in the Books of Chronicles*, Cambridge 1977, p.135.

29. So W. Rudolph, 'Problems of the Books of Chronicles', *V*, 4 (1954), p.404.

30. On the development of eschatology in the Qumran community see H. Ringgren, *The Faith of Qumran*, Philadelphia 1963, pp.152–98; D. E. Aune, *The Cultic Setting of Realized Eschatology in Early Christianity* SNT, 28: Leiden 1972, pp.29–44. On Qumran as an apocalyptic community see Cross, *Canaanite Myths and Hebrew Epic*, pp.326–42.

6. The Limits of Prophecy

1. See Crenshaw, *Prophetic Conflict*; F. L. Hossfeld and I. Meyer, *Prophet gegen Prophet. Eine Analyse der alttestamentlichen Texte zum Thema: Wahre und falsche Propheten*, Biblische Beiträge 9: Fribourg 1973; H-J. Kraus, *Prophetie in der Krisis. Studien zu Texten aus dem Buch Jeremia*, Neukirchen-Vluyn 1964; I. Meyer, *Jeremia und die falschen Propheten*, OBO, 13: Freiburg 1977; E. Osswald, *Falsche Prophetie im Alten Testament*, SGVSGTR, 237: Tübingen 1962; T. W. Overholt, *The Threat of Falsehood. Studies in the Theology of the Book of Jeremiah*, SBT 2: 16: London 1970. I have not yet seen S. J. de Vries, *Prophet against Prophet*, Grand Rapids 1978. Cf. also A. S. van der Woude, 'Micah in dispute with the pseudo-prophets', *VT*, 19 (1969), pp.244–60; Sanders, 'Hermeneutics in True and False Prophecy', *Canon and Authority*, pp.21–41.

2. Cf. 'In sum, the authority of a prophet was a vulnerable, shifting social reality – closely tied to acceptance and belief. It was supported by verbal appeals to transcendent commission, and by concrete deeds of power, even momentary claims of special status, removed from bearing ultimate responsibility for one's words. But the authority rested upon acceptance of those appeals. It was reinforced by deeds taken as proof of legitimacy, and by telling legends of such deeds. But it *depended* upon attributing truth to the "sign" or to tales of such signs. The prophet's authority was likely maintained and supported in groups, and reinforced by his conformity with social expectations. But it was made real insofar as his behavior was accepted by others.' B. O. Long, 'Prophetic Authority as Social Reality', in *Canon and Authority*, p.19.

3. The motif of falsehood (*šeqer*) is a dominant one in the book of Jeremiah, see especially Overholt, *The Threat of Falsehood*, passim.

4. Cf. Bright, *Jeremiah*, p.152.

5. On this point see Carroll, 'A Non-Cogent Argument in Jeremiah's Oracles against the Prophets', *ST*, 30 (1976), pp.43–51.

6. Crenshaw, *Prophetic Conflict*, pp.56–61.

7. The heavy deuteronomistic editing of Jeremiah has produced a paradigm of prophetic conflict, reflecting its own theological understanding of prophecy, in Jer.28.

8. The charge occasionally made against Hananiah (e.g. Osswald,

Falsche Prophetie, p. 21) that he applied an old message in a new situation, i.e. he was incapable of orientating himself to a new set of circumstances, will hardly do in view of the deuteronomistic presentation of Jeremiah as a representative of an old tradition of prophetic preaching (cf. Jer. 28.8; 7.12).

9. Buber, *The Prophetic Faith*, p. 178. Cf. Overholt, *The Threat of Falsehood*, p. 62. Duber offers no evidence of how a community might have determined whether a period was one of false security or great adversity, hence his analysis is unhelpful at this point because it describes, by virtue of hindsight, what happened without recognizing the great difficulty for the contemporary community of determining precisely which prophet had made the correct analysis.

10. Eichrodt (*Ezekiel*, p. 157) makes the observation: 'Prophetic assurance, like all assurance of faith, cannot be comprehended or proved from any point outside itself, but carries its authentication within itself. It can do nothing but appeal back to itself and to the fact of its own existence, as a fact which calls for a decision about it, and advise men for once to begin to be really serious about what they see there.'

11. Eichrodt, ibid., p. 176. He (p. 177) regards faith as the only judge of the truth or falsehood of prophecy. On the lack of a valid criterion for separating true from false prophets see especially Crenshaw, *Prophetic Conflict*, pp. 49–61.

12. For Jonah as a satire see M. Burrows, 'The Literary Category of the Book of Jonah', in H. T. Frank and W. L. Reed (eds), *Translating and Understanding the Old Testament*, Essays in honour of H. G. May: Nashville-New York 1970, pp. 80–107. In spite of the many difficulties involved in categorizing Jonah the treatment of it as satire may contribute to an understanding of the decline of prophetic status in the post-exilic community. The presentation of Nineveh as a community too stupid to know their right hand from their left yet capable of instant repentance (3.6–9) may well have been a scornful satire on the prophetic call for repentance: what kind of repentance is open to morons? Furthermore the repentance of Nineveh did not prevent its ultimate destruction in 612 so perhaps the satirist was lampooning the prophet as both vicious and pointless in his activities. On the negative assessment of prophecy in Jer. 23.33–40; Zech. 13.2–6 see D. L. Petersen, *Late Israelite Prophecy: Studies in Deutero-Prophetic Literature and in Chronicles*, (SBLMS 23: Missoula 1977), pp. 27–38.

13. Cf. Overholt's judgment (*The Threat of Falsehood*, p. 93) 'In a deeper sense, the fall of Jerusalem in 586 was less a vindication of Jeremiah than a clear indication of his failure to get his message across persuasively enough for the people to take the proper steps to avert the disaster.'

14. Sanders (*Canon and Authority*, p. 40) regards this approach as part of 'the canonical monotheizing process'.

15. Cf. *The Iliad*, Loeb Classical Library: London 1924, Book II, 1–83 (the baneful dream given to Agamemnon by Zeus and believed by Nestor), Book IV (the agreement between Hera and Zeus, against the better

judgement of Zeus, to destroy the city of Ilios), Book XIV, 153–522 (the seduction of Zeus by Hera thus allowing Poseidon to aid the Danaans during the sleep of Zeus).

16. On this see Crenshaw, *Prophetic Conflict*, pp. 77–90. G. Quell (*Wahre und falsche Propheten: Versuch einer Interpretation*, BFCT 46; Gutersloh 1952, p. 100) states 'the demonic stands in the place of truth, and the demon is God himself' (also quoted in Crenshaw, p. 90). W. Eichrodt (*Theology of the Old Testament*, 1, p. 262) also makes the point that the attribution to Yahweh of the causation of all events 'gave the divine nature something of a demonic character'.

17. Cf. Levine, *In the Presence of the Lord*, pp. 77–91, especially pp. 80–2. The only point where demonology actually penetrated the cult was in the day of atonement ritual where provision was made for the demon Azazel (Lev. 16.8, 10, 26). See also Eichrodt, *Theology of the Old Testament*, 2, pp. 224–6.

18. There is a growing literature on I Kings 13; see especially Crenshaw, op. cit. pp. 39–46; Hossfeld and Meyer, *Prophet gegen Prophet*, pp. 21–7; also K. Barth, *Church Dogmatics*, Edinburgh 1957, II/2, pp. 393–409.

19. Barth, ibid., p. 399.

20. Crenshaw, op. cit., pp. 47–8.

21. Hanson, *The Dawn of Apocalyptic*. In a paper (as yet unpublished) 'Twilight of Prophecy or Dawn of Apocalyptic?' I have provided a critique of Hanson's thesis which is the basis for what follows in this section.

22. *Dawn of Apocalyptic*, pp. 11–12. Hanson distinguishes between the two sets of activists by terming the apocalyptists 'visionaries' as distinct from 'prophets'.

23. M. Weber, *The Sociology of Religion*, London 1966; K. Mannheim, *Ideology and Utopia. An Introduction to the Sociology of Knowledge*, London 1960; E. Troeltsch, *The Social Teaching of the Christian Churches*, New York 1960, 2 vols. See Hanson, *Dawn*, pp. 211–20.

24. Ibid., p. 218.

25. On this see A. Cody, *A History of Old Testament Priesthood*, AB 35: Rome 1969, especially pp. 146–74; E. Rivkin, *The Shaping of Jewish History. A Radical New Interpretation*, New York 1971, pp. 21–41.

26. *Dawn*, pp. 274–9. For a similar point about the Chronicler's lack of interest in eschatology cf. Plöger, *Theocracy and Eschatology*, pp. 39–45.

27. Cf. *Dawn*, pp. 368, 400.

28. Hanson (ibid., p. 29) offers four results as the summary of his thesis: (1) the sources of apocalyptic eschatology lie solidly within the prophetic tradition of Israel; (2) the period of origin is in the sixth to the fifth centuries; (3) the essential nature of apocalyptic is found in the abandonment of the prophetic task of translating the vision of the divine council into historical terms; (4) the historical and sociological matrix of apocalyptic is found in an inner-community struggle in the period of the Second Temple between visionary and hierocratic elements.

29. For the intervention of God at the climactic point of history as the

apocalyptic myth see Lindars, 'The Apocalyptic Myth and the Death of Christ', *BJRL*, 57 (1975), pp.366–87.

30. *Dawn*, pp.402–3.

31. This is defined by Hanson (*Dawn*, p.29) as follows: 'In order to trace the history of the relation between vision and reality in prophetic Yahwism we developed what we call the contextual-typological method. It seeks to interpret the apocalyptic compositions within the context of the community struggle discernible behind the material studied, and it applies typological tools in analyzing the material. The typologies traced are those of poetic structure and meter, of prophetic oracle types (genres), and of the prophetic eschatology – apocalyptic eschatology continuum.' (Cf. ibid., pp. 291–2.)

32. *Dawn*, pp.400–1.

33. Cf. J. Bloch, *On the Apocalyptic in Judaism*, JQRMS 2: Philadelphia 1952, pp.28–39; D. S. Russell, *The Method and Message of Jewish Apocalyptic*, OTL: London 1964, pp.88–100. For a much earlier association of apocalyptic with prophecy in relation to unfulfilled predictions and the development of tendencies within prophecy by apocalyptic see R. H. Charles, *A Critical History of the Doctrine of a Future Life in Israel, in Judaism, and in Christianity or Hebrew, Jewish, and Christian Eschatology from Pre-prophetic Times till the Close of the New Testament Canon*, London 1913², pp.184–90.

34. On one occasion (*Dawn*, p.29 note 26) Hanson does admit that his typology is overly simplified.

35. For criticisms of his *RB* paper on this score see J. J. M. Roberts, 'Myth *versus* history: Relaying the comparative foundations', *CBQ*, 38 (1976), pp.1–13. It is hardly surprising that Hanson (*RB* 78, p.41) should be dismissive of Albrektson's important work *History and the Gods*, for it poses a serious problem for his analysis of history as a distinctive concept in Israelite thought. Perhaps it is time to call for a moratorium on the use of such weasel words as myth and history in biblical studies (unless their treatment becomes more reflective and less biased against non-Israelite sources).

36. So H. Butterfield, *Christianity and History*, London 1949, p.81. Cf. the treatment of the will of God as the creation of a new myth by the Israelites in H. Frankfort and others, *Before Philosophy. An Essay on Speculative Thought in the Ancient Near East*, London 1949, pp.241–8.

37. Cf. E. Shils, 'Ideology', *IESS*, 7, pp.66–75.

38. That is, the activities of the Fourth Philosophy men in the Roman era; cf. A. R. C. Leaney in *Israelite and Judaean History*, pp.636–63.

39. Bloch, *On the Apocalyptic in Judaism*, p.153 (my italics). For recent work on apocalyptic see K. Koch, *The Rediscovery of Apocalyptic. A polemical work on a neglected area of biblical studies and its damaging effects on theology and philosophy*, SBT 2: 22: London 1972; W. Schmithals, *The Apocalyptic Movement. Introduction and Interpretation*, Nashville and New York 1975; also J. Barr, 'Jewish Apocalyptic in Recent Scholarly Study', *BJRL*, 58 (1976), pp.9–35; R. North, 'Prophecy to

Apocalyptic via Zechariah', *SVT*, 22 (1972), pp. 47–71. Hanson's account of apocalyptic can be found in briefer form in his articles 'Jewish Apocalyptic against its Near Eastern Environment', *RB*, 78 (1971), pp. 32–58; 'Old Testament Apocalyptic Reexamined', *Interpretation*, 25 (1971), pp. 454–79; 'Zechariah 9 and the Recapitulation of an Ancient Ritual Pattern', *JBL*, 92 (1973), pp. 37–59.

Conclusions

1. The term 'conventionalist stratagem' or 'conventionalist twist' is Karl Popper's (*Conjectures and Refutations*, p. 37). The New Testament treatment of prophecy is a good example of the strengths and weaknesses of transformational reinterpretation of prophecy and also illustrates Popper's argument (ibid., p. 38 n. 3; *The Poverty of Historicism*, London 1966, pp. 12–17) about the Oedipus effect of prophecy, i.e. predictions have an influence on the predicted event. Thus much of the synoptic picture of Jesus is constructed from prophecy without constituting a fulfilment of prophecy.

2. Cf. Matt. 24.6–8, 14, 34; II Thess. 2.2; Gager, *Kingdom and Community*, pp. 43–8. Some confusion arises when the New Testament is treated as a holistic work rather than a collection of diverse theologies relating to Jesus but with discrete views about the future, e.g. a second coming (synoptics, early Paul, the Apocalypse) or his presence in his body the church (John, Ephesians, Colossians). However the structures of dissonance response relate to Christianity in so far as the parousia did not happen.

3. For the range of possible meanings see Kaiser, *Isaiah 13–39*, pp. 252–4.

4. Little serious analytical work has been done on these sects so extant literature tends to be partisan journalism. I have extracted the above data (adding my own evaluation of them in terms of dissonance response) from K. W. Carden and R. W. Pelton, *The Persecuted Prophets. The Story of the Frenzied Serpent Handlers*, London 1976.

5. On the utopian in prophecy see B. Albrektson, 'Prophecy and Politics in the Old Testament' in H. Biezais (ed.), *Symposium on the Myth of the State*, Stockholm 1971, pp. 45–56.

6. We know very little about how the prophets were viewed in their time but for later views that rejected them as soothsayers, sorcerers and diviners see J. Macdonald, *The Samaritan Chronicle No. II* (or: *Sepher Ha-Yamim*). *From Joshua to Nebuchadnezzar*, BZAW 107: Berlin 1969, pp. 163–4, 184, 187–8. The technique of describing the prophet as 'claiming for himself that he was a prophet' (e.g. Jeremiah) is obviously a dismissive one and illustrates the principle that one community's prophets are another community's deceivers.

7. It is assumed here that the roots of the later Pharisaic view of prophecy as commentary on Torah were in this period. For the concept of theological streams see O. H. Steck, 'Theological Streams of Tradition', *Tradition and Theology in the Old Testament*, pp. 183–214.

Select Bibliography

R. P. Abelson, *et al.*, *Theories of Cognitive Consistency: A Sourcebook*, Chicago 1968

P. R. Ackroyd, *Exile and Restoration. A Study of Hebrew Thought of the Sixth Century BC*, OTL: London 1968

B. W. Anderson and W. Harrelson, *Israel's Prophetic Heritage*, London 1962

J. L. Austin, *How To Do Things with Words*, Oxford 1976²

J. Barr, *Old and New in Interpretation. A Study of the Two Testaments*, London 1966

W. Beyerlin (ed.), *Near Eastern Religious Texts Relating to the Old Testament*, OTL: London 1978

J. Bloch, *On the Apocalyptic in Judaism*, JQRMS 2, Philadelphia 1952

J. W. Brehm and A. R. Cohen, *Explorations in Cognitive Dissonance*, New York 1962

J. Bright, *A History of Israel*, London 1972²

— *Covenant and Promise*, London 1977

— *Jeremiah*, Anchor Bible 21: New York 1965

R. Brown, *Social Psychology*, New York 1965

M. Buber, *The Prophetic Faith*, New York 1960

R. P. Carroll, 'Ancient Israelite Prophecy and Dissonance Theory', *Numen*, 24, 1977, pp. 135–51

— 'A Non-Cogent Argument in Jeremiah's Oracles against the Prophets', *ST*, 30, 1976, pp.43–51

— 'Eschatological Delay in the Prophetic Tradition?', *ZAW*, forthcoming

— 'Inner Tradition Shifts in Meaning in Isaiah 1–11' *ExpT*, 89, 1978, pp.301–4

— 'Prophecy and Dissonance: A Theoretical Approach to the Prophetic Tradition', *ZAW*, forthcoming

— 'Prophecy, Dissonance and Jeremiah XXVI,' *TGUOS*, 25, 1976, pp.12–23

— 'Second Isaiah and the Failure of Prophecy', *ST*, 32, 1978, pp.119–31

B. S. Childs, *Exodus. A Commentary*, OTL: London 1974

— *Isaiah and the Assyrian Crisis*, SBT 2: 3: London 1967

G. W. Coats and B. O. Long (ed.), *Canon and Authority. Essays in Old Testament Religion and Theology*, Philadelphia 1977

R. G. Collingwood, *The Idea of History*, Oxford 1973

J. L. Crenshaw, *Prophetic Conflict. Its Effect Upon Israelite Religion*, BZAW, 124, Berlin 1971

W. Eichrodt, *Ezekiel. A Commentary*, OTL: London 1970

— *Theology of the Old Testament*, OTL: London, vol. 1, 1961; vol. 2, 1967.

L. Festinger, *A Theory of Cognitive Dissonance*, Evanston 1957

— *et al.*, *When Prophecy Fails. A Social and Psychological Study of a Modern Group that Predicted the Destruction of the World*, Minneapolis 1956

G. Fohrer, *History of Israelite Religion*, London 1973

— *Introduction to the Old Testament*, London 1970

— *Studien zur alttestamentlichen Prophetie (1949–1965)*, BZAW, 99, Berlin 1967

H.-G. Gadamer, *Philosophical Hermeneutics*, (ed.) D. E. Linge, Berkeley 1976

— *Truth and Method*, London 1975

J. G. Gager, *Kingdom and Community. The Social World of Early Christianity*, Englewood Cliffs 1975

P. D. Hanson, *The Dawn of Apocalyptic*, Philadelphia 1975

G. F. Hasel, *The Remnant. The History and Theology of the Remnant Idea from Genesis to Isaiah*, Andrews University Monographs V, Berrien Springs 1972

J. H. Hayes and J. M. Miller (eds), *Israelite and Judaean History*, OTL: London 1977

H. W. Hoffmann, *Die Intention der Verkündigung Jesajas*, BZAW, 136, Berlin 1974

E. Jenni, *Die politischen Voraussagen der Propheten*, ATANT, 29, Zürich 1956

O. Kaiser, *Introduction to the Old Testament*, Minnesota 1975

— *Isaiah 1–12. A Commentary*, OTL: London 1972

— *Isaiah 13–29. A Commentary*, OTL: London 1974

Y. Kaufmann, *The Religion of Israel*, New York 1972

D. A. Knight (ed.), *Tradition and Theology in the Old Testament*, London 1977

K. Koch, 'Ezra and the Origins of Judaism', *JSS*, 19, 1974, pp. 173–97

B. Levine, *In the Presence of the Lord. A Study of Cult and Some Cultic Terms in Ancient Israel*, SJLA, 5 Leiden 1974

J. Lindblom, *Prophecy in Ancient Israel*, Oxford 1962

J. L. Mays, *Amos. A Commentary*, OTL: London 1969

— *Hosea. A Commentary*, OTL: London 1969

— *Micah. A Commentary*, OTL: London 1976

J. Milgrom, *Cult and Conscience. The ASHAM and the Priestly Doctrine of Repentance*, SJLA, 18, Leiden 1976

T. W. Overholt, *The Threat of Falsehood. Studies in the Theology of the Book of Jeremiah*, SBT 2: 16: London 1970

J. B. Payne, *Encyclopedia of Biblical Prophecy. The Complete Guide to Scriptural Predictions and Their Fulfilment*, London 1973

O. Plöger, *Theocracy and Eschatology*, Oxford 1968

K. R. Popper, *Conjectures and Refutations. The Growth of Scientific Knowledge*, London and Henley 1972[4]

G. von Rad, *Old Testament Theology*, Edinburgh and London, vol. 1, 1962; vol. 2, 1965

I. T. Ramsey, *Religious Language. An Empirical Placing of Theological Phrases*, London 1967

D. S. Russell, *The Method and Message of Jewish Apocalyptic 200 BC—AD 100*, OTL: London 1964

M. Smith, *Palestinian Parties and Politics that Shaped the Old Testament*, New York and London 1971

M. Weinfeld, *Deuteronomy and the Deuteronomic School*, Oxford 1972

C. Westermann, *Isaiah 40–66. A Commentary*, OTL: London 1969

H. Wildberger, *Jesaja 1. Jesaja 1–12*, BKAT X/1, Neukirchen-Vluyn 1972

L. Wittgenstein, *Philosophical Investigations*, Oxford 1972

— *Tractatus Logico-Philosophicus*, London 1966

H.-W. Wolff, *Hosea. A Commentary*, Hermeneia: Philadelphia 1974

— *Joel and Amos. A Commentary*, Hermeneia: Philadelphia 1977

R. B. Zajonc, 'Cognitive Theories in Social Psychology', in G. Lindzey and E. Aronson (eds), *The Handbook of Social Psychology*, Massachusetts 1968[2], 1, pp. 320–411

W. Zimmerli, *Ezechiel*, BKAT, XIII, Neukirchen-Vluyn 1962ff.

Index